(Continued)

PLAY

and the Social Context of Development in Early Care and Education

Edited by
BARBARA SCALES
MILLIE ALMY
AGELIKI NICOLOPOULOU
SUSAN ERVIN-TRIPP

Teachers College, Columbia University
New York and London

Published by Teachers College Press, 1234 Amsterdam Avenue, New York, NY 10027

Copyright © 1991 by Teachers College, Columbia University

Proceedings of an Institute of Human Development symposium, University of California, Berkeley, May 1988.

Grateful acknowledgment is extended for permission to reprint material in Chapter 14 from the following sources:

Friendship and Peer Culture in the Early Years, by W. Corsaro. Copyright © 1985 by Ablex Publishing Corporation, Norwood, NJ. Reprinted by permission of the publisher.

Reprinted by permission of the publishers from *Siblings: Love, Envy, and Understanding,* by Judy Dunn and Carol Kendrick. Cambridge, Mass.: Harvard University Press. Copyright © 1982 by Judy Dunn and Carol Kendrick.

Library of Congress Cataloging-in-Publication Data

Play and the social context of development in early care and education
    / edited by Barbara Scales . . . [et al.].
        p.   cm.—(Early childhood education series)
    Includes bibliographical references and index.
    ISBN 0-8077-3067-X.—ISBN 0-8077-3066-1 (pbk.)
    1. Play.   2. Education, Preschool—United States.   3. Education.
Preschool—California—Case studies.   4. Cognition in children.
I. Scales, Barbara, 1930–   .   II. Series.
LB1137.P53   1991
372.21—dc20   90-2234

ISBN 0-8077-3065-3
ISBN 0-8077-3066-1

Printed on acid-free paper
Manufactured in the United States of America

98 97 96 95 94 93 92 91   8 7 6 5 4 3 2 1

Contents

Part II. Language, Literacy, and the Social Worlds of Children

Part III. Play, Cognitive Development, and the Social World

Part IV. Play and the Social Worlds of Children

Foreword

PAUL MUSSEN

Research on the origins, nature, and functions of play—topics of speculation since ancient times but only recently the foci of systematic investigation—can yield critically important information about cognitive, social, and emotional development. The findings of such research may also be applied practically and effectively in preschool education and child care, settings in which play is the central activity. The conditions or contexts in which play occurs are governed not by researchers but by educational professionals—indirectly by policy makers and directly by teachers and administrators.

Although practitioners and developmental researchers share a fundamental goal—the promotion of the welfare of children—they operate virtually independently of each other and with minimal communication between them. Yet it seems obvious that both groups could benefit enormously from continuing communication: Policy decisions and early education programs should be guided by scientific knowledge, while research would become richer and more relevant if it took into account the educational professional's everyday activities and goals that shape the social context of play.

A multidisciplinary symposium on "Play and the Social Context of Development in Early Care and Education," held at the Harold E. Jones Child Study Center of the University of California in May 1988, was designed to stimulate this kind of communication. In the editors' words, it was intended to "provide a forum for a dialogue between researchers interested in studying play in context and educational professionals struggling with the new and conflicting demands of the growing institutionalization of early care and education." Almost all the thoughtful and thought-provoking chapters in the present volume are based on papers given at that symposium. Even a cursory review of the contents reveals that a wide net was cast and a broad spectrum of perspectives was represented. No other publication provides such a clear picture of the complex problems practitioners confront—for example, analyses of the social-economic-political issues of public policy relating to child care, the establishment of standards for optimal child care institutions, responding sympathetically to the individual needs of young children, and the taxing workloads of teachers. The lucid accounts of research findings offer compelling evidence that play of all sorts—free play, constructive play, peer interactions, guided expression, and play with blocks—can be highly effective in promoting the development of manual skills, language, empathy, thinking and reasoning, and social and emotional adjustment. Furthermore, the research chapters offer many novel insights into the meaning of play, and the authors carefully spell out the practical implications, illuminating the ways teachers can stimulate children's play in order to achieve educational goals.

Yet in a real sense, these highly informative and challenging chapters demonstrate the need for more and more focused dialogue between practitioners and researchers, for each chapter is written from the perspective of *either* the context of play—that is, major social and educational factors affecting the work of child care institutions—*or* the nature of play in its impacts on learning. Only a few chapters deal with relationships between these parameters.

The unique, invaluable contribution of this volume is its *consciousness raising:* It informs researchers, theorists, and practitioners of one another's accomplishments, goals, and problems. This reciprocal awareness will stimulate interactions that will ultimately produce deeper insights into the links between aspects of the social contexts of child care institutions and the educational, development-enhancing activities of those institutions. Furthermore, by specifically defining the many needs for further research and by evaluating the contributions and limitations of current theories, the authors indicate ways to make investigations more sophisticated and comprehensive and to formulate more integrative theories, leading to more fruitful educational applications of scientific findings in the future.

Acknowledgments

This book and the symposium from which it originated owe their existence to the support of the Institute of Human Development, University of California, Berkeley. Special thanks go to Paul Mussen, who as the Institute's director at the time, provided initial support, guidance and advice for the Symposium. Thanks are also due Joseph Campos, the Institute's current director, who provided support for the preparation of this publication. Acknowledgments must also go to their assistant, Susan Cardwell, a resource of inestimable worth.

We are also indebted to all of those who participated in the symposium, as well as to those who contributed chapters to the book.

The Child Study Center, its director, Jane Hunt, and its staff contributed to the project in many ways. The Center provided the setting for the symposium. Secretaries Sheila Bradley, Amy Udisches, Alice Engle, and Patrice Parame took care of myriad details for the symposium and for preparation of the manuscript. La Shonda Spencer and Carol Heller, student assistants, helped with some of the tasks of editing. Hannah Sanders, former head teacher in the Center, took over in the classroom when Barbara Scales's editorial responsibilities seemed about to eclipse those of teaching.

Marcy McGaugh was the ever efficient typist for much of the manuscript. Acknowledgment should also be made to the Teachers College Press editorial staff. Sarah Biondello and Nina George provided initial and continuing encouragement. Faye Zucker's developmental editing helped to sharpen and focus the editing, while Myra Cleary's copy editing elicited favorable comments from many of the authors.

Introduction

BARBARA SCALES
MILLIE ALMY
AGELIKI NICOLOPOULOU
SUSAN ERVIN-TRIPP

This book, and the symposium on which it is based, grew out of concerns for the effects that the increasing institutionalization of child care and early education may have on the role of play in the development of the young child. As early care (once exclusively the domain of the home) is increasingly ceded to the public domain of schooling, conceptions and demands about it shift, depending on what perspective one adheres to at the moment or on the issue of concern.

On the one hand, schooling is traditionally associated with learning and education. When early care is seen from this perspective, both parents and teachers demand that early learning be continuous with and vital to later learning. Some want the academic skills of elementary school to be taught in kindergarten or preschool. Others want programs to concentrate on the young child's natural and playful propensities for learning. All believe that young children now need a head start to meet the increasing demands of our highly literate society. On the other hand, when early care is viewed from the perspective of the home it is replacing, then most parents and teachers want to make the settings for early education and care homelike, nurturing environments where learning is usually informal and often playful.

While teachers attempt to provide an environment that supports play, they are also compelled to justify the educational goals of their daily classroom activities, whether playful or not, to parents, administrators, and other teachers. Among teachers, there is a growing recognition that early childhood curricula need to be articulated more clearly (see Chapters 3 and 13). Some preschool teachers respond to conflicting demands by adapting curricula from kindergarten and early grades, trying to change the pace to fit younger children. Others continue to encourage spontaneous play, and attempt to justify its place in the curriculum by citing the learning that they see in it. Some teachers experiment with new ways of structuring or intervening in children's play to incorporate goals appropriate to their ages. Unfortunately, teachers often lack sufficient time to make and record systematic observations, and later to evaluate whether what they did was successful or not. Also, they have little time to compare and discuss their observations with others who work in similar settings. Such concerns as these suggested to us that teachers might enjoy contributing to a dialogue with researchers who are also interested in play.

From the research arena, we were interested in engaging researchers who share a framework with educational practitioners; that is, researchers who attempt to study development in its sociocultural context—a group that has been growing in recent years. The increasing interest in this approach is reflected, for example, in the current resurgence of the sociocultural theory of L. S. Vygotsky; the growing concern with cultural, educational, and psychological studies; and the expanding acceptance of ethnographic research as an appropriate method for studying socialization. This approach has allowed researchers to study socialization in such places as homes, classrooms, and playgrounds.

Given these important trends in both the professional and academic communities, it seemed an opportune moment to provide a forum for a dialogue between researchers interested in studying play in context and educational professionals struggling with the new and conflicting demands of the growing institutionalization of early care and education.

It also seemed an appropriate time to include in the dialogue individuals who could speak to issues of policy affecting this institutionalization. In the United States, research, policy, and practice often develop independently of each other. Yet, in the present instance, it is clear that the provisions made for children's play in child care centers will depend not only on the evidence that teachers and researchers can bring to bear on the importance of play, but also on their ability to share their findings with the public, parents, and especially policy makers. All need to understand that play is unlikely to flourish in settings that are overcrowded and understaffed.

Bringing together differing professional groups promised to provoke some lively dialogue. It also seemed that as the participants learned of each other's realities, goals, and aspirations, some interest in collaboration might eventually emerge. But the initial goal was simply to provide a forum for the dialogue. The Institute of Human Development at the

University of California at Berkeley, which has for over 50 years researched the effects of early experience on later development, sponsored a symposium around this convergence of interests in play and, appropriately, provided the Harold E. Jones Child Study Center as its setting.

The lively interchange in the symposium among presenters and between presenters and other participants, including a small number of researcher colleagues and early childhood teachers, indicated that the topics stimulated mutual interest. The dialogue had begun. Our book attempts to extend it.

Three Views of Play

A major portion of the dialogue centered around play's place in the curriculum, reflecting three different views. The child, of course, is impelled to play as a "whole" child, at once an affective, cognitive, social, and physical being. The researcher, looking at the child's play, may, however, categorize it as belonging to a particular domain of behavior as social, or cognitive or motor. The researcher who stays in the classroom long enough to observe developmental changes, may attribute them to the child's play experiences.

The teacher, privy to a tremendous amount of information about each child and the group of which each is a part, views play somewhat differently from most researchers. The teacher asks whether play activities, so indigenous and so absorbing to children, must be curbed in order to teach them, or whether the play activities, in themselves, constitute opportunities for learning. Knowledgeable teachers are aware that an increasing body of research and theory, beginning perhaps with Piaget, exists to substantiate the latter view.

The belief that play activities have a legitimate and fruitful place in the early childhood curriculum prevails in this book, and influenced our selection of the views of play that are presented. Thus, Part II of the book is devoted to discussions of play from the view of language and literacy. Connections between the playful aspects of children's symbol manipulation and their later literacy learning have recently been recognized in holistic approaches to literacy.

Language and literacy, usually described as "learning to read" at the early childhood level, may be the hottest issue early childhood teachers confront. It is an issue that has grown hotter as general dissatisfaction with elementary schooling has increased. It is also an area where research, much of it done in classrooms with the collaboration of teachers, has begun to pay off. Countering the narrow and long prevailing emphasis on reading readiness workbooks and primers with controlled vocabulary, the efficacy of capitalizing on young children's interests in print and of drawing on their play life for themes to write about has been demonstrated. Accordingly, a number of state education departments and school systems are already working to change their approach to teaching reading. Research has also shown how children's play contributes to their language development. We believe that the collaborative efforts of teachers and researchers, as well as their findings, have much to offer early childhood educators. The justification of play in other curriculum areas might well evolve through the use of similar strategies.

Another view of the role of play in the curriculum looks specifically at its cognitive aspects. Here the guiding question for the teacher may be, What concepts do children reveal or are they acquiring through play? For many years, early childhood teachers have been able to draw on the work of Piaget and of researchers inspired by him, for assistance in looking at these kinds of questions. Part III of this book discusses cognition, but it moves beyond questions related to the nature of children's concepts to examine, again from the viewpoint of the educator, the processes involved as children "learn through their play." Here the theory of Vygotsky extends that of Piaget and illuminates the role of the child's social world, including the teacher's part in it. This appears to be a promising area for teachers and researchers to explore together. It is not yet nearly as well developed as the area of language and literacy.

The third view of play, taken up in Part IV of this book, is equally promising, but even less well developed than that of cognition as it relates to the social world. This view looks directly into that social world and tries to ascertain how children view themselves, each other, and the adults around them. It is concerned, in the largest sense, with the ways children use their play to construct their own humanness. Play from this view is the work children must do to establish who they are and how they are like and how they differ from their peers and from adults, and to test their own powers. More narrowly, it has to do not only with social development but also with moral development. As this area of research and theory expands, it promises early childhood education a powerful argument for the importance of play in the curriculum. At the same time its very nature seems to demand collaboration between researchers and teachers.

Contributors to the Dialogue

The reader may have noted from the list of editors and contributors at the back of this book that some of the authors are described as researchers in child development and others as teachers or early childhood educators. A word about the selection of the authors seems in order. All of the researchers, both those who made presentations and those who wrote "the research perspectives" chapters that introduce Parts II–IV of the book, were invited to contribute chapters because of their identification with one of the three views on play delineated.

The authors of the "perspectives from the field" chapters that end each part of the book are all individuals with long experience as teachers in varied early childhood programs. All, who are also active in early childhood organizations, responded enthusiastically to the invitation to describe the concerns and commitments from which they view research.

The Editors' Views

Having finally and gratefully assembled and perused 17 chapters from authors known to be much too busy to write another word, let alone an article of some length, we marvelled at the richness and diversity of the ideas presented. Surely every reader will find here something to expand and illuminate what he or she already knows about young children's play, some insight to modify or extend curricular provisions, or some question to which an answer can be sought.

Perhaps that is enough said. On the other hand, the reader may welcome some further guidance to the content of the chapters, and some pointing to the issues that are raised. Our debates among ourselves raised the possibility that adding our voices to the diversity of voices already speaking in the different chapters might only create further cacophony. Despite that risk we choose to be heard.

Framing Our Concerns

The first part of the book provides background by delineating issues that surround policy for early education and care. Chapter 1 considers play and its place in early education and care from an historical perspective, showing that today's issues are deeply rooted. It considers the contradictions that have arisen when early childhood teachers have taken strong positions on the importance of play but have failed to buttress their positions with strong scientific evidence. While some pioneer nursery school teachers were able to collect systematic evidence about play from their own classes, such collection in the face of other demands on the teachers' time and energy, often coupled with inadequate child development preparation, has become increasingly difficult. Underpaid and overworked, as has long been the case in women's occupations, many early childhood teachers have experienced a sense of powerlessness that has made the assumption of true professionalism difficult. In an occupation that is so highly labor intensive the issue of how to advance professionalism and the related recognition deserved by practice based on scientific knowledge remains persistent and crucial.

Chapter 2, by Grubb, considers some of the history and concerns raised in Chapter 1 but in the larger focus of public policy. He shows, on the one hand, what is involved in quality programs and, on the other hand, the areas where negotiation must take place, if such programs are to come into being.

Early childhood educators, researchers, and parents reading this chapter may well ask themselves which of their own favorite ideas serve as shibboleths that can block progress in negotiating resolutions to policy issues. An examination of the negotiations that eventually led to a coalition of organizations that backed the proposed Act for Better Child Care Services, which came before Congress in 1988, 1989, and 1990, might also be instructive.

In Chapter 3, attention shifts to a single policy issue and the way it has been dealt with in a single state, California. Smith reports on her experience as a member of a state task force on school readiness. Its recommendations eventuated in a new policy for programs for 4- to 6-year-olds. The chapter raises many questions. How do the various protagonists in the story define play? Why do the views of so many teachers appear so contradictory? Is "experiential instruction" a euphemism for play? If so, how is the curriculum for 6-year-olds to differ from that for 4-year-olds? How do parents of varying backgrounds view such school policy shifts?

Beardsley provides information on some of these questions in Chapter 4. She describes the ways in which many teachers have responded to the new California policy and points out the factors that may impede progress. These include inadequate preparation for the new kind of teaching, insufficient funding, and problems of articulation between preschool, kindergarten, and first grade. Most important, she considers another group of stakeholders in the policy's success, parents.

This chapter is the only one in the book that devotes a section to parents although references are made to them throughout. Since the institutionalization of child care means that an important aspect of the child's life—play—may be transformed, it seems strange that so little early childhood literature and research have given consideration to the views of parents. One suspects that too often parents are expected to collaborate with teachers in promoting children's play before sufficient attention is given to the cultural diversity that affects the role of play in the child's life and development.

Language, Literacy, and Social Worlds

Part II moves away from background factors in shaping early childhood programs to research addressing specific aspects of play and its social context. Considering that language and literacy are areas where research has moved forward rapidly during the 1980s, and where applications to practice are well underway, the reader may consider the possible sources of such success. Perhaps it lies in the severity of dissatisfaction with traditional language arts teaching. It may also stem from the direct nature of the research results often relying on case studies and the clarity of their communication.

Genishi, in Chapter 5, which introduces the material in this part of the book, points to the usefulness of the case study while also showing how its findings must be anchored in logic. Early childhood teachers are familiar with case studies; such studies enable them to protect the integrity of the individual, something they miss in the generalizations of other kinds of research. Implicitly, Genishi proposes that case studies, collected systematically and with reference to a specific aspect of play, can enhance the teacher's position in dialogues with other researchers, with parents, and presumably with administrators and policy makers.

In Chapter 6 Ervin-Tripp compares the roles of peers and adults in facilitating the language development of preschool children and examines the role of play in that development. She gingerly avoids applying her findings to practice. Nevertheless, they challenge the traditional elementary school view that language learning requires direct instruction and underscore the preschool teacher's assertion that "children learn through play." Questions as to the most effective proportions of child play and adult instruction and at what ages they apply remain as topics for future research. They are questions appropriate for early childhood staffs, given time and support, to investigate.

Dyson, reporting in Chapter 7 on her investigation of the roots of literacy development, shows how closely language, play, and literacy are intertwined, even as children move into first and second grades. Her observations were made during "journal time" when the children drew on their play and the social worlds they were building in it, for the sketches and the texts they produced. The journals, as Dyson shows, were more than assignments. They revealed the children's concerns, their interests, their fantasies, and their imagination. What are the ingredients for such production? How do teachers maintain the necessary balance between "experiential and didactic instruction" here?

The case study of their own performances, offered by Altman and Fong in Chapter 8, provides some leads. Their children may not be journal artists and writers, but the teachers have found ways to protect some of their time for pursuits of their own interests. Altman and Fong's accomplishment takes place amidst a welter of other obligations, to the state and local school systems, to individual children and their parents, and to their community. Nevertheless, they are open to the resources that become available through research. We wonder whether teachers like Altman and Fong would happily engage in a research project of the researcher's choosing. On the other hand, how would such teachers respond to an offer of collaboration on a project of mutual interest?

Play, Cognition, and the Social World

Part III turns from language and literacy to cognitive development. In Chapter 9, the introduction to this part, Nicolopoulou shows how examination of the social context of play illuminates the nature of the child's cognitive functioning. Her discussion of the influence of the theories of Piaget and Vygotsky on play research traces the influences that affected them and the aspects of their thinking that researchers have overlooked or misinterpreted. Her analysis leads her to posit a new view of play, one that enables practitioners and researchers to share their understanding of what play is. This view has great promise for their collaboration and for the eventual resolution of problems such as determining the most effective balance between play and direct instruction.

The first research presentation in this part is concerned not with play but with early number development. Chapter 10, by Saxe, Gearheart, and Guberman, illustrates how developmental psychologists studying cognition proceed to investigate the influence of the social context in the child's functioning. Here the authors look at the influence of mothers, not peers, but the children's cognitive processes may not be dissimilar to those involved when children learn from their negotiations in play.

Considerations of Chapter 10 may raise further questions about the balance between direct instruction and play at the preschool level. Furthermore, from the perspective of child care the question of whether teachers provide the kinds of intimate negotiations that the authors describe as characteristic of the mothers deserves consideration.

The next two chapters in Part III do deal with play, particularly constructive play. Reifel and Yeatman (Chapter 11), in their collaborations, used videotape to record the action and talk in the block center of their preschool. From these records they inferred the thought of the children. They provided focus for their study by embedding it in a curriculum devoted to pets. They could then study the way this theme was reflected in the children's play. Nicolopoulou (Chapter 12), interested in similar questions about constructive play, thought that the classroom presented too many confusing variables and so designed an "experiment" in which children playing individually made constructions from cardboard blocks with systematically varied color and shape. She could then study the relationships between the properties of the blocks and the symbolic meanings the children attached to them.

The reader will find that the two studies are thought provoking. Assume first, as early childhood educators have for many decades, that spontaneous play is an integral part of the curriculum. Assume, too, that the opportunity for spontaneous play, in which the child is free to fantasize, to act or not to act, to share or not to share, is essential to the child's development. It appears that the teacher has great responsibility for protecting such play, but, much as is the case with language development, we know very little about the possible effects of decreasing or increasing the ratio of opportunities for spontaneous play to teacher-directed instruction, or even to guided play. Although teachers have long experimented with various ways of intervening in children's play, such as supplying themes, suggesting roles, providing different props, changing the composition of the group of children playing together, the effectiveness of such strategies for individual children and for different groups of children are largely unknown.

The perceptive reader may well ask, "Effective for what?" Some tough issues of concern to parents as well as to teachers arise. For example, what do we want the children's experiences in preschool or in a child care center to contribute to their long-term and all-round development? Are the experiences they have inherently worthwhile?

Monighan Nourot considers these and other questions in Chapter 13 as she brings the reader vignettes from contemporary early education classrooms. She reiterates the complexities of the teacher's job and asserts the need for artistry as well as scientific knowledge.

Nicolopoulou, as one of the authors of this introduction, suggests that some new activities may be emerging in certain nursery schools, in response to current conflicting perspectives on the needs of children and the demands of society. New forms of guided play extend the character and values of homes while incorporating educational goals appropriate to the ages of the children. She suggests that these new play forms, initiated by a few creative teachers, need study to determine how best to guide and enrich play without driving it out of the classroom. Such study would be most effective if it combined the expertise of researchers and the vision of teachers. From the viewpoint of researchers, such studies would also be helpful in elucidating the character of play.

The Social Worlds of Children

In Part IV we move directly into the social worlds of children. Information about this world, particularly from the viewpoint of the children themselves, has only recently begun to be incorporated into the literature of child development, although certain aspects of its nature have been inferred from studies of language, of thought, and of social interaction.

Cook-Gumperz, in Chapter 14, inquires into how "childness" is seen by children, that is, how they define themselves. She considers the factors that contribute to this definition and also describes the different ways children and their social worlds are seen by social scientists from different disciplines. For example, Nucci and Killen, psychologists and authors of Chapter 15, rely on interviews with individual children to gain information about their moral and social concepts. But this information is supplemented with direct observation of their social interaction.

Corsaro, a sociologist, and coauthor with Schwarz of Chapter 16, also observes social interaction, but in a different way. Corsaro tries to be more of a participant observer, videotaping the play while becoming, in effect, a "big child" and remaining in regular attendance in a particular preschool for a matter of months. Chapter 16 is enriched by the fact that his extended observations have been made in different countries, the United States and Italy.

Chapters 15 and 16 are complementary in that both deal implicitly with aspects of play that often present themselves to teachers as "discipline" issues. Both also explore the implications of their research for teachers.

As noted previously, research that enables the teacher to see more clearly into what may be described as an emerging peer culture offers much promise for the validation of play in the early childhood curriculum. A keener understanding of and a closer view into their own classrooms should enable teachers both to plan more effectively for children's play and to assess the children's developmental progress.

Finally, in Chapter 17, Tracy discusses the hazards that impede teachers' full use of the research that is already available to them. It is a plea for the kind of educational preparation, support, and time that early childhood educators need if they are to become full-fledged professionals engaged in vigorous support of young children's play.

Part I
FRAMING OUR CONCERNS

CHAPTER 1

Defending Play
in the Lives of Children

BARBARA SCALES
MILLIE ALMY
AGELIKI NICOLOPOULOU
SUSAN ERVIN-TRIPP

Play, that absorbing activity in which healthy young children participate with enthusiasm and abandon, has been declared one of a child's basic rights (United Nations Declaration of the Rights of the Child, 1948) and takes its place along with such other rights as nutrition, housing, health care, and education. Many children, even in the United States, are deprived of these rights; moreover, other, more-favored youngsters, also lack the time, opportunity, and suitable settings for their play.

Many adults consider children's play a mere time filler, not an essential component of healthy development. In contrast, teachers and researchers who have examined what children do when they play see it as a special activity with features that set it apart from other behaviors. Such features include self-directed interest and active engagement, and experimentation with possibilities in the realm of ideas, in the physical world, and in their relationships with their peers. In their play children generate rules for conduct, establish roles and plots, and engage in complex negotiations. They make longer utterances and use more varied vocabulary than when they are not playing (Rubin, Fein, & Vandenberg, 1983).

This chapter begins with consideration of the place that play has held in early education and care in the United States from the introduction of kindergartens during the nineteenth century to the present, and describes current developments and their potential for changing the nature of children's play in ways that may affect them in the long term.

Historical Perspectives

Play has long been the centerpiece of the early childhood curriculum. Its position, beginning with the establishment of the first kindergartens in Germany over a century ago, is often attributed to the philosophy of Friederich Froebel.

According to Weber (1984), "Froebel saw play as the perfect medium for self-activity—for the release of the child's inner powers. He was not content to accept the happy exuberance of play, but he watched for evidences that symbolized the awakening of the child's inner nature" (pp. 37–38). Furthermore, Froebel, who emphasized the importance of the earliest play between mother and child, saw school as an extension of the family setting and a place for disciplined social development. For Froebel, "benevolent social relationships were expected outcomes of family and school life" (p. 39).

Following their introduction in the United States, Froebel's ideas for the education of children younger than 6 years flourished. By 1873, kindergartens began to shift from private or philanthropic support to support within the public schools (Osborn, 1980). Froebel's influence gradually waned, to be replaced by the ideas of John Dewey, G. Stanley Hall, and E. L. Thorndike (Weber, 1984). In response, the curriculum, that is, the kinds of experiences in which children engaged, changed over the years. Some changes may also be attributed to the initiation of morning and afternoon sessions, enabling more children to attend and often doubling the responsibility of teachers. Precise ages for admission were also established, generally limiting kindergarten to 5-year-olds. Nevertheless, play remained an essential element, at least in kindergarten ideology, if not always in performance, for many years.

Meanwhile, nursery schools, appearing on the scene in the first quarter of the twentieth century, gradually became available for 2-, 3-, and 4-year-olds. Initially affiliated mostly with universities and colleges, nursery schools tried to exemplify an approach to early education based on scientific knowledge. From the beginning, nursery schools gave play a crucially important role in the curriculum, emphasizing spontaneity and encouraging self-direction.

Play: A Child-Centered Activity

Kindergartens and nursery schools, as they were established, presented a striking contrast to traditional elementary school programs. The children were younger, of course, but, of more significance here, they were also freer. They were not constrained to sit in rows, to speak only when spoken to (by an adult), and to refrain from sharing other children's materials or ideas. They were expected to learn not only from the teacher and from books, but also from each other and from their experiences while manipulating a variety of objects.

Such programs have often been described as "child centered" and different from those that are "teacher centered" or "subject-matter centered." These terms, often appearing in the rhetoric of early childhood education, are misleading. A child-centered program emphasizes play in the belief that it is the child's way of coming to terms with personal experience in and knowledge of the physical and social world. But play, unfettered by adult awareness or response, is insufficiently educative for groups of young children. Adults are needed not only to ensure safety and security but also to attend to the play and what it reveals about the children's development and learning. Teachers provide ever-expanding opportunities, paced to the children's advancing knowledge, for them to learn, both from their own actions and observations, and from being told or shown about themselves, about people, and about the physical environment. Accordingly, an effective child-centered program demands as much, or more, activity and thought on the part of the teacher as does a so-called teacher- or subject-matter-centered program. The emerging science of child development, from the 1940s onward, provided nursery schools and kindergartens with justification for programs that were child centered and play-oriented.

Early observational studies conducted in nursery schools furnished norms that enabled teachers to consider whether the children's play behavior was typical or unusual. Beginning in a few schools in the 1930s and expanding in influence through the 1940s and 1950s, psychodynamic views of children's play became predominant. The major developmental theorists, and especially Freud, Erikson, and Piaget, emphasized the ways that play contributed to the children's social, emotional, and cognitive development. Meanwhile, the Soviet sociohistorical school showed how play constitutes the leading activity in the development of the young child (e.g., El'konin, 1966; Leontiev, 1981; Vygostsky, 1966). Through play, the young child progresses from one level of development to the next. Unfortunately, the Soviet material did not become available in the United States until the 1960s and is only now becoming familiar to educators.

By the 1960s many nursery school teachers seem to have used psychoanalytic theory to justify the emotional and social benefits of play while disregarding its cognitive benefits. This is ironic since it suggests a disregard for the "whole child" concept that had long been part of the ideology of early childhood education. This concept emphasized the interrelatedness of development and suggested that the teacher should take into consideration all aspects of the child's development, usually phrased as "physical, mental, emotional, and social." The tendency to overemphasize emotional development became especially apparent during the so-called "renaissance" of early childhood education that began in the United States in the late 1950s.

Renaissance and Debate

A number of factors contributed to the rediscovery of early education and particularly of nursery schools. Nursery schools had come briefly into the public eye under the aegis of the Works Projects Administration (WPA) in the 1930s, where they provided jobs for unemployed teachers, and under the Lanham Act, where they offered child care to women in World War II defense industries. In the years following they increased steadily but not rapidly in numbers, serving mostly parents who could afford to pay for them. Kindergartens were available in public schools in many states. In 1965, however, when the rediscovery was well under way, only 27 percent of 3-, 4-, and 5-year-olds were enrolled in public or private programs. The bulk of the enrollment (60.6%) was among 5-year-olds (National Center for Education Statistics, 1988).

One important factor in the rediscovery was the renewed interest in cognitive development on the part of psychologists, especially Benjamin Bloom (1964), Jerome Bruner (1960), and J. McV. Hunt (1961). The increasing availability of translations of Piaget's work paralleled this interest. Recognition that an overwhelming number of children living in poverty areas were failing in school, and would be unable to compete for jobs, began to take on political importance.

The next 20 years saw the initiation, proliferation, and attempted evaluation of dozens of experimental nursery schools (most of them by then significantly called preschools). Head Start, with a "whole child" orientation on the part of its founders, came into being and like other experimental programs was evaluated on cognitive accomplishments. Cognitive achievement, at least of an elementary sort, is relatively easy to assess, in striking contrast to accomplishments in the social and emotional realms.

Many debates centered around these burgeoning early childhood programs. Of particular interest here is the debate about play. Many nursery school teachers reacted adversely to the notion that their so-called "traditional" programs emphasized play, and social and emotional development to the detriment of the children's cognitive development. They noted that some of the experimental programs emphasized cognition at the complete expense of play. Other experimental programs attempted to capitalize on the children's propensities for play in various ways. In some the teachers sought clues to the children's interests and concerns and tried to enrich their experience accordingly. In others the teachers in effect became authors as well as directors or stage managers of the children's play. According to Sutton-Smith (1971) their efforts represent the imposition of cognitive child labor into play.

Those who believed that young children's play provides cognitive, social, and emotional benefits to children and that play should remain the centerpiece of early childhood programs, were gratified when the long-term (14 years or more) evaluations of some programs were completed. For example, according to one widely cited study, poor children who had participated in high quality, well-run programs compared with children of similar backgrounds who had not participated, not only were less often retained in a grade or assigned to special education classes, but also were less often delinquent and more likely to hold jobs after leaving high school (Berrueta-Clement, Schweinhart, Barnett, Epstein, & Weikart, 1984).

As Haskins (1989) points out in a review of other studies of preschool programs, the programs varied in a number of ways, including long-term results. Nevertheless,

> taken as a group, they demonstrate unequivocally that quality preschool programs provide an immediate boost to children's intellectual performance and reduce their rate of placement in special education classes. The studies also provide moderate evidence that quality preschool programs decrease grade retention and increase the likelihood of high school graduation. (p. 276)

The attention given to cognitive development in the period of rediscovery and debate about early childhood education had its effect on kindergartens as well as nursery schools. The young child's propensities for many kinds of learning were often interpreted as mere readiness for earlier academic work. Workbooks and drills often moved downward from first grade into kindergarten, where they replaced opportunities for direct experience with materials. A curriculum that had been based on play became a 3 R's curriculum.

Thoughtful kindergarten teachers, aware of changes in the backgrounds and home experiences of many children, often complained that the children had as much need as ever for spontaneous play. However, they felt constrained by pressures for academic achievement coming from parents and the media. Competition with the Soviets had already highlighted the inadequacy of the public schools. Many parents felt that if special early childhood programs were to benefit disadvantaged children, would not all children be helped by greater emphasis on academics in the early years, the supposed "prime time" for learning?

The societal factors that were of concern to teachers affected all early childhood programs. One such factor was the increase of employment of women outside their homes and the consequent need for child care in addition to the hours spent in nursery school or kindergarten.

Child Care and Education

Traditionally, and most commonly, employed mothers in the United States have turned to relatives or neighbors for child care. A smaller number have used child care institutions—the philanthropic day nursery going back as far as the Civil War; more recently the child care center, sometimes philanthropic, sometimes under the aegis of state or local government, sometimes proprietary. Unlike nursery school or kindergarten, these institutions were open from early morning to beyond the end of the mother's working day.

As early as the 1930s some day nurseries began hiring nursery school teachers, bringing to the children a play curriculum similar to that of the nursery school. Many child care centers continued this trend. Often, however, questions arose as to whether centers could afford the expense of qualified teachers. This was one issue underlying the later and persistent difficulty in implementing Federal Interagency Day Care Requirements intended to set minimal standards for staffing child care centers.

A possible solution to the problem of staffing and also of space eventually came from the American Federation of Teachers, suggesting that child care come under the aegis of the public schools. In some states and cities schools had successfully taken on such responsibilities, but as Grubb describes in Chapter 2, the proposal met with considerable opposition. Other issues hampering the development of child care centers were the identification of child care with welfare, and resistance to providing something for families that they had traditionally provided for themselves.

For many years responsibility for the licensing of child care institutions has rested with welfare departments. Child care outside the home, and especially in centers, has been seen as something that might be needed by the poor, but as not necessary for the typical American family. Further, that family is regarded as inviolate, not to be intruded upon by society, even for its own good. Such attitudes appear to reflect the strong tradition of individual responsibility and competitiveness that has characterized our society.

Child Care: Whose Responsibility?

Public policy in the United States has never been strongly committed to either early education or early care. Only in the past two decades have all states come to support kindergarten as part of the public schools. In most states attendance is not compulsory, but about 90 percent of all 5-year-olds attend, and 80 percent of those are in public school, suggesting how much parents value such education (Spodek, 1986).

Some change in the attitude of reluctance to impose on families began to be apparent beginning in the 1960s. Early education programs directed specifically to disadvantaged children increased during the 1960s and early 1970s. Child care funds also became available to the states under the Title XX Social Services Act. Tax credits were extended for child care but brought help only to those families above the poverty level. What could have been a major step toward more effectively meeting the needs for both care and education was the Comprehensive Child Development Act, passed by both houses of Congress in 1971. This act, which "enjoyed the highest degree of consensus yet developed on child care legislation, . . . was the result of tough compromises by myriad organizations . . . and by numerous sponsors in the house and senate" (Beck, 1982, p. 326). Unfortunately, President Nixon, responding to right wing pressure, vetoed the proposed legislation. The veto marked the beginning of a long period in which federal support for child care declined, and responsibility for it shifted to states and local communities.

The long-term reluctance of government in the United States to assume much responsibility for its young children contrasted strongly with attitudes in many other countries. For example, 10 European countries, Canada, Australia, and New Zealand provide universal access to health care and a basic income support system for families with children (Children's Defense Fund, 1988, p. 26). Furthermore, most industrialized countries have a policy that provides maternal care for infants in the first months of life. Their mothers are granted leaves with cash benefits and assurance of return to their jobs. In addition, most European countries have free preschool programs for children from the time they are 2½ years old (Kamerman, 1989).

In the 1970s a number of American scholars visited, studied, and reported on child care and early education programs around the world, including those in such European countries as Belgium, France, Germany, the United Kingdom, and Sweden (Almy, 1975). The spate of publications that resulted appears to have strengthened the convictions of child care advocates in this country. More recently the first report from a study of the child care and education of young children in 14 countries became available (Olmstead & Weikart, 1989). Much, it seems, can be learned from the experience of other countries, but the question of why the United States has moved forward so much more slowly remains puzzling.

Undoubtedly, important factors in the reluctance in the United States to come to terms with child care are its size and its diversity, and, related to the latter, various myths about families. The years following Nixon's veto of the Comprehensive Child Development proposal were marked by steadily increasing employment of women, paralleled by increasing numbers of single-parent families. As the demand for day care grew, states and communities found themselves hard put to even begin to meet the needs. This was true despite a 30 percent increase in the number of day care centers for 3- to 5-year-olds from 14,000 in 1970 to 18,300 in 1976 (Levine, 1982). Increasing scarcity and the inability to enforce standards led to chaos and sometimes tragedy.

On the other hand, ingenuity sometimes led to solutions worth continuing. An example is the development of systems of information and referral where parents can find out what kinds of child care are available. Scarce resources also led community agencies, child care advocates, and concerned parents to make sure that facilities were being used to the fullest and were offering services that parents desired. Further, to a greater extent than ever before, those groups learned to work together cooperatively, rather than competitively, sharing the goal of adequate care for all children.

Proof of the effectiveness of this sort of collaboration was evident in the growing attention the media gave child care and in demands for legislation at local, state, and eventually federal levels. Proposed bills came from both sides of the political spectrum. Especially noteworthy at the federal level was the Act for Better Child Care Services (ABC) which, according to Kahn (1988), had no major defects and received "extraordinary support." As Kahn predicted, the coalition of organizations supporting ABC held through 1989 and continued through 1990, when both houses of Congress passed Child Care bills. By late October the two houses had reached agreement but the outcome at the hands of the President was uncertain.

Whatever the outcome of further efforts to provide more support for child care, it is clear that children will be affected. Their opportunities for play and the nature of their play can be expected to reflect the kinds of early care and education available to them.

In retrospect, in the years since Froebel brought children's play to the attention of educators, interest in it has grown slowly but steadily. Those who have valued it have done so for a variety of reasons. Some value its spontaneity and creativity. Others see it as a channel for influencing various aspects of development. At the same time it has never been without some detractors, including those who see it as appropriate only for the youngest children. Now, in the last decade of the twentieth century, new questions about play arise even as social changes precipitate possible new dangers to it.

Current Realities

As the 1990s begin, the need for more child care facilities continues unabated. More than half of all married mothers with infants younger than 2 years are in the labor force, as are 50 percent of all mothers of preschool children. Estimates indicate that by 1995 two-thirds of preschool children and four out of five school age children will have mothers who are employed outside the home (Children's Defense Fund, 1988).

As more and more mothers go to work, care for children in the homes of relatives or neighbors becomes less available. Waiting lists for subsidized child care grow longer and longer. The pinch affects middle class families as well as those in poverty. These factors are reflected in changing attitudes toward child care. The pressures for child care and early education that brought the ABC coalition together at the federal level are equally apparent in many states. As Grubb describes in Chapter 2 of this volume, some 20 states have recently passed legislation relating to early education.

One source of pressure has been the fact that "businesses are finding their productivity affected by workers' child care needs" (Quality Child Care, 1989, p. 6). Some corporations are not only establishing resource and referral services, offering child care benefits, and funding community projects, but also "forming partnerships with other business, civic groups, and the public sector to improve community child care systems and to spread awareness that *this is a social imperative*" (p. 6, emphasis added).

While the United States has until recently been laggard in facing the problem of child care, it should be noted that what appears to be an acute crisis is by no means limited to this country. "Worldwide, as in the U.S., the expanding need for child care is related to an increase in labor force participation by women and to an increase in the number of single parent households" (Olmstead, 1988, p. 1). Later phases of the study of child care and education in 14 countries (Olmstead & Weikart, 1989) will consider how 3½- to 4½-year-old children spend their time away from their parents and examine the effects of variations.

As more and more children participate in early education and care for extended periods of the day, the traditional context for their development and socialization is changing. Formerly much early socialization was informal, based largely on interaction with parents and in spontaneous play with siblings. Such play was monitored more or less indirectly by parents, relatives, neighbors, and teachers, who could reasonably ensure children's safety at home, on neighborhood streets, and in parks and playgrounds.

The possible effects of increased time in child care institutions are largely unknown. Certainly, however, much will depend on the kinds of experiences the children have in their extended hours in school or center. To what extent will it be child centered and to what extent adult directed? Will it build on or run counter to the experiences children have in their limited time with their parents?

Consideration of the possibilities must take into account the complex diversity that characterizes present-day American society. In any one classroom, children may represent cultures from all over the world. For example, children in one San Francisco school come from homes where as many as 30 different languages are spoken.

In some homes play is the prerogative of young children. In other homes, very young children contribute to the work of the family as soon as they have the most elementary skills. Religion makes a difference in many family living patterns and in what parents expect from child care. Parents may, for example, not wish their children to be exposed to fantasy in books or stories. They may forbid the celebration of holidays and birthdays.

How the issue of diversity is dealt with constitutes a major challenge in the extension of child care to more and more children. It is, however, but one of many challenges that are apparent when resources and apparent needs are examined.

Research Evidence

Child care centers are not new, nor have they lacked the examination provided by scientific research. Clarke-Stewart (1987) comments that the research has come in waves. The first wave considered possible harm or benefit from such care. The second wave asked abut the effects of different kinds of care. The third, or contemporary, wave considers

how child care qualities in combination with family characteristics produce effects in children's development.

Wave 1 research showed that *quality* child care (measured by ratings
of child care environments) is not harmful and may, in the case of children from low income families, be associated with cognitive gains. Wave
2 research appears to have alerted researchers to the importance of variables not previously considered or measured. Accordingly, Wave 3 research has given some attention to measures of children's social competence and adjustment as well as their cognition and language. It has
considered children's interactions with their care-givers and peers, and
has gone beyond group size and child/care-giver ratios to look at care-
givers' experience and stability as well as their education and training.
These studies affirm the importance of quality in child care, but they
also raise many questions and suggest the need for new kinds of research
to address them.

Relatively few studies, for example, have used direct observation of
group settings, and fewer still have continued observation over a long
period. Few have been concerned with the direct influence of the social
and ecological features of group setting on children's play. The importance of the social processes at work as children interact with peers and
teachers and as they engage in organized learning experiences is increasingly recognized. However, few researchers have been able to give
detailed attention to such processes.

As Phillips (1987) points out, most studies have been limited to a
single site (or often a single program). Considering the diversity in child
care programs and family backgrounds, this fact seriously restricts the
generalizations that can be made.

Since child care represents a collaboration between the staff and the
parents, it is surprising to find that neither group's concerns are specifically represented in most of the research. Teachers and care-givers are
most instrumental to programs. What parents want for their children and
how they see its realization in a program are also essential factors in the
program's success and presumably its influences on the children.

While child development research has not yet addressed many of
the questions that need to be answered as center day care becomes more
widespread, certain changes in the assumptions underlying the research
bode well for the future. Hetherington (1983), as editor of the volume of
the *Handbook of Child Psychology* dealing with socialization, personality, and social development, comments on the nature of these changes.
She notes that in contrast to the 1970 volume of the *Handbook*, "children are no longer seen as passive objects of socialization" but as "active

participants in shaping their life experiences and social development"
(p. ix). At the same time psychologists are increasingly aware that "human development can be understood only in terms of the social, cultural, and historical context of the child's life" (p. ix). Finally, she states that scientific method no longer rests as exclusively on experimental and laboratory studies. Rather, "more diverse methods and varied settings are being used in the study of children" (pp. viii, ix).

Hetherington might have added that a chapter on children's play appeared in the *Handbook* for the first time, reflecting increasing interest in play as a topic for research. The conveners of the symposium on Play and the Social Context of Development in Early Care and Education knew that play was also a topic of great concern to many practitioners of early education and care. Many teachers, frequently pushed to support their play curricula, were asking good, often researchable, questions about play, but they did not find the help they sought in the child development resources available to them (Monighan-Nourot, Scales, Van Hoorn & Almy, 1987, pp. 7–10). Perhaps the time had come to bring researchers, with their recently found flexibility, together with teachers who had questions.

The Status of Early Childhood Teachers

Since the democratization of the nursery school began under WPA in the 1930s the requirements for employment in early education and care have varied widely. Certification standards that apply to kindergarten and primary teachers in the public schools are usually not applicable to child care workers and nursery school teachers.

The safety of children younger than elementary school age and the length of the child care day necessitate the presence of one or more adults, who may or may not be qualified to act as head teachers, in addition to the head teacher. The National Association for the Education of Young Children (1984), in an attempt to clarify different roles and related training, has described four levels of early childhood staff. These range from "teacher assistant," a high school graduate trained on the job, to "associate teacher" holding an associate degree in Early Childhood Education or Child Development, or a National Child Development Associate credential, to "early childhood teacher" holding a baccalaureate degree in Early Childhood Education or Child Development. The latter assumes chief responsibility for a group of children. With three years' experience in the field and/or an appropriate advanced degree, an early childhood teacher may qualify to be an "early childhood specialist."

In practice, because of the great demand for child care personnel and the lack of consistent state standards, many centers function with "teachers" who lack appropriate qualifications. Some states require only a high school diploma, while others are specific about early childhood education and development backgrounds. States also vary widely in expectations for teacher performance. For example, "Texas requires only one adult for every seven 3- or 4-year-olds" (Lewin, 1989, p. 91).

Considering the wide variation in standards, and the fact that child care is often considered women's work of little economic value, it is not surprising to find that child care workers rank, along with gas station attendants, near the bottom of the occupational scale. The National Child Care Staffing Study (Whitebook, Howes, & Phillips, 1989), examining the quality of care in 227 centers in five metropolitan areas, found that the average hourly wage in 1988 was $5.35. On an annual basis this would amount to a total income of a little less than the poverty level for a family of three. Nevertheless, child care workers are, on the average, better educated than women workers at other low occupational levels. Unfortunately, more years of education do not pay off very well even for teachers and directors, who, on the average, earn only $1.03 more per hour than assistant teachers and aides.

In the circumstances, frequent turnover of staff is also characteristic of many child care centers, creating frustration for other staff and confusion for children. The National Child Care Staffing Study revealed an average annual turnover rate of 37 percent, and found that children in centers with high turnover rates spent more time in aimless wandering and less time in social activities with peers than did children in centers with stable staffs (Whitebook, Howes, & Phillips, 1989).

This is a grim picture. It contrasts sharply with the optimistic views held by well-qualified nursery school teachers when that field began to expand in the 1930s. According to Finkelstein's examination of the heritage of today's early childhood educators, they

> are the recipients of a problematic professional legacy mired in a historical tradition of child advocacy; economic unselfishness; political powerlessness; commitment to interdisciplinary research (having marginal interests in several fields and making the realization of common goals complicated); and narrow concepts of moral, cultural, political, and economic possibility for women. (1988, pp. 24–25)

This heritage need not be questioned, but there is evidence that changes are under way.

NAEYC: *Advocate for Children and Teachers*

The recent history of the National Association for the Education of Young Children (NAEYC) shows that early childhood educators are becoming more aware of the "definitional and professional bind" (Finkelstein, 1988) in which they have been caught. NAEYC, growing from 200 to 60,000 members in the 60 years of its existence, is not the only organization in which early childhood teachers participate. However, it probably most accurately represents the field's diversity.

Finkelstein describes the double bind faced by early childhood teachers:

> On the one hand they identify professionalism with the scientific application of child development principles to formal educational settings for the very young—kindergartens, child care centers, Head Start programs— thus linking practice to professional knowledge. On the other hand, they fail to identify professionalism with the acquisition of power and status, thus failing to transform clinical authority into humane and just environments for young children. (1988, p. 25)

In the last decade NAEYC has pushed harder than before in its efforts to link practice to knowledge. Examples are its examination of teacher roles (described above), the setting of standards for teacher education, and the establishment of the National Academy of Early Childhood Education Programs, which enables child care programs to initiate self-study assessment leading toward accreditation.

At least some of these efforts appear to be paying off in increased power and status. The number of programs seeking accreditation in the National Academy is growing steadily. NAEYC's criteria for developmentally appropriate practice in early childhood programs serving children from birth through age 8 have been well received in a period when federal and state standards have been missing or disregarded.

The concept of developmental appropriateness, as defined by NAEYC, has two dimensions. One relates to age and derives from human development research indicating "universal, predictable sequences of growth and change that occur in children during the first nine years of life" (Bredekamp, 1987, p. 2). Knowledge of these sequences as they occur in physical, emotional, social, and cognitive development provides a framework for teachers to use in making provisions for learning environments and experiences. The second dimension of the concept of developmental appropriateness has to do with the individual child:

> Each child is a unique person with an individual pattern and timing of growth, as well as individual personality, learning style, and family back-

ground. . . . [Appropriate] experiences should match the [individual] child's developing abilities, while also challenging the child's interest and understanding (p. 2)

NAEYC spells out appropriate and also inappropriate practice in fairly concrete terms; for example, "adults provide many opportunities for 3s to play by themselves, next to another child [parallel play] or with one or two other children," contrasted with "adults expect children [3-year-olds] to expect to participate in whole group activities. . . . They do not allow children to leave the large group activity" (Bredekamp, 1987, p. 48). Similarly explicit and detailed criteria are applied to all aspects of education and care beginning with infancy and extending through age 8. The criteria, representing the suggestions of hundreds of early childhood professionals, have been well received. Grubb commented during the symposium discussion that "developmentally appropriate has become a common phrase in Washington" and in some states has also begun to influence early elementary school programs.

The concept of developmental appropriateness has great potential for improving practice, but realization of the concept will not be easy. A teacher who has a good understanding of age appropriateness must also make many subtle judgments about the developing abilities of individual children and about those emerging abilities as they relate to other children in the group. The teacher must also establish constructive relationships with parents to facilitate development. To deepen and strengthen the knowledge and practical skills of teachers and directors now in the work force as well as those who are yet to be recruited presents a great challenge even in the unlikely circumstance of truly adequate funding.

Nevertheless, NAEYC seems positively inclined toward moving ahead. It has even begun to consider its power and status problems somewhat more directly than before. Issues related to the financial inequities of child care workers are being discussed in its journal, *Young Children,* and in sessions at the annual conference.

With all its diversity, all its problems, and all its proposed solutions the field of early education and care is dynamic and vital. It was this impression that led to the Symposium, "Play and the Social Context of Development in Early Care and Education."

References

Almy, M. (1975). *The early childhood educator at work.* New York: McGraw-Hill.
Beck, R. (1982). Beyond the stalemate in child care public policy. In E. F. Zigler &

E. W. Gordon (Eds.), *Day care: Scientific and social policy issues* (pp. 307–337). Boston: Auburn House.

Berrueta-Clement, J., Schweinhart, L. J., Barnett, W. S., Epstein, A. S., & Weikart, D. P. (1984). Changed lives: The effects of the Perry Preschool Program on youths through age 19. *Monographs of the High/Scope Educational Research Foundation, 8.* Ypsilanti, MI: High/Scope Press.

Bloom, B. (1964). *Stability and change in human characteristics.* New York: Wiley.

Bredekamp, S. (Ed.). (1987). *Developmentally appropriate practice in early childhood programs serving children from birth through age 8* (expanded ed.). Washington, DC: National Association for the Education of Young Children.

Bruner, J. (1960). *The process of education.* Cambridge, MA: Harvard University Press.

Children's Defense Fund. (1988). *A call for action to make our nation safe for children: A briefing book on the status of children in 1988.* Washington, DC: Children's Defense Fund.

Clarke-Stewart, K. A. (1987). In search of consistencies in child care research. In D. A. Phillips (Ed.), *Quality in child care: What does research tell us?* (pp. 105–120). Washington, DC: National Association for the Education of Young Children.

El'konin, D. (1966). Symbolics and its function in the play of children. *Soviet Education, 8,* 35–41.

Finkelstein, B. (1988). The revolt against selfishness: Women and the dilemmas of professionalism in early childhood education. In B. Spodek, O. N. Saracho, & D. Peters (Eds.), *Professionalism and the early childhood practitioner* (pp. 10–25). New York: Teachers College Press.

Haskins, R. (1989). Beyond metaphor: The efficacy of early childhood education. *American Psychologist, 44*(2), 274–282.

Hetherington, E. M. (1983). Preface. In P. H. Mussen & E. M. Hetherington (Eds.), *Handbook of child psychology: Vol. 4. Socialization, personality and social development* (pp. viii, ix), New York: Wiley.

Hunt, J. M. (1961). *Intelligence and experience.* New York: Ronald Press.

Kahn, A. J. (1988, December). The ABC legislative approach should be preserved in 1989. *CDF Reports* (monthly newsletter of the Children's Defense Fund).

Kamerman, S. B. (1989). An international overview of preschool programs. *Phi Delta Kappan, 71*(2), 135–137.

Leontiev, A. N. (1981). *Problems of the development of the mind.* Moscow: Progress Publishers.

Levine, J. A. (1982). The prospects and dilemmas of child care information and referrals. In E. F. Zigler & E. W. Gordon (Eds.), *Day care: Scientific and policy issues* (pp. 378–401). Boston: Auburn House.

Lewin, T. (1989, January 29). Small tots, big biz. *The New York Times Magazine,* 30–31, 89–92.

Monighan-Nourot, P., Scales, B., Van Hoorn, J., & Almy, M. (1987). *Looking at children's play: A bridge between theory and practice.* New York: Teachers College Press.

National Association for the Education of Young Children. (1984). Position statement on nomenclature, salaries, benefits, and the status of the early childhood profession. *Young Children, 40*(1), 52–55.

National Center for Education Statistics, Offices of Education Research and Improvement. (1988). *Digest of education statistics.* Washington, DC: U. S. Department of Education.

Olmstead, P. (1988, Spring/Summer). The many worlds of today's preschoolers. *High/Scope Resource: A Magazine for Educators, 7*(2), 1, 10–12.

Olmstead, P. P., & Weikart, D. P. (Eds.). (1989). *How nations serve young children: Profiles of child care and education in 14 countries.* Ypsilanti, MI: High/Scope Press.

Osborn, D. K. (1980). *Early childhood education in historical perspective.* Athens, GA: Education Associates.

Phillips, D. A. (Ed.). (1987). *Quality in child care: What does research tell us?* Washington, DC: National Association for the Education of Young Children.

Quality child care: It's a business issue. (1989, January/February). *The International Child Resource Bulletin,* p. 6.

Rubin, K., Fein, G., & Vandenberg, B. (1983). Play. In P. H. Mussen & E. M. Hetherington (Eds.), *Handbook of child psychology: Vol. 4. Socialization, personality, and social development* (pp. 693–774). New York: Wiley.

Spodek, B. (1986). *Today's kindergarten: Exploring the knowledge base, expanding the curriculum.* New York: Teachers College Press.

Sutton-Smith, B. (1971). The playful modes of knowing. In *Play: The child strives toward self-realization. Proceedings of a conference.* Washington, DC: National Association for the Education of Young Children.

United Nations. (1948). *Declaration of the rights of the child.* (Adopted 1959).

Vygotsky, L. S. (1966). Play and its role in the mental development of the child. *Soviet Psychology, 1,* 16–18.

Weber, E. (1984). *Ideas influencing early childhood education: A theoretical analysis.* New York: Teachers College Press.

Whitebook, M., Howes, C., & Phillips, D. (1989). *Who cares? Child care teachers and the quality of care in America: Executive summary, National Child Care Staffing Study.* Oakland, CA: Child Care Employee Project.

CHAPTER 2

Policy Issues
Surrounding Quality and Content
in Early Care and Education

W. NORTON GRUBB

The recent upsurge of interest in early childhood programs is both welcome to children's advocates and, given the hostility toward children in the 1980s (Grubb & Lazerson, 1988), somewhat unexpected. At the federal level, more than 80 bills related to early childhood have been introduced (Robins, 1988), some of them—notably the Act for Better Child Care Services (the ABC bill, HR3660/S 1885)—with considerable support; and new federal funds supporting child care for "workfare" participants have been authorized by the Welfare Reform Act of 1988. Since 1979, at least 20 states have enacted some form of early childhood education, and a few others have used their existing school aid mechanisms to fund early childhood programs in the schools (Marx & Seligson, 1988). Even the business community, long indifferent or even hostile to social programs, has added its support of early childhood programs as valuable "investment strategies" (Committee for Economic Development, 1987).

Still, many issues surrounding early care and education remain undecided. Issues surrounding funding have not yet been resolved; even if major federal legislation such as the ABC bill does pass, the resources it provides will be tiny compared with the need. Substantial confusion persists about early childhood programs—about their basic purposes, their costs and effects, and what constitutes good quality. The content of early childhood programs—the mix of "care" and "education," the balance of play and more "school-like" activities, the appropriate roles for teach-

This paper is drawn in part from earlier papers, including Grubb, 1988, 1989a, and 1989b.

ers—is the subject of continuing battles. Even if they are resolved, the issues are particularly difficult to influence through public policy.

Here I examine some basic policy issues in early childhood educa-tion, particularly those surrounding quality and content, including the appropriate role for play-oriented activities, which are the focus of this volume. I first review the different purposes of early childhood programs both historically and currently. The content of early childhood programs poses critical choices both for federal policy and for states, with some resolution necessary of the substantive differences between preschool and child care programs, and between elementary educators and early childhood educators—differences that are examined next. Finally, I out-line the policy options available, particularly those that might influence the quality and content of programs.

The Strands of Early Childhood Education:
Historical and Current Manifestations

The proposal to extend schooling downward to younger children is an idea that every generation seems to rediscover. Different motives—in turn, educational, economic, and reformist, sometimes stressing the needs of children and sometimes forgetting the child in favor of adult concerns—have prompted these proposals. Many have died, but their legacies have included models that continue to influence and confuse us.

One of the earliest justifications for educating young children was the compensatory rationale. In the growing cities of the early nineteenth century, philanthropists began to support charity schools to provide po-litical and moral education for poor children whose parents "seldom keep any government in their family" and who therefore "unavoidably contract habits of idleness and mischief and wickedness" (Kaestle, 1983). Others, intent on rescuing poor children from their allegedly harmful parents as early as possible, instituted infant schools for those as young as 18 months. The infant school movement, most active in the 1830s and 1840s, died out as the view spread that mothers should care for their own children. But its essential vision—that schools should take in children as young as possible, to teach them and protect them from the evil influences of home—lived on in many forms. The movement for the kindergarten, began in the 1880s, also developed as part of urban reform to teach poor children the values of industriousness, cleanliness, discipline, and cooperation, and was then incorporated into the public schools as a way of expanding their funding and scope (Grubb & Lazer-son, 1977; Lazerson, 1972). More recently the institution of Head Start represents yet another attempt to compensate for the deficiencies of parents by educating their children earlier, and most of the recent state preschool programs also have an explicitly compensatory purpose.

A very different institution for young children developed at the turn of the century, again in response to the wretched conditions of urban slums. The day nurseries established by settlement houses were, like the charity kindergartens, directed at low income children. They had two purposes: "to provide a shelter for the children of mothers dependent on their own exertions for their daily bread; [but] also to rear useful citizens among the class represented by the children we reach" (Steinfels, 1973, Chapter 2). However, mothers were supposed to be caring for their own children rather than working, and the day nurseries therefore became associated with pathological families and the problems of the "unworthy poor." While the day nurseries themselves declined under this stigma, their legacy has been the "welfare" or "custodial" model of child care, providing extended care so that mothers of poor children can work (Grubb & Lazerson, 1977).

The "developmental" model of programs for young children was born in the nursery school movement of the 1920s. Nursery schools emerged as complements to mothering rather than "mother substitutes" like the day nurseries; the nursery schools were part-day rather than full-day programs and were directed at the cognitive enrichment of middle class children (National Society for the Study of Education, 1929). Because of their firm links to parents and to middle class children, the nursery schools avoided the stigma of the day nurseries and provided a strong institutional image of what early childhood programs should be. With their success and the decline of the day nurseries, the split widened between self-consciously "developmental" programs for young children and more obviously "custodial" programs.

Other institutional developments for young children were temporary responses to specific crises. During the Depression, the Work Projects Administration (wPA) established a series of federally funded nursery schools, primarily to provide employment for teachers. Since they were administered through state departments of education and local school boards, they developed an educational orientation. But they ended when the Depression was over and federal funds ceased. During World War II the Lanham Act provided funding for day care centers to facilitate the employment of mothers for the war effort. While some of these centers were run by schools, care of children during working hours was their central purpose. Like the wPA nurseries, they folded as soon as the crisis was over, with no pretense that what had been acceptable during wartime might continue.

Once the kindergarten had become part of the public schools, the idea of extending schooling to even younger children kept reappearing. In 1945 the Educational Policies Committee of the National Education Association recommended that schooling be extended to 3- and 4-year-olds, "closely integrated with the rest of the program of public education," especially to provide education for children "whose parents are not able by circumstance, nature, or training to give them the values inherent in a carefully directed program" (Educational Policies Committee, 1945). These proposals failed to have any general influence, as they were blocked by the ideology that mothers should remain in the home. In the 1960s, however, programs for young children went through a renaissance. New research—especially J. McVickar Hunt's *Intelligence and Experience* (1961) and Benjamin Bloom's *Stability and Change in Human Characteristics* (1964)—was widely cited as confirming that the early years are critical and that slow development in those years may be irremediable. Another "crisis"—once more, the recognition of poverty—spurred the federal government to action. The Head Start program, a centerpiece of the War on Poverty, was explicitly educational and compensatory (Zigler & Valentine, 1979). Others proposed a similar model for all children; for example, the Education Policies Commission of the National Education Association recommended in 1966 that "all children should have an opportunity to go to school at public expense at the age of four," relying on the convention of how crucial the first five years of life are to subsequent development (Frost, 1969).

Other federal programs of the 1960s aimed at young children were more obviously attempts to provide child care. Part of the War on Poverty was the "services strategy," to provide various training, counseling, and social services to help children escape poverty. The child care programs funded, which were explicitly intended to reduce poverty, became the archetype of the "welfare" approach to child care, with low costs and custodial care more important than education. Thus the major federal programs of the 1960s left the division between "developmental" programs and welfare-related "custodial" programs intact.

With early childhood programs now established and increasing numbers of women working, proposals and legislative initiatives multiplied during the 1970s. Major federal legislation to expand support for child care was introduced in 1971, 1975, 1976, and 1979; all proposals were defeated, partly because of attacks from anti-feminist conservatives and partly because of reactions against government intervention and the Great Society. In the midst of battles over federal funding, the American Federation of Teachers (AFT) proposed that the public schools should control federally subsidized early childhood and day care pro-

grams, arguing that the schools were dedicated to education, that professionalism would improve the low quality of existing care, and that the
schools already had a well-developed organizational structure (AFT,
1976). However, with a surplus of teachers looming, many interpreted
this argument as a self-serving attempt to put unemployed teachers back
to work. The early childhood community rose to the attack, arguing that
elementary teachers were inappropriately trained for young children
and that the schools were rigid, uncommitted to young children, and hostile to parents (Fishhaut & Pastor, 1977; Grubb & Lazerson, 1977). The
episode revealed the deep rift between educators and the early childhood community, though the demise of federal legislation made the debate moot.

The legacy of this history, then, was fragmentation and paradox.
The historical division continued between developmental programs for
young children and custodial programs providing care while parents
worked. Another split emerged between custodial care associated with
efforts to reduce welfare costs, and therefore of the lowest possible cost
and quality, and the ideal of high quality child care that most working
parents seek. Still another division, between elementary educators and
early childhood educators was reopened for the first time since the kindergarten movement. With more women working, the need for more
child care of better quality has been generally acknowledged, but has
also been fought bitterly by those arguing that mothers belong at home.

In many ways, the recent interest in early childhood programs rep-
licates these historical strands. One source of support, of course, has
been the continued increase in working mothers. In 1986, 54.4% of
mothers with children under 6 were in the labor force, up from 46.8% in
1980, 38.8% in 1975, and 25.3% in 1965 (Hayghe, 1986; U.S. Bureau
of Labor Statistics, 1986). To be sure, these trends are hardly novel,
since the participation of women in the labor force has been increasing
at least since 1890; but passing the magical 50% has clarified that the
trend is irreversible and working is now the norm for women rather than
an aberration. About two-thirds of women with children under 6 work
full time, so that part-time programs—like traditional preschools and
nursery schools—are insufficient.

A different strand of support has emphasized the wisdom of educating children earlier, particularly low income and other disadvantaged
children—the legacy of the compensatory rationale. The movement for
"excellence" with its emphasis on higher academic standards has coex-
isted with a growing alarm about dropout rates and illiteracy. Earlier
schooling promises one way of meeting simultaneously the needs of re-
mediation and the demands for excellence. The link between the two

had been made most explicit by those states adopting preschool programs as part of more general educational reforms and by the National Governors' Association Task Force on Readiness to Meet the New Standards (NGA, 1986).

Finally, the "welfare" approach to child care—providing care so that women can work to support their families—has emerged once again in the Family Support Act of 1988. As part of a range of social services, job training, and education to enable welfare recipients to move into employment, the legislation provides expanded funds for child care—a welcome source of resources in a system that has been chronically underfunded. However, as welfare-to-work programs have been implemented in a number of states, the pressures on such child care programs have become clear: Programs to prepare welfare mothers (and some fathers) for employment typically aim to get them into relatively low-skilled work, paying near the minimum wage; but at such wage levels independence requires them to use child care of relatively low cost. Caught between the high cost of child care and the low wages considered "realistic" for welfare clients, the welfare system is likely to replicate once again the low quality, custodial approach to care.

Thus the major reasons for current interest in young children replicate the historical divisions among early childhood programs. Those concerned with middle class working parents are the heirs of both the custodial model and the developmental model, seeking to serve those needing care but wanting high quality programs. Those concerned with the independence of welfare recipients replicate the arguments of the custodial approach. Those promoting the compensatory education of young children continue to argue the benefits of earlier intervention for poor and other disadvantaged children. But right away there is a conflict between these strands of thought. The compensatory strand usually promotes half-day programs, lasting 2½ to 3 hours a day during the school year; but these are of little help to full-time working parents. Purely custodial programs may not provide the self-consciously developmental experiences envisioned by early childhood educators and proponents of the Perry Preschool, and they do not provide the array of services included in the Head Start model.

But in many ways it is no longer appropriate to maintain these distinctions. One reason is that the reality of working mothers has undermined the usefulness of the older developmental model; nursery schools, which used to be half-day programs, have generally evolved into full-day programs for working parents. Many children—especially most "at-risk" children, whose mothers are more likely to be single, poor, and working full time—can no longer attend half-day programs. (For example, in

Texas many superintendents felt that the required prekindergarten programs would be underenrolled because working mothers would find it impossible to have their children attend a half-day program; see Grubb et al., 1985, Chapter 8.) Conversely, the view that the early years are important to development has become conventional wisdom. In my experience, most child care centers have some conscious policy about a developmental curriculum; many devote some time during the day to formal instruction, and most state a variety of developmental goals for children. There is no real difference between the activities in *good* child care facilities—both day care centers and family day care homes—and self-consciously developmental preschool programs. Many child care workers call themselves teachers and consider themselves professionals, resenting deeply the common notion that they are merely "babysitters." The notion that child care is intrinsically custodial is badly out of date.

Above all, the idea that early childhood programs are either developmental or custodial can only limit these programs. After all, schools are rich, multipurpose institutions, with economic, political, moral, and avocational purposes coexisting. Early childhood programs at their best are similarly rich and multifaceted, providing cognitive, physical, social, and emotional development for children; security and full-time care, which are important for working parents; substantial cooperation between parents and care-givers; and parental education for those seeking different ways of interacting with their children. The best programs provide early, noncompetitive, and supportive experiences for children of different races and class backgrounds, rather than segregating children. To search for a single purpose for early childhood programs is to destroy this vision of what early childhood programs can be.

One laudable goal of both federal and state policy, therefore, would be to bridge the deep divisions among different conceptions of early childhood programs. Of course, a variety of fiscal, philosophical, and administrative barriers to integrating the strands of early childhood programs exist, none of them easy to topple. But the goal of integration is important, since the alternative is a limited vision of what programs for young children can be and programs that are less effective than they could be.

Philosophy and Turf:
The Split Between Early Childhood and
Elementary Education

Another split in approaches to young children has been replicated in recent developments. At least since the turn of the century and the kindergarten movement, a division has existed between teachers and administrators in programs for young children and those in the elementary schools. This split emerged with some force in the 1970s, and the early childhood community still fears that public school control of programs for young children could ruin early childhood education (Bredekamp, 1987; Morgan, 1985; NAEYC, 1986).

Not surprisingly, one argument between the two camps has involved turf—control over jobs and revenues. However, the turf issues should not be as serious at the moment, because there is a shortage rather than a surplus of school teachers. Instead, the deepest differences are those of philosophy, method, and purpose. They are difficult to reconcile because practices deeply embedded in the schools and resistant to change are anathema to early childhood educators.

To be sure, there is enormous variety in both early childhood programs and elementary education. There are rigid and didactic forms of early childhood programs, as well as informal, child-oriented elementary classrooms associated with "open classrooms" and the free school movement. But the differences between the two approaches to education are real, and they can be readily seen by contrasting a typical early childhood classroom with an elementary classroom. In child care, children are likely to be moving among different activity centers, with a relatively high noise level. Periodically a teacher will gather all the children for instruction, reading, or some version of assembly (chapel, temple, or a talk by a visitor, such as a firefighter), but instruction is limited to perhaps a half-hour a day and children are usually free to choose their own activities. The progression of activities throughout the day is geared to the abilities and attention spans of small children and the rhythms of child care: Early and late periods tend to be absorbed in free play because the arrival and departure of children can be disruptive; instruction is limited to short periods, usually in mid-morning when young children are most alert; and scheduling is generally flexible. Teachers circulate to make sure that all children are engaged, to provide guidance and informal instruction to individual children (rather than large groups), and to prevent disruptions; they are "guides and facilitators," rather than instructors. Rooms are arranged so that there are areas for privacy as well as "public" areas with different activities. To the untrained observer, there seems to be little planning or structure to the classroom, but in fact structure is pervasive if covert: in the arrangement of the classroom, in the constant monitoring of the teacher and interaction with children, and in the progression of activities throughout the day.

In contrast, elementary classrooms are dominated by lessons taught by teachers to children: "Teacher talk" is pervasive (Sirotnik, 1983). Children are at individual desks, sometimes in "islands" but often in rows; there may be some freedom for children to go to activity centers when they have finished lessons, but children are much less free to choose what to do. In general the noise level is much lower than in early childhood classrooms; order and quiet are intrinsically much more important goals, not merely instrumental to learning. The day begins and ends at prescribed times, and the scheduling of subjects is much more regular and rigid than in child care.

Of course, class size is usually much smaller in early childhood programs compared with the elementary grades. Smaller classes are not simply more pleasant; large classes force upon the teacher an attention to control and order rather than interaction and guidance, and they force instruction to be more formal, group-oriented, and didactic than informal, individualized, and interactive. Large classes also make child-initiated activities more difficult to manage.

The appearance of different classrooms is not simply happenstance; the basic philosophy of teaching and learning in the two settings varies dramatically. (See position statement of the NAEYC, 1986; Bredekamp, 1987.) Most child care centers and preschool programs in this country adopt, even if not consciously, a Piagetian model of children: Children are active learners, who learn by initiating activity and by experimenting (including playing); the teacher's role is to facilitate rather than to direct the child's learning. In contrast, most elementary teachers implicitly follow a behaviorist model, in which the child is a *tabula rasa,* a blank slate onto which lessons are written by the teacher. With the importance of rewards and punishment in the behaviorist model, the schools have developed highly formalized assessment mechanisms, including grades and tests. One deep fear of early childhood educators is that the emphasis on formal evaluation and assessment in the elementary classroom would, if extended to earlier years, bring the devastating experience of failure to young children, with detrimental consequences, including poor self-esteem, lower expectations of subsequent teachers, and placement in lower tracks. Partly because black children so often experience this kind of treatment in the schools, the National Black Child Development Institute (1985) has condemned school sponsorship of early childhood programs as an "incubator for inequality."

Another division involves the scope of education. The elementary grades have focused on basic cognitive skills emphasizing the manipulation of symbols and the mastery of facts. In contrast, early childhood programs uniformly place cognitive skill development—"pre-reading" and "pre-math"—alongside social skills (especially behavior appropriate for group settings), the ability to recognize and control emotions, and the development of fine and gross motor skills. Early childhood advocates generally fear that educators would convert programs for young children into more "school-like" settings by reducing the importance of noncognitive goals and by emphasizing one kind of learning (epitomized by the 3 R's and memorizing facts) over more creative, independent, and active forms of cognition. Certainly the current attention to preschool programs as mechanisms of compensatory education can only strengthen this fear, since the most important criterion of success in compensatory programs is later success in school.

Early childhood advocates place great value on flexibility and variety in programs, since parent schedules, preferences about types of curricula, and the learning styles and personalities of young children vary so much. There is a similar ethic within elementary education: The ideals of local control and individualized instruction express the view that variation within and among classrooms should respond to local conditions, parental preferences, and student differences. But despite these claims, elementary classrooms look remarkably the same across the country, with little variation in teaching methods or content (Sirotnik, 1983). Certainly hours of operation—a crucial issue to working parents—vary only in trivial ways. As a result, early childhood advocates have complained that school control of preschools would standardize and rigidify current practices.

Finally, early childhood educators and elementary educators differ on the roles of parents. A shibboleth of early childhood practice is that parents must be involved in the care of their children, because parents know their children best and because consistency and support between home and program are crucial. Many advocates like to cite evidence, from early Head Start evaluations and other sources, that parental involvement enhances the development of children. Early childhood advocates fear that if the public schools, with weak commitment to parental involvement and a history of demeaning some parents (especially parents of poor and minority children), ran preschool programs, they would abandon any pretext of including parents. On the other hand, parent participation in child care and preschool programs has been difficult to develop because working parents are pressed for time, some administrators resent the additional burdens parents impose, and some facilities—especially proprietary day care centers—will brook no intrusions on their operations.

In sum, the differences between elementary education and early childhood education reflect basic differences in conceptions of learning, in the roles of parents and teachers, in the training necessary for teachers, and in purposes. The question for policy is not whether these differences exist, but whether they can be contained and narrowed. Then it would be possible to use the institutional structure of the educational system—certainly the best-developed structure available, and the only institution now providing social programs to large numbers of children—to administer early childhood programs while still ensuring that the content of these programs is appropriate to young children.

One way of answering this question is to examine early childhood programs operated by the public schools. The programs recently initiated by states provide some evidence. Most of these programs have at least two elements crucial to the success of early childhood programs: Their teacher–pupil ratios are high, around 1:10 (with the conspicuous exceptions of Texas, Maine, and New Jersey); and most of them require or prefer teachers with early childhood training. In addition, most of them require some form of parental involvement, consistent with good practice in early childhood programs (Gnezda & Robinson, 1986). Once in operation these programs may bend in the direction of elementary goals and methods, but at the outset they indicate that programs for young children controlled by the schools are not just downward extensions of kindergarten.

Other evidence comes from early childhood programs that have been operated by the public schools for longer periods of time. About 20 percent of Head Start programs are administered by school districts, and there are few differences between the programs run by school districts and by other agencies. School district-based programs more often require a B.A. degree of their teachers and tend to pay higher salaries because they often use a school teacher salary scale, but no other differences seem to emerge. Instead, because of the great variety of Head Start programs, inter-group differences are small compared with intra-group differences (Esther Kresh, Administration for Children, Youth, and Families, oral communication). Over the past two decades, some local districts have incorporated a variety of early childhood programs, including preschool programs, funded with Chapter I revenues, after-school programs, and parent education programs, indicating that schools can be flexible and imaginative in their approaches to young children. A study of exemplary school-based programs concluded that they displayed the same range of quality as those run by other agencies, suggesting that the institutional sponsorship of early childhood programs is less important than the qualifications of teachers and the quality of leadership (Mitchell, 1988).

California provides the best evidence about the ability of schools to develop good early childhood programs. School districts have operated full-day programs for children aged 2 to 5 ever since World War II. The Children's Centers are relatively well funded, with higher teacher salaries and teacher–child ratios (and therefore higher costs) than most child care centers. They provide full-day child care, but they also emphasize cognitive development and usually have well-developed curricula and assessment methods. Compared with community-based child care programs, the Children's Centers are more cognitively oriented, are more consistently pulled in the direction of school-like practices (like curriculum development and more formalized assessment mechanisms), and have slightly less parental involvement. But the potential excesses of school-based programs are generally held in check, because teachers must have a Children's Center permit requiring early childhood education and because an active early childhood community monitors and advises the Children's Centers (Grubb & Lazerson, 1977, updated by conversations with Jack Hailey and June Sale).

At the other extreme, the Texas prekindergarten program enacted in 1984 illustrates the worst fears of early childhood advocates. The legislation, drafted with no consultation from the early childhood community, requires prekindergarten programs in every district with at least 15 eligible children. Districts were generally unprepared for this aspect of the comprehensive reform legislation; many administrators were hostile to early childhood programs as mere "babysitting," very few districts had any experience with early childhood programs, and the Texas Department of Education had no personnel to offer guidance. The maximum class size of 22 children is far in excess of the ratios recommended by early childhood education groups, and a preference for teachers with "teacher of young children" certificates was relaxed because of shortages. Some districts may be able to use state funds to develop strong programs on their own, but the state's legislation does not encourage exemplary programs (Grubb et al., 1985).

Evidently, then, it is possible for the schools to operate exemplary early childhood programs; and it is also possible to legislate inappropriate programs of low quality. Despite the difficulty in legislating quality some legislative direction—ratios, teacher qualifications, and purposes in particular—is absolutely crucial, both as a way of reconciling the conflicts between elementary educators and early childhood advocates and as a way of realizing the benefits of exemplary programs.

Policy Options Affecting the Quality and Content of Early Childhood Programs

Early childhood policy stands at the brink of potentially crucial developments. The intense interest at both the federal and state levels is unmistakable, and most observers feel there will be legislative break-throughs in the next few years. It is impossible to make policy *de novo,* because of existing programs like Title XX and Head Start, but most states and the federal government will have a rare opportunity to estab-lish policies on the basis of sound principles.

Governments at all levels face a variety of policy choices, including decisions about which children to serve, the duration of programs (par-ticularly half-day versus full-day) the funding levels and ancillary ser-vices provided, the specific funding mechanisms used, the choice of ad-ministrative mechanisms, and policies surrounding quality and content, including those related to teacher certification and preparation (Grubb, 1988, 1989b; Schweinhart & Koshel, 1986). However, for those most concerned about the opportunities for play and about play-oriented con-ceptions of development that are the focus of this volume, a variety of policies are crucial for their influence on the quality and content of early childhood programs.

Right at the outset, decisions about quality are embedded in mech-anisms of funding. Over the past few years there has been an active debate about whether federal policy should provide tax credits to par-ents for child care (as President Bush proposed), enabling parents to make all decisions about which programs they use, or whether federal funding should provide direct funding to establish early childhood facil-ities, as the ABC bill does. Advocates of tax credits and other voucher mechanisms like to rely on rhetoric about parental choice, since no one would deny that parents should have a choice about their child's care and education. *If* parents are fully informed about child care options, and *if* sufficient choice exists in a neighborhood, then voucher mechanisms may work well, and parents can choose the quality of care that is most appropriate. But both those assumptions underlying voucher mecha-nisms are problematic: Parents are often badly informed and do not know what to look for in early childhood programs; and in many neigh-borhoods (particularly low income areas) there is a dearth of options. Under these conditions tax credit and voucher mechanisms cannot pos-sibly ensure the quality of programs. In contrast, direct funding of pro-grams can regulate quality directly, and so—from the viewpoint of those who care about content—they are infinitely superior.

Still other choices about quality are embedded in legislative pre-scriptions about adult–child ratios, teacher salaries (which may affect the caliber of teachers and turnover rates), and costs per child. One of the most important aspects of quality, and one of the few that is easily quan-tified, is the adult–child ratio. The National Day Care Study (ABT Asso-ciates, 1979) found that ratios between 1:5 and 1:10 made little difference to program quality, and recommended ratios between 1:8 and 1:10. Above the 1:10 level, however, the study found that quality would deteriorate, and in particular that children showed less persistence and less interest in activities. Consistent with these recommendations, the National Association for the Education of Young Children recommended a ratio of no more than 1:10 for 4- and 5-year-olds, with gradual increases in this ratio as children move into the primary grades. Despite the diversity in practice, some consensus has emerged about acceptable ratios, with a standard of 1:10 the outer limit of most recommendations.

Another crucial aspect of program quality is determined by costs, including teacher salaries (which influence both the quality of teachers and their turnover). In this area a powerful inconsistency has persisted: The greatest excitement about early childhood education has been generated by the Perry Preschool Program and its 7:1 benefit–cost ratio (Berrueta-Clement, Schweinhart, Barnett, Epstein, & Weikart, 1984); but an understanding of its quality and costs—over $6,000 (in current dollars) per child per year for a part-day program, extraordinarily expensive by any standard—has lagged. The benefits of exemplary programs cannot be expected for very different programs or those of low quality: *It is senseless to cite evidence from exemplary, high quality programs and then to enact a program with low spending, low ratios, low salaries, and inadequate teacher preparation.* For those who care about content and quality, therefore, there must be consistency between the evidence about high quality programs and public pressure for high quality programs on the one hand and the level of public resources on the other.

Unfortunately, higher adult–child ratios, higher teacher salaries, and ancillary services are relatively expensive. However, there is at least one aspect of quality that does not require higher expenditures. The National Day Care Study determined that smaller class sizes enhance quality, regardless of the adult–child ratio, because smaller groups reduce distractions and chaos and increase the interaction between teachers and children; thus two classes of 20 are better than one class of 40 children, even with the same number of teachers. Thus a common recommendation is for federal and state standards to incorporate limits on class sizes independently of limits on adult–child ratios.

Still another mechanism for guiding the content of early childhood programs is teacher certification, specifying the education requirements for those working in child development agencies. In this area, there is one unanimous recommendation from the early childhood community and from research on the quality of care: Teachers of young children must have specific training in early childhood development. Such a requirement—without waivers for teachers with elementary teaching certificates—is one way to prevent elementary teachers from being placed in such programs without retraining, as was proposed in the 1970s, and to ensure that programs are not simply downward extensions of kindergarten. A more controversial certification issue emerges from the National Day Care Study finding that the quality of care is a function of specific training in early childhood, not of the number of years of education, implying that individuals with community college certificates and degrees, or with Child Development Associate (CDA) credentials, are appropriate teachers.

The dimensions of quality mentioned so far—ratios, class sizes, expenditure levels, and teacher requirements—are relatively easy to quantify and therefore to regulate in either federal or state policy. Unfortunately, many aspects of good practice in early childhood education cannot be so easily specified; they require sensitivity in working with young children, an ability to understand and react appropriately to the different stages of child development, and a level of energy and a kind of "informed caring" that can be recognized but not regulated. (For an excellent description of the interactions in good and bad early childhood programs, identifying the aspects of state policy that can affect these interactions, see Beardsley, 1990.) To be sure, the purpose of high adult–child ratios and small class sizes is to provide the conditions in which good practices can take place; higher salaries can attract better teachers and allow them to accumulate experience; and requiring specific preparation in child development is intended to teach good practice. Still, the more subtle aspects of quality are difficult to regulate in conventional ways, and other approaches are necessary.

One method is to enhance program quality through the actions of the federal, state, and local administering agencies, through licensing requirements and technical assistance. Licensing is usually interpreted as ensuring minimum health and safety standards rather than enhancing program quality. Technical assistance—consultation, workshops, information about model programs, and access to a network of early childhood practitioners concerned about quality—is a better way to encourage the development of good programs. Of course, technical assistance requires a competent state agency, or some parallel institution with legitimacy. In California, for example, a good deal of technical assistance to early childhood programs is provided by state-supported but privately operated resource and referral agencies.

Publicly funded resource and referral agencies can also provide data to parents, to help them become informed about the facilities available and to educate them about what to look for in a good quality program. With this kind of data parents can also play an *informed* role in ensuring quality—not, as advocates for vouchers would have it, placing the entire burden on parental choice, but rather providing parents information so that they can influence quality along with the regulatory mechanisms of government.

Still another alternative is to adopt the model of accreditation that has been developed for higher education and medical facilities. The National Association for the Education of Young Children has recently established voluntary accreditation involving guidelines for good practice, self-study, and a site visit by "validators" who present their findings to facilities they visit (Bredekamp, 1984). In contrast to licensing, which is associated with requirements and coercion, the accrediting procedure emphasizes advice from peers and can cover aspects of good practice more complex and subtle than those that can be codified in the simpler licensing regulations.

Finally, if early childhood policy is to be integrative, then it must take care not to replicate the divisions that now plague early childhood programs. In particular, early childhood programs should encompass child care during the working day for parents who need that and should also maintain a developmental focus and avoid the indifferent care of much mediocre child care; neither half-day preschool programs nor low quality, custodial child care programs are adequate. It is equally important to support a variety of institutions providing such programs, rather than school districts alone. Formula-based mechanisms for allocating funds to school districts are therefore inappropriate; a better approach would be to develop grants to a variety of public and private agencies, to provide a range of child care programs designed to meet the varying needs of parents—for family day care as well as center-based care, after-school care, sick child care, care for handicapped children and those whose parents have unusual schedules, as well as the more familiar kinds of child care centers. Such an approach would also facilitate the exercise of parental choice, which can be just as readily provided through direct spending mechanisms as through vouchers.

Above all, it is clear that policy toward the quality and content of early childhood programs must be carefully considered and crafted, rather than being left to chance and mischance. Even in states, like California, with relatively well-developed early childhood programs, policy toward quality is weak, inconsistent, and limited by resources, a nonpolicy made up of uncoordinated bits and pieces (Grubb, 1989a). A more coherent approach would be a vast improvement, with a clear delineation of appropriate public measures and those that are best left to parents, providers and their professional associations, and other advisory groups.

It is not hard to see what is good for young children. The accumulated experiences of early childhood programs, the research on program effects and quality, and the broad areas of consensus among parents and those professionals who have thought the hardest about young children provide the materials for knitting together the divisions in the arena of early childhood programs. Then it will be possible to make good on our rhetoric about children as "our most precious natural resources," rather than leaving that rhetoric as evidence of broken promises.

References

ABT Associates. 1979. *Final report of the National Day Care study: Children at the center* (5 vols.). Cambridge, MA: Author.

American Federation of Teachers Task Force on Educational Issues. (1987). *Putting early childhood and day care services into the public schools*. Washington, DC: Author.

Beardsley, L. (1990). *Good day/bad day: The child's experience of child care*. New York: Teachers College Press.

Berrueta-Clement, J., Schweinhart, L. J., Barnett, W. S., Epstein, A. S., & Weikart, D. P. (1984). Changed lives: The effects of the Perry Preschool Program on youths through age 19. *Monographs of the High/Scope Educational Research Foundation, 8*. Ypsilanti, MI: High/Scope Press.

Bloom, B. (1964). *Stability and change in human characteristics*. New York: Wiley.

Bredekamp, S. (1984). *Accreditation criteria and procedures of the National Academy of Early Childhood Programs*. Washington, DC: National Association for the Education of Young Children.

Bredekamp, S. (Ed.). (1987). *Developmentally appropriate practice in early childhood programs serving children from birth through age 8* (expanded ed.). Washington, DC: National Association for the Education of Young Children.

Committee for Economic Development. (1987). *Children in need; Investment strategies for the economically disadvantaged*. New York: Author.

Educational Policies Committee. (1945, December). *Educational services for young children*. Washington, DC: National Education Association.

Fishhaut, E., & Pastor, D. (1977, November). Should the schools be entrusted with preschool education: A critique of the AFT proposals. *School Review, 85,* 38–49.

Frost, J. (1969). *Early childhood reconsidered*. New York: Holt, Rinehart, & Winston.

Gnezda, T., & Robinson, S. (1986, October). *State approaches to early childhood education*. National Conference of State Legislatures, Denver, CO.

Grubb, W. N. (1988, October). *Choices for children: Policy options for state provision of early childhood programs*. Finance Collaborative Working Paper #5,

Education Commission of the States and National Conference of State Legislatures.

Grubb, W. N. (1989a). The conundrums of early childhood and child care programs
in California. In *The conditions of children in California* (pp. 65–95). University of California, Berkeley: Policy Analysis for California Education.

Grubb, W. N. (1989b). Young children face the state: Issues and options for early
childhood programs. *American Journal of Education, 97,* 358–397.

Grubb, W. N., & Lazerson, M. (1977, November). Child care, government financing, and the public schools: Lessons from the California Children's Centers.
School Review, 86, 5–37.

Grubb, W. N., & Lazerson, M. (1988). *Broken promises: How Americans fail their
children.* Chicago: University of Chicago Press.

Grubb, W. N., et al. (1985). *The initial effects of House Bill 72 on Texas public
schools: The challenges of equity and effectiveness.* Austin: LBJ School of Public Affairs, University of Texas.

Hayghe, H. (1986, February). Rise in mothers' labor force activity includes those
with infants. *Monthly Labor Review, 109,* 43–45.

Hunt, J. M. (1961). *Intelligence and experience.* New York: Ronald Press.

Kaestle, C. (1983). *Pillars of the Republic: Common schools and American society.*
New York: Hill & Wang.

Lazerson, M. (1972). The historical antecedents of early childhood education. In I.
Gordon (Ed.), *Early childhood education, Seventy-first yearbook of the Na-
tional Society for the Study of Education* (pp. 33–54). Chicago: University of
Chicago Press.

Marx, F., & Seligson, M. (1988). *The state survey.* The Public School Early Childhood Study, Bank Street College of Education.

Mitchell, A. (1988). *The case studies.* The Public School Early Childhood Study,
Bank Street College of Education.

Morgan, G. (1985, May). Programs for young children in the public schools? Only if
. . . *Young Children, 4*(4), 54.

National Association for the Education of Young Children. (1986, June). *Position
statement on developmentally appropriate practices in programs for 4- and 5-
year-olds.* Washington, DC: Author.

National Black Child Development Institute. (1985, January). *Child care in the
public schools: Incubator for inequality.* Washington, DC: Author.

National Governors' Association. (1986, August). *Time for results: The governors'
1991 report on education.* Washington, DC: Author.

National Society for the Study of Education. (1929). *Twenty-eighth yearbook: Preschool and parental education.* Bloomington, IN: Public School Publishing Co.,
312–313.

Robins, P. (1988). *Federal financing of child care: Alternative approaches and economic implications.* University of Miami; prepared for the Child Care Action
Campaign.

Schweinhart, L., & Koshel, J. (1986). Policy options for preschool programs. *High/
Scope Early Childhood Policy Papers, 5.*

Sirotnik, K. (1983, February). What you see is what you get—consistency, persistency, and mediocrity in classrooms. *Harvard Educational Review, 53,* 16–31.

Steinfels, M. O. (1973). *Who's minding the children? The history and politics of day care in America.* New York: Simon & Schuster.

U.S. Bureau of Labor Statistics. (1986, August). Half of mothers with children under 3 now in labor force. USDL 86–345, Washington, DC.

Zigler, E., & Valentine, J. (Eds.). (1979). *Project Head Start: A legacy of the War on Poverty.* New York: Free Press.

CHAPTER 3

Here They Come: Ready or Not!
Report of the California
School Readiness Task Force

DORIS O. SMITH

In the 1980s a new kind of crisis beset many early childhood classrooms across the country. A California parent's despairing comment reflected its nature: "My child just finished kindergarten and *hates* school."

It was becoming increasingly evident that kindergarten, once a pleasant, playful introduction to "real" school, had become a source of boredom—if not active dislike—for many children. A proliferation of popular books with such titles as *The Hurried Child* (Elkind, 1981), *The Erosion of Childhood* (Suransky, 1982), *The Disappearance of Childhood* (Postman, 1982), and *Children Without Childhood* (Winn, 1983) addressed the larger background issues.

Concern about the effects of pushing more and more academic learning into kindergarten led to re-examination of early childhood curricula in many states. This chapter considers the work of the School Readiness Task Force formed in California in 1987. I served as chair of its curriculum subcommittee. The chapter begins with a description of the context from which the Task Force arose, describes how it operated, and examines the recommendations it made.

The Context

In the early 1980s I conducted a summer workshop at California State University, Fresno, entitled Children of the '80s. The goal set for the class was to discover to what extent young children in that geographic area were experiencing the travails described in the literature of the time. Developmental psychologists, social workers, counselors, child care directors, parents, teachers, and principals were invited to speak to the class about children of the '80s from their own perspectives.

Students in the class also developed a survey instrument designed to reflect the findings from the literature. This survey was distributed in the local community. The summer workshop participants and I devoted at least two nights to discussing the findings. By the end of the class it was verified that the insights and findings described in the literature had been confirmed by the speakers and the survey results. The class agreed that the following statement accurately and succinctly reflected the work they had done together: *"Children of the '80s perceive or feel a lack of involvement of significant others in their lives."* It does not matter so much if there really is or is not a lack of involvement, but it does matter that children feel or perceive that important people in their lives are not paying serious attention to them.

A Balance of Instruction?

Children's feelings that adults lacked significant involvement in their lives could stem in part from instruction that they found boring, repetitious, or meaningless.

Perhaps the California state legislature recognized this when it passed SB813, which, among other things, called for "a balance of direct instruction and cognitive instruction" in all classrooms in California. This balance should occur between skill learning requiring direct instruction and the practice of cognitive instruction for promoting critical thinking, problem solving, self-awareness, self-expression, and cooperative learning.

In the spirit of this legislation two California professors of early childhood education, Michael Ballard-Campbell and Judith Wagner, joined me in developing an instrument to investigate the balance or imbalance of cognitive instruction and direct instruction in California kindergartens (Smith, 1986). We took the pedagogical position that problem solving and critical thinking develop in young children through experiential activities (NAEYC, 1986).

The survey instrument compared five didactic activities exemplifying direct instruction (reading workbooks, math workbooks, whole group direct instruction, small group direct instruction, and diagnostic testing) with five experiential activities exemplifying instruction in which the child's own cognitive activity is the source for learning (painting, blocks, dramatic play, science/cooking, and math manipulatives). The survey

asked how often children did the various activities, how many participated each time, how the children were selected for the activities, why
these activities were chosen, how children seemed to feel about what
they did, and how children reacted to the activities.

When the number of times an activity was offered was combined
with the number of children participating, the results showed a prepon-
derance of didactic experiences over experiential activities for each kindergarten child over time.

The open-ended item "List your three major concerns about teaching kindergarten today," showed that 62 percent of the kindergarten
teachers in California who answered the survey said there is too much
academic pressure in kindergarten. Responses included: "There are too
many paper and pencil tests." "I don't have time to do the things I want."
"There's too much asking the kids to do things they can't do."

Surprisingly, the survey results also indicated that the teachers selected activities for the children—even the experiential activities—a
majority of the time. In other words, the teacher said, in effect, "Johnny,
it's your turn to paint now. Whether you want to paint or not, it's your
turn to paint." This is how the ubiquitous rotation system works in kindergarten. This unexpected finding means that children in their first
school experience are being treated as passive receivers of the "system."
Because they are still formulating their ideas of how institutions work,
the children could mistakenly conclude that something is wrong with
them and their thinking because they are not being asked for their opinions. They then become less involved, less interested, and less confident.
Could it be that this practice of assigning activities is one reason children
say or feel that significant others are not paying serious attention to
them?

Another surprising finding was that 55 percent of the teachers who
answered the survey indicated they would continue doing what they
were doing in their classrooms even though they had said that there is
too much academic pressure in kindergarten. Informal follow-up conversations with kindergarten teachers elicited the following possible explanations for such a response:

1. *It's too hard to change.*   A review of the literature on the tenacity of
   teacher belief systems is relevant here (Katz & Raths, 1985; Sigel,
   1986; Smith & Shepard, 1988; Spodek, 1987).
2. *Teachers don't know how to teach in any other way.*   It was suggested that the kindergarten curriculum has changed so much in recent years that kindergarten teachers have become conditioned to
   using teaching manuals and textbook approaches. If they ever knew

how to teach differently, they have forgotten now, and many teachers never knew. They just don't know what is meant by developmentally appropriate curriculum. Because of this critical gap between what is and what is needed, the State Department is currently producing a California Kindergarten Curriculum Manual to reflect developmentally appropriate, integrated experiential instruction.

3. *Teachers don't feel empowered to make changes.* There seems to be a pervasive feeling that "curriculum comes down from above." It is fixed and cannot be changed.

4. *There's not enough time or money to teach in an experiential way.* During hearings task force members were told that teachers who want to change might need to spend up to $1,000 a year of their own money to purchase manipulatives and materials to enhance their kindergarten teaching. If a teacher can't do this, perhaps it is easier to continue to use a worksheet.

5. *Parental pressure to teach the basics.* From the Kindergarten Survey and from task force hearings evidence was given that many kindergarten teachers do not feel supported by parents, administrators, or colleagues. Some kindergarten teachers seem very lonely in their schools.

The School Readiness Task Force

Supported by mounting evidence of a serious problem and by the literature and research, the California Department of Education formed the School Readiness Task Force to investigate how school readiness was assessed and how extensive the problem of kindergarten retention was in California. The 18-member task force included preschool teachers, a child care director, kindergarten teachers, an administrator, a pediatrician, a school board representative, a PTA representative, a legislative representative, and others.

The task force was asked to describe creative program options to meet the needs of the diverse groups of children ages 4 through 6 in the state and to look at the preparation and certification of teachers for programs serving these children. The process of developing recommendations included listening to testimony from teachers, parents, and administrators at hearings across the state and synthesizing the work of five task force subcommittees on developmental needs, curriculum, assessment, articulation, and governance. The task force members discovered early on that one cannot just "fix" kindergarten. Kindergarten is the way it is because of what comes before and after. Thus, the focus of the task force expanded to include prekindergarten and first grade, as well as kindergarten.

The task force recommendations affect a broad range of programs for children and families in California. Because of the particular organization of programs that serve children ages 4 through 6 in California, the work of this task force required communication and cooperation across several agencies. For example, the Child Development Division serves most state-funded programs for children prior to kindergarten, and the Elementary Curriculum and Instruction Division of the Department of Education serves children in K–12 classrooms. Title V legislation regulates public school programs, but Title XXII legislation regulates ratios and health and safety measures in the private sector. Pre-K, kindergarten, and after-school child care licensing issues involve the Department of Education and the Department of Social Services. Furthermore, children may enter kindergarten with no prior group experience or with experience from federal, state, or private programs. The interests of children and their families from ethnic perspectives, health perspectives, and special needs perspectives had to be monitored constantly. In addition to representation on the task force, representatives from various subgroups served as observers or as guest speakers at task force meetings.

One task force member commented that practically every early childhood issue surfaced at some time during the meetings. Complicated administrative, legislative, and funding issues involving the Child Development Division, the State Department of Education, and the Department of Social Services, including private and public sectors, were addressed. The need for articulation among pre-K, kindergarten, primary, and child care teachers and administrators was raised. The problem of early introduction of skills regardless of a child's developmental capacity to respond was discussed. The importance of positive communication with parents and of being sensitive to issues relating to diversity was raised repeatedly. The work of the task force resulted in two reports: *Here They Come: Ready or Not!—A Summary Report* (1988b) and *Here They Come: Ready or Not!—Full Report* (1988a).

At the press conference announcing the release of the reports, California Superintendent of Schools Bill Honig said,

> Among the most far reaching of the recommendations is the Task Force's recommendation to change fundamentally the way in which young children are taught. The Report calls for a halt to the use of workbooks and ditto sheets which are frequently employed to teach skills such as counting and learning the alphabet. While it is important for children to learn basic skills

the teaching techniques and the curriculum must be balanced between child centered activities and content centered approaches that are appropriate for each child. (1988)

Recommendations

Curriculum

The most important recommendation made by the task force is a call for an appropriate, integrated, experiential educational program for all children ages 4 through 6. In making its recommendations, the task force leaned heavily on the work of the National Association for the Education of Young Children (NAEYC) regarding developmentally appropriate curriculum (Bredekamp, 1987). Furthermore, it recommended that the State Department of Education make available to every elementary school in the state copies of NAEYC's position statements on "Good Teaching Practices for 4- and 5-Year-Olds" (1988) and "Appropriate Education in the Primary Grades" (1988). Additionally, it noted that the curriculum recommendation was completely consistent with the California English-Language Arts and Mathematics Model Curriculum Guides (1987 b & c) and State Frameworks (1987a, 1985). The implementation of language experience, thematic teaching, and the use of manipulatives is highlighted throughout these state documents, but many teachers and administrators are not aware that such documents exist.

The task force recognized the importance of addressing the difficulties regarding implementation of the recommendations. Since the Symposium on Play over 100 presentations on the task force report have been given to school districts, professional organizations, and interested groups. In June 1989 a Leadership Training Institute prepared between 75 and 80 facilitators to disseminate and interpret the task force recommendations. Also in June 1989 State Department of Education advisories on curriculum, retention, and assessment practices for programs that serve children from ages 4 through 6 were distributed to every elementary school and child development program in California. Many school districts have formed early childhood task forces to study, interpret, and implement the recommendations at local levels.

Class Size

The task force recommended reducing class size for programs that serve children ages 4 through 6 in early primary programs to 24 children with two adults. Because of the complicated political and fiscal implications of this recommendation, the task force recommended working toward this goal while beginning at other points, such as making curricular changes. Evidence was presented and documented that, although it would be difficult and not optimal, aspects of developmentally appropriate curriculum could be implemented while working toward reduction of class size.

Two-Year Kindergartens

The task force recommended that the organization and teaching methods for programs that serve children ages 4 through 6 should reflect the heterogeneous skills and abilities of children in the prekindergarten, kindergarten, and primary grades. This recommendation resulted from serious concerns over the proliferation of two-year kindergartens, junior kindergartens, transitional kindergartens, and/or developmental kindergartens. The practice of testing and placing children in special classes or of advising parents to keep their children out of school for another year because the children were not "ready" for school was addressed frequently in the task force hearings.

The word "developmental" was used with a variety of meanings by various groups. Some call the first-year kindergarten a developmental kindergarten because it is essentially an activity-based program. The second-year kindergarten becomes a skill and drill program for which the child is now presumably "ready." (Some reports indicate that some developmental kindergartens are drill and practice—thus the child gets two years of drill instead of one!) The practice of two-year kindergartens in effect adds an entire school year to a child's school life. Instead of being in school 13 years (kindergarten plus 12 years) these children are in school for 14 years. The task force report cites research data indicating that the profile of the typical California retained kindergarten child in 1983 was "boy," "low income," and "minority." Since 1983, a steady increase in kindergarten retentions has occurred in the form of two-year kindergartens.

Those who started the movement for two-year kindergartens are given recognition and credit for drawing attention to the mismatch of children's development with school curriculum. With the best of intentions to prevent children from being hurt emotionally and damaged psychologically because of inappropriate school practices, these educators designed programs to help the children. Based on the assumption that the curriculum for kindergarten was fixed, the initial solution was to create an extra kindergarten year. This year would give children more time to develop readiness for an academic, skill-specific first grade. However, when some kindergarten teachers began to question the necessity for a fixed curriculum, it became apparent that to ensure developmentally appropriate instruction, changes must occur in the primary grades as well as in kindergarten. Thus, the task force recommendation was to change the curriculum to ensure developmentally appropriate instruction in all pre-K, kindergarten, and first-grade classrooms—that is, to make the schools fit the children and cease trying to fit the children into existing programs.

Wide Age Grouping

In order to break away from a narrow, homogeneous model based on testing and placing children, the task force recommended the consideration of wide age groupings such as 4's and 5's, kindergarten-firsts, or even K/1/2 classes. Teachers who have used wide age grouping have observed that young children characteristically have learning spurts and plateaus. It is not clear just when the spurts will come. However, over a period of two years, a teacher knows that a majority of children will experience considerable growth. Wide age grouping does not add a year to a child's school life. Rather, it provides for a flexible approach to curriculum to meet the various developmental levels of the children being served. However, the task force also recognizes that excellent programs can and should continue with developmentally appropriate curriculum practices in separate, self-contained classrooms for 4's, 5's, and 6's.

Standardized Testing and Placement

Because of the high risk of misplacement of young children when standardized test scores are used for placement decisions, the task force recommended a drastic change in testing practices. Children are ready for school when they are the legal age for school. Thus, it is unnecessary to test to see if they are "ready" for school. The position of the task force is that no standardized test score alone should be used to make decisions regarding placement in pre-K, kindergarten, or primary programs. An increasing number of school districts have stopped using paper and pencil tests in kindergarten. It is true that accountability measures are required for Chapter One monies, but these measures do not have to be standardized tests in kindergarten. The task force supports accountability and calls for multiple alternative measures to be used, including observations and teacher assessments.

Demonstrated Articulation Among Programs

One of the strengths of the California programs for young children is the variety of program options that exist. In California there are state-funded Children's Centers, state preschools, Head Start programs, family child care homes, as well as private nonprofit and for-profit schools and child care centers. The task force recommendation calls for demonstrated articulation among all programs that serve a particular kindergarten. Thus, parents, teachers, and administrators should meet together to promote continuity among programs. Of equal importance is the articulation between the kindergarten and first-grade teachers, parents, and administrators. The task force described the programs being discussed as the early childhood programs or the lower primary unit. The intention of identifying this "unit" conceptually is to designate someone to be responsible for articulation among the programs and for the implementation of consistent and developmentally appropriate curricula in the classrooms.

Teacher Training:
Child Development/Early Childhood Education

The task force discovered kindergarten/primary credentialed teachers in California who have never had a course in child development or early childhood education. To correct this condition the task force recommended that every kindergarten and primary teacher must have at least one course in child development/early childhood education through staff development inservice or institutions of higher education. Because of the feedback from administrators who say that teachers do not know how to teach experientially, the task force called for an emphasis on child development/early childhood education theory in preservice and inservice training. The intention is effectively to merge the school's expectancies with child development/early childhood education principles.

Public Awareness Campaign

Other recommendations called for a public awareness campaign to educate the media, legislators, parents, and school personnel regarding the importance of developmentally appropriate practices.

Conclusion

The Symposium on Play focused on the importance of facilitating child-centered experiences for young children. Children must feel or perceive that significant others are paying serious attention to them. The mismatch between school expectations and the actual development of young children has resulted in frustrated and angry teachers, confused parents, and children with damaged dispositions to learn (Katz & Raths, 1985).

Through the work of subcommittees on developmental needs, curriculum, assessment, articulation, and governance, California's Task Force on School Readiness developed far-reaching recommendations to restructure programs that serve young children. A balance of didactic and experiential instruction in California kindergartens is essential if children are to be treated with respect, their experiences valued, and their school days made positive ones.

The experience of the task force also reveals the complexity of interrelated factors that can influence the social context of children's development.

References

Bredekamp, S. (Ed.). (1987). *Developmentally appropriate practice in early childhood programs serving children from birth through age 8* (expanded ed.). Washington, DC: National Association for the Education of Young Children.

California State Department of Education. (1985). *Mathematics framework for California public schools.* Sacramento, CA: Author.

California State Department of Education. (1987a). *English-language arts framework for California public schools.* Sacramento, CA: Author.

California State Department of Education. (1987b). *English-language arts model curriculum guide.* Sacramento, CA: Author.

California State Department of Education. (1987c). *Mathematics model curriculum guide.* Sacramento, CA: Author.

California State Department of Education. (1988a). *Here they come: Ready or not!—Full report.* California Department of Education. Sacramento, CA: Author.

California State Department of Education. (1988b). *Here they come: Ready or not!—Summary report.* California Department of Education. Sacramento, CA: Author.

California State Department of Education. (1989). *Program advisory: Educating young children: Next steps in implementing the School Readiness Task Force Report.* Sacramento, CA: Author.

Elkind, D. (1981). *The hurried child: Growing up too fast too soon.* Menlo Park: Addison-Wesley.

Honig, B. (1988, March 24). *Here they come: Ready or not!* (News Release). Sacramento, CA.

Katz, L. G., & Raths, J. D. (1985). Dispositions as goals for teacher education. *Teaching & Teacher Education, I*(4), 301–307.

National Association for the Education of Young Children. (1986). NAEYC position statement on developmentally appropriate practice in early childhood programs serving children from birth through age 8. *Young Children, 41*(6), 3–19.

National Association for the Education of Young Children. (1988). Appropriate education in the primary grades. Washington, DC: Author.

National Association for the Education of Young Children. (1988). Good teaching practices for 4- and 5-year-olds. Washington, DC: Author.

Postman, N. (1982). *The disappearance of childhood.* New York: Delacorte.

Sigel, I. E. (1986). Human development and teacher education or what teachers are not taught about human development. In D. D. Dill & P. K. Fullager (Eds.), The knowledge most worth having in teacher education: An exploration of the knowledge, values, and skills essential to teaching in the middle and secondary schools (pp. 38–46). *Proceedings of the Chancellor's Invitational Conference.* Chapel Hill: University of North Carolina, Office of the Chancellor.

Smith, D. (1986). *California kindergarten survey.* Fresno: California State University, School of Education.

Smith, M. L., & Shepard, L. A. (1988). Kindergarten readiness and retention: A qualitative study of teachers' beliefs and practices. *American Education Research Journal, 25*(3), 307–333.

Spodek, B. (1987). Thought processes underlying preschool teachers' classroom decisions. *Early Child Development and Care, 29,* 197–208.

Suransky, V. P. (1982). *The erosion of childhood.* Chicago: University of Chicago Press.

Winn, M. (1983). *Children without childhood.* New York: Pantheon.

CHAPTER 4

Perspectives from the Field
Teachers and Parents Respond to the Call for Developmentally Appropriate Practice in the Primary Grades

LYDA BEARDSLEY

A teacher friend of mine, whom I'll call Brendan, recently asked me to recommend some materials to supplement his manipulative-based math curriculum. When I suggested that I could think of nothing more appropriate for his first graders than a set of hardwood unit blocks, he replied, "But if I have blocks in the classroom, when will the kids ever get their work done?"

I found Brendan's reply particularly disturbing because he is a recent graduate of a well-respected teacher training program that emphasizes an understanding of child development as a foundation to teaching. The concerns he expresses are indicative of the many contradictory demands that even the most sensitive and effective teachers must consider when making decisions about the best way to structure learning experiences for their students.

Brendan recognizes the immense attractiveness of blocks to children of this age, in that block activities offer endless possibilities for open-ended, self-directed, failure-proof play. He is also aware that block play is not idle or aimless, but rather offers children rich opportunities for integrated exploration of many of the same spatial, numerical, and social concepts that the traditional elementary curriculum focuses on as isolated areas of skill development. Nevertheless, he hesitates, worried about the negative consequences of introducing a clearly play-based learning material into his modern, academically oriented first-grade classroom.

Brendan's first concern centers around his ability to supervise 32 children who would all be happy to zip through their other work in order to get a chance to play with the blocks. The very appeal of the blocks is problematic in that their presence alone is likely to divert the children's interest from other, more "educational" materials. Brendan is also uncomfortable at the thought of having to justify his decision in response to the inevitable concern of parents, colleagues, and school administrators at the appearance of "preschool toys" in a first-grade classroom.

Another concern arises when Brendan realizes that he is not sure how to reveal and make concrete the connection between the children's learning in the block area and the rest of the curriculum. It's not as easy to quantify the kind of complex conceptual learning that emerges through child-directed play as it is to measure the discrete skills that are illuminated when teachers deliver, rather than facilitate, learning.

As always, Brendan worries about complying with his principal's request that the children be prepared to score well on their yearly standardized tests. He knows that these tests are inadequate to measure the broad understandings that are revealed through the kind of integrated learning activities he would like to offer his students, but he is unaware of any other child assessment procedures that would satisfy his district's demand for teacher accountability.

Brendan's situation is not unique, although his interest in providing "developmentally appropriate" materials (see Chapter 1 for definition and discussion) for his students may be ahead of his time. Brendan's dilemma illustrates many of the key issues that have emerged with the recent movement toward implementation of developmentally appropriate curricula, particularly in the primary grades.

The Call for Developmentally Appropriate Practice

In California, early childhood education is in the midst of an especially exciting transition, one that promises to relieve Brendan of some of his worries and that may predict the future of the field as well. In June 1989, California's Superintendent of Public Instruction issued a program advisory (California State Department of Education, 1989) commending and accepting the recommendations of the School Readiness Task Force Report (see Smith, Chapter 3, this volume).

The program advisory urges school districts and the providers of preschool and early primary programs (kindergarten through third grade) to "make a firm commitment to the quality and the continuity of the educational experiences of their young children, particularly those ages four through six" (California State Department of Education, 1989, p. 1). The advisory then proceeds to provide specific direction and assistance toward implementing the task force recommendations regarding the provision of developmentally appropriate curriculum and instruction, child assessment techniques, parent involvement, and staff development.

The report and the program advisory are especially impressive because they represent a landmark effort by a public agency to utilize the recommendations of early childhood professionals (practitioners *and* researchers) to shape educational policy. This phenomenon is by no means limited to California. Since the National Association for the Education of Young Children (NAEYC) issued its powerful position statement defining developmentally appropriate practice in preschool through the primary grades (Bredekamp, 1987), several national school reform reports have endorsed these quality standards. The Child Care Action Campaign (1988), the National Association of State Boards of Education (1988), and the National Black Child Development Institute (1987) called for a new partnership between public schools and early childhood programs in which curriculum, instruction, and child assessment would be culturally sensitive and appropriate to the child's level of development.

Teachers Respond to the Call

Because of the proliferation of recent reports and editorials regarding the inadequacies of the American educational system, teacher morale in general is at a low point. Thus, any administrative mandate that is perceived by teachers as saying, in effect, "We've discovered that the way you've been teaching for the last 2, 10, or 25 years is ineffective and we want you to change," threatens to demoralize teachers further. Educators are understandably resistant to conform to yet another bureaucratic shift in policy that guarantees a tremendous amount of rethinking, retraining, and rearranging on the part of teachers, with the promise of very little reward.

Happily, though, the task force report and accompanying advisory have been enthusiastically received by most preschool and many primary-grade teachers in California, particularly because the recommendations provide validation for the way many of these early childhood educators have been trying to teach throughout their careers. In fact, many teachers report a great sense of relief, especially over issues of readiness and retention, now that the California State Department of Education has endorsed the notion that early childhood classrooms should be child centered and that curricular and instructional goals should be determined by the developmental level, age, and individual needs of each child (Susan Thompson, Administrator, Child Development Division, personal communication, August 23, 1989). In other words, concerns about the *child*'s readiness to do kindergarten or first-grade work have shifted to a focus on the *educational program*'s readiness to accommodate the child.

There is strong concern, however, about teachers' ability to implement the recommendations at the K–1 level without additional funds to purchase developmentally appropriate materials and to reduce class size (a key recommendation of the task force). Although no new funding to support the recommendations is forthcoming so far, the advisory does provide direction in addressing those recommendations that can be readily achieved. Nevertheless, a number of serious issues threaten to impede the movement to implement developmentally appropriate early childhood programs at the primary level.

Acknowledging Parental Concerns

One of the most pressing problems of implementation concerns how well the plan addresses and accommodates parents' priorities for their young children's education. Certainly, the movement away from standardized texts, workbooks, and "skill and drill" learning is a welcome change for many parents of young children. These individuals have for many years vocalized their concerns about both the lack of intellectual substance and the level of stress their children were experiencing in overly academic and competitive kindergarten and first-grade classrooms.

On the other hand, many parents are concerned about the plethora of recent reports citing the decline in excellence in America's schools. These parents believe that any reform other than a "back to basics" approach is doomed to failure. For some, these attitudes represent a reaction to what many perceive as the failure of the educational "experiments" of the 1960s and early 1970s and an ignorance of the sound educational principles that fostered those and earlier reform movements. Other parents are uncomfortable whenever their children's early academic experiences do not resemble the kind of desk-bound, skill-specific learning that they experienced and that educational psychologists now argue is suitable, if at all, only for much older children (e.g., Elkind, 1986; Zigler, 1987).

These concerns are voiced by parents at both ends of the economic spectrum. Poor parents often see academic success as a key to breaking the cycle of poverty and are thus more concerned about their children learning to sit still at a desk filling in worksheets than expressing themselves creatively in the art corner. Economically successful parents often share a similar vision and are determined that their children be nurtured in the same competitive academic spirit that has served them so well in the world of commerce.

As an increasing number of young children have some kind of preschool experience, parents are often disappointed when kindergarten and first grade appear to offer the same kind of playful environment that their children already experienced in preschool. These parents expect teachers to provide concrete and quantifiable evidence that the children's learning is advancing beyond preschool and thus are further concerned when teachers eschew traditional devices like textbooks and spelling tests. Ongoing parent education, along with improved assessment procedures, is essential if parents are to recognize, for example, that a young child's spontaneous interest in estimating, comparing, and manipulating numbers of objects is greater evidence of comprehension of mathematical concepts than is the ability to repeatedly provide rote answers to drills of addition and subtraction facts (Beardsley, 1990).

Educators and policy makers alike recognize that successful implementation of developmentally appropriate curricula requires that K–3 programs encourage the kind of partnerships with parents that are typically seen in high quality preschool and child care programs (Beardsley, 1990). In these high quality prekindergarten programs, there is ongoing reciprocal communication between school and family about long-term goals, day-to-day activities, and children's progress. Parents are provided with the relevant skills, information, and access to community support services to nurture and strengthen their children's learning at school and at home. Parents are encouraged to take on decision-making, advisory, and advocacy roles. This kind of school–home collaboration requires a more comprehensive and reciprocal relationship with parents than most elementary teachers have heretofore experienced. It is also far more difficult to achieve when the ratio of children to teachers is two to five times greater in elementary than in preschool settings.

In addition, cultural and socioeconomic factors remain powerful determinants of parents' receptiveness to educators' efforts to provide the kind of school environment in which parents are valued as essential partners in the education of their children. It is difficult enough for teachers to promote ongoing communication with parents whose lives are busy and often filled with stress, but tougher still to break down the suspicion and resistance many parents feel as a result of their own unpleasant school experiences.

A strong parent involvement and education component is advocated by NAEYC (Bredekamp, 1987), the National Association of State Boards of Education (1988), the National Black Child Development Institute (1987), and the California State Department of Education (1988, 1989). Their recommendations offer hope that the impediments to constructive collaboration between parents and teachers can be eliminated in favor of a movement to further parental understanding and support for teachers' efforts to implement developmentally appropriate curricula in the primary grades.

Articulation Among Programs That Serve Young Children

Another impediment to successful implementation of developmentally appropriate early childhood practice is the lack of alignment among programs that serve young children as they progress through preschool, kindergarten, first grade, and beyond.

Not long ago, my 6-year-old daughter arrived home from her after-school child care program complaining, "I lost that dumb contest again because Carole says I spelled one of the words wrong!" Upon inquiry, I discovered that the children had been participating in a contest in which they had to identify the contents of a "feely box" using only their sense of touch. The winners were those who were able to correctly name the items by writing them on a slip of paper judged by their teacher, whom I'll call Carole. My daughter and her friends lost the contest repeatedly because they had written their correct answers using "invented spelling" (e.g., "catn bals") as they were permitted to do by their first-grade teacher, whom I'll call Beverly, rather than "dictionary spelling" ("cotton balls"), the only form of spelling that their after-school teacher, Carole, would accept.

Beverly, long committed to using her knowledge of child development as a basis for structuring her literacy curriculum, encourages her first graders to use their phonetic knowledge to write. She believes that invented spelling provides a method for youngsters to express their thoughts with fluency and without fear of censure (because there is no need to replicate some absolute standard) and thus demonstrate what they already know about word formation. Beverly then aims her teaching toward enriching and expanding this knowledge base by continuing to expose the children to the correct forms of spelling in a variety of other reading and writing activities.

Carole, who received her teacher training more than a decade before Beverly and has received little staff development since then, uses her contest as a way of encouraging the children to learn to write using dictionary spelling. She feels strongly that when teachers fail to correct misspelled words, bad habits are reinforced that will interfere with the children's eventual mastery of the correct forms of spelling. It has never occurred to Carole to question whether or not her expectations about the children's learning effectively accommodate the interests and abilities of 6-year-olds.

Although both Carole and Beverly are employed by the same school district, neither is aware of the educational philosophy and curriculum in the other's classroom or has made any attempt to coordinate the children's experiences across the learning day. In my daughter's experience, her teachers had structured educational experiences that had similar goals (i.e., learning to write), but that used very different criteria to measure success. To be successful in each setting, the children had to learn to adapt their responses to conform with each teacher's quite different requirements. In other words, the child had become the interpreter of the curriculum. Of necessity, the *child* had to be able to translate the criteria for success in each setting. Since 6-year-olds are generally not capable of or interested in performing this metacognitive feat, many of the children exhibited confusion throughout the school year about the rules for writing in each context.

My daughter and some of her friends were able to come up with a solution of sorts, although it entailed just the kind of compliance with adult learning priorities that early childhood experts caution may interfere with the spontaneous, self-directed process that characterizes young children's learning (Bredekamp, 1987; Elkind, 1986). "Yea, we never lose any more," my daughter explained some weeks later. "We just ask Kay (the aide) to spell the words for us before we write them down for Carole to check." Of course, what she learned had little to do with writing, but a lot to do with relying on adults rather than her own abilities to come up with the right answer. And this was exactly the kind of lesson that her first-grade teacher, Beverly, was trying to avoid.

My daughter's dilemma highlights how children are adversely affected by a lack of articulation between primary-grade classrooms and the school age child care programs that serve them before and after school. The discontinuity that often exists between preschool and early primary programs gives rise to similar concerns and is at the root of the difficult transition many children experience when entering kindergarten (Beardsley, 1990). Poor alignment between the kind of educational programs offered in kindergarten and first-grade classrooms can create additional stress and confusion for the child. For these reasons, many experts have come to believe that continuity between early childhood programs is a key element in ensuring children's continued success through the elementary years (e.g., Bredekamp, 1987; California State Department of Education, 1988, 1989; National Association of State Boards of Education, 1988).

These experts argue that a key to achieving continuity across early education programs is a common teaching philosophy, founded in an understanding of child development, to which all teachers turn when they make decisions about designing learning experiences for children. This entails ongoing communication and coordination among teachers and early childhood programs. Once this dialogue is established, it will be possible for teachers like Carole and Beverly to work together to assess each child's readiness to move toward dictionary spelling, and to support that learning both in the classroom and in child care, across what the child will then experience as a "seamless" learning day.

Are Early Childhood Educators "Real" Teachers?

The lack of articulation among early childhood programs is not surprising given the lack of respect or understanding that continues to exist among preschool, elementary, and child care teachers. Work with very young children is particularly devalued in our society, probably because of its association with traditional women's roles, and is generally compensated poorly and accompanied by low prestige and high turnover rates (Child Care Action Campaign, 1988; Grubb, 1989; Scarr, 1984; Whitebook, Howes, & Phillips, 1989; Willer, 1987).

Elementary teachers and even many preschool teachers are often tempted to demean the care-giving aspects of work with young children. This attitude gives rise to the notion that the traditional teacher role, with its focus on stimulating the child's intellectual development, is somehow superior to that of the early childhood educator, which, because of its emphasis on the importance of supporting the child's development in all areas, is often dismissed as more "babysitting" than "real" teaching. Even many preschool teachers are reluctant to relinquish their cognitively oriented curricula in favor of the wholistic approach advocated by early education experts (e.g., Bredekamp, 1987), in which *all* aspects of the child's development—physical, social, and emotional, as well as intellectual—are considered equally deserving of the teacher's attention (Beardsley, 1990).

The inferior status of early childhood teachers is particularly ironic in California, where those who hold a Child Development Programs Permit (required for all who teach in state-funded child care programs) are required to have significantly more training specific to child development and its application to early childhood curriculum and instruction than are those who possess regular elementary teaching credentials. Nevertheless, certain educational organizations (the California Teachers Association in particular) continue to oppose the use of state educational improvement funds for cost-of-living increases for state-subsidized child development programs, contending that these programs are not "educational" in the sense that the K–12 system is (Legislative Snips, 1989).

Conclusions

It is unlikely that meaningful articulation among early childhood programs will be achieved until issues of parity in training, accountability, and compensation are addressed. Increased resources for education would improve low morale, increase understanding, and encourage cooperation rather than competition among those who educate young children.

Correspondingly, despite tremendous enthusiasm for the recent spate of early childhood policy reports that advocate developmentally appropriate practice, it is unlikely that successful implementation will be effected at the primary level until other key issues are resolved. Specifically, parental concerns must be recognized and addressed, class size or teacher–child ratios must be significantly reduced, new assessment tools must be developed to supplant standardized, norm-referenced tests and to provide more sensitive monitoring of student progress and teacher effectiveness, and both preservice and inservice teacher training programs need to be improved so that teachers are kept abreast of current research findings and given assistance and support in applying the new information to their work with young children.

These are difficult, but not impossible, tasks to accomplish, especially at a time like this when so many educational leaders, researchers, teachers, and parents have come together to articulate a common vision of the education of today's young children. Implementation of these new policies and curricula will succeed as long as the educational process is understood as an interaction among developing individuals (educators and parents as well as children), and teaching practice acknowledges and celebrates the special nature of the early childhood years.

References

Beardsley, L. (1990). *Good day/bad day: The child's experience of child care.* New York: Teachers College Press.

Bredekamp, S. (Ed.). (1987). *Developmentally appropriate practice in early childhood programs serving children from birth through age 8* (expanded ed.). Washington, DC: National Association for the Education of Young Children.

California State Department of Education. (1988). *Here they come: Ready or not!—Full report*. Sacramento, CA: Author.

California State Department of Education. (1989, June). *Program advisory: Educating young children; Next steps on implementing the School Readiness Task Force Report*. Sacramento, CA: Author.

Child Care Action Campaign. (1988). *Child care: The bottom line. An economic and child care policy paper*. New York: Author.

Elkind, D. (1986, May). Formal education and early childhood education: An essential difference. *Phi Delta Kappan*, pp. 631–636.

Grubb, W. N. (1989). Child care and early childhood programs. In M. Kirst & J. Guthrie (Eds.), *The conditions of children in California* (pp. 63–95). Berkeley: Policy Analysis for California Education (PACE).

Legislative snips. (1989, September–October). *Bananas Newsletter*, p. 3.

National Association of State Boards of Education. (1988). *Right from the start: The report of the NASBE Task Force on Early Childhood Education*. Alexandria, VA: Author.

National Black Child Development Institute. (1987). *Safeguards: Guidelines for establishing programs for four-year-olds in the public schools*. Washington, DC: Author.

Scarr, S. (1984). *Mother care/other care*. New York: Basic Books.

Whitebook, M., Howes, C., & Phillips, D. (1989). *Who cares? Child care teachers and the quality of care in America. Executive summary of the National Child Care Staffing Study*, Oakland, CA: Child Care Employee Project.

Willer, B. (1987). Quality or affordability: Trade-offs for early childhood programs? *Young Children, 42*(6), 41–43.

Zigler, E. (1987). Formal schooling for four-year-olds? No. *American Psychologist, 42* (3), 254–260.

Part II

LANGUAGE, LITERACY, AND THE SOCIAL WORLDS OF CHILDREN

CHAPTER 5

The Research Perspective
Looking at Play Through Case Studies

CELIA GENISHI

The chapters in this volume address issues related to both play and the contexts in which it occurs. One striking motif throughout is the vulnerability of children (and childhood) and play. Children are part of a society that fails to provide support for the most economically needy (Grubb, Chapter 2, this volume); and in centers or schools, children may encounter situations that fail to accommodate their ways of learning (Beardsley, Chapter 4, this volume). Also striking are the contrasts and potential tensions from chapter to chapter: The voices of some researchers contrast with teachers' voices in both tone and goals; society's aims contrast with some educators' and children's aims. Yet in this second part, researchers and practitioners share similar goals—ones that value children's ways of learning.

Here I comment on the three chapters in Part II from the point of view of a teacher educator and classroom researcher concerned with how practitioners and researchers can collaborate on behalf of young children's learning. My comments center around the usefulness of case study research as a way of understanding children's play and development, as well as a way of continuing dialogues among the diverse groups who contributed to this volume. The chapter is divided into sections on case studies, a focus on the language of play, the need to look at the classroom and the broader contexts beyond it, the need to value equally voices and perspectives from practice and research, and conclusions.

Case Studies: Close Looks at Playful Situations

As contributors Ervin-Tripp, Dyson, and Altman and Fong develop their respective themes of language learning, literacy development, and practitioner concerns, they assume that play is a fundamental way in which children make sense of situations. So although play appears endangered in published curricula and academically oriented classrooms, the authors present it as a clearly empowering setting for children. We get a direct sense of this power because of the way the authors present their information, often through dialogue and *stories*. In researchers' terms, these stories are *case studies,* close looks at individuals in particular places.

Case studies are not new. They are a tradition in medicine and business for purposes of record keeping and teaching (Yin, 1989). In developmental psychology the most widely known might be Piaget's studies (1937/1954) of his own children. Within the last 10 to 15 years, case studies have also become a familiar approach in educational research (Stake, 1988). Associated with qualitative, single-subject, or "small-number" studies, the approach is responsive to a growing interest in information missing in data about groups. Case studies, then, can answer many questions: What happens in the classrooms of experienced teachers whose "methods" are not captured in published curricula or children's test scores? And what are the stories of these teachers (Ayers, 1989) and of the children themselves (Dyson, 1989; Kelly-Byrne, 1989)?

There now seems to be a convergence of theorists', researchers', and practitioners' interest in a focus on individuals. Feminists, for instance, support the need to make public the voices of individuals who are not socially or politically dominant, such as women and children. In a theoretical discussion of feminism and political theory, Joan Cocks (1989) posited the human need to sense vitality in theories about social and political relationships. When she critiques theory in general, she sympathizes with those who have little patience with it. She claims that there is a vast distance between "felt experience," which for many of us is "life," and "abstract understanding," which for many of us is "theory": "However loyally theory works off concrete life as its original material and ground, it has for its own governing principle not life but logic" (Cocks, 1989, p. 107).

Accordingly, theory should have some of the feeling of lived lives, especially if it is meant to illuminate the world it explains. For example, a theory of learning has far more value if it can somehow evoke in an audience the way it feels to learn. (Contributors Altman and Fong are well aware of this when they challenge traditional theories of evaluation: They ask, "How do you evaluate 'learning how it feels to do something well'?") Cocks discussed one way of illuminating theory—the historical example, or in other words, the case study. Cases, examples of particular events and situations, can enliven theory (though Cocks cautions that they should link with the inner logic of theory, a point to be considered later). The stories told in this part about particular people learning enliven what has come to be called *constructivist* theory, which is compatible with Piagetian principles and assumes that each individual constructs what she or he knows about reality in interaction with others.

Psychologist Michael Cole has long been an advocate of looking beyond the individual to social contexts (Cole, Gay, Glick, & Sharp, 1971). But he also sees the importance of understanding individuals' experiences, citing novelist Walker Percy as a source of support:

> There is a secret about the scientific method which every scientist knows and takes as a matter of course, but which the layman does not know. . . . The secret is this: Science cannot utter a single word about the individual molecule, thing, or creature in so far as it is an individual but only in so far as it is like other individuals. (cited in Paley, 1986b, p. vii)

In adhering only to scientific quantification based on large numbers of subjects, psychology, the discipline devoted to understanding *individual* behavior and consciousness, may ultimately avoid its own goal.

Cole included the above quotation in his introduction to Vivian Paley's *Mollie Is Three* (1986a), a teacher's look at children in her own classroom learning through interaction, conversation, and play. Paley, a teacher-researcher, seems to know the scientist's secret; and through close looks at individuals like Mollie, she demonstrates not only how Mollie's thinking and learning are like her peers' but also how they are unique and how the uniqueness flourishes in play.

Closer Looks Through Language

An unusually sensitive listener, Paley illustrated children's learning through tape-recorded examples of their talk (see also Paley, 1981, 1986b). Susan Ervin-Tripp and Anne Haas Dyson also use children's language, both spoken and written, as the most direct form of evidence of development. Both researchers focus on spoken language—talk—as well as important features of the situation that nourish talk among peers. Ervin-Tripp describes a number of studies that show that particular kinds of conversational or discourse activities, such as role play, narration, cooperative action, and argument, become sites for using new vocabulary and complex language structures for both first- and second-language learners. Ervin-Tripp presents a child's example from role play: "*When* I grow up and you grow up, we're going to be the bosses." The use of a temporal conjunction (*when*) in forming a complex sentence, is prompted by children's need to describe future events or plan the course of play. The cooperative action of reading might prompt another complex sentence: "You listen *while* I read." Ervin-Tripp argues that such structures are less likely to occur in adult-child conversation, which is often adult controlled.

Similarly, Dyson demonstrates the fluidity of child-controlled settings in a primary-grade classroom. In this situation, where the teacher encourages talk and cooperation, children create drawings and stories as they rely on what they know from prior experience and on what they can imagine. The talk of children like Chiel and Manuel that surrounds their actions is a critical part of the social world in which the children's growing literacy is embedded. Thus, learning to read and write is not detached from playful situations; in fact, play is an important *resource* for the reader/writer. And the constant overlapping of playful talk, prior experience, and imagined worlds illustrates Dyson's point that literacy learning is a highly *contextualized* process. It requires social support embedded in peer talk, not the removal of such support in decontextualized settings.

Looks at the Broad Context

The close looks at language by Ervin-Tripp and Dyson display the artfulness of researchers as they reveal structure and regularity in talk among individual children. The looks also show the artfulness of children in portraying themselves as individuals, as well as integral parts of ongoing groups. The child within the "ongoing group" of school and the community beyond is the concern of principal Marian Altman and teacher Wendy Fong. Their story from the primary grades complements those from researchers: Here are children becoming storytellers and writers, artists, English speakers; and this development occurs because the enabling situations that Ervin-Tripp and Dyson describe are present in this school.

Altman and Fong clearly favor classroom approaches that value individual ways of learning. Altman, for example, discusses with teachers every one of their students. Fong arranges for times in each day when children choose their own activities. Both refer to play and holistic uses of language as foundations of the curriculum, and both use actual talk from children and teachers to illustrate the points they make. Further, they highlight the pressures that practitioners feel in their daily work lives: economic pressures (which materials should be replaced first?), pressure from parents, pressure from state requirements, and so on. All of these impinge on administrators' and teachers' abilities to develop curricula based on the playful and child-controlled talk that researchers describe.

A consideration of the broad context brings us to a reflection on Cocks' (1989) caution that the case studies we select should not be atypical or chance events. While representing "life," developmental stories should also link with the inner logic of theory. They should, in other words, expand our understanding of theory, and not reduce it by presenting too narrow an example. Through documentation of specific settings, Ervin-Tripp and Dyson expand constructivist theories of language and literacy development, respectively, particularly the aspects of these theories related to peer interaction. The researchers also contribute, though less directly, to a theory of how learning and teaching work, an overarching "theory of practice" (Fein & Schwartz, 1982).

With respect to this broader theory, we might ask how stories about children link with stories of teachers and others in the child's world. What other contexts, in addition to those controlled by children, add to sound theory? One context outside the scope of this volume is the home. Studies like those of Tizard and Hughes (1984) of young British children learning at home and school demonstrate the importance of *adult*–child talk in working class and middle class homes. Tizard and Hughes make several important points: First, the adult, not peers, may facilitate certain kinds of dialogue about concepts with which the child has little experience (money, for example). Second, any presumption that middle class families provide richer sites for dialogue than working class families is questionable. Third, mothers may provide a much richer learning environment than the children's preschool teachers. Like Dyson and Ervin-Tripp, Tizard and Hughes provide examples of children's talk from case studies as evidence for their arguments, though they do not come to firm conclusions. Instead their findings prompt critical questions for educators in the United States, where there are many more working mothers than in Great Britain. We have only begun to answer questions like these: What are the stories of children in day care? How does peer talk compare with teacher talk there? How do teachers compare with mothers? What sorts of "spaces" for play might adults leave in their talk with children? Further, what is the role of the teacher in enriching children's play? These questions are no more important than those the authors in this part have raised, but they imply the need for complementary studies that will link to a comprehensive theory of well-examined practice.

Hearing Varied Voices

A comprehensive theory requires a fair hearing for the voices of those who most directly benefit from and shape early childhood education: children, parents, teachers, administrators. In volumes like this, all those voices are valued. Researchers like Dyson, Ervin-Tripp, Corsaro and Schwarz (Chapter 16, this volume) and Reifel and Yeatman (Chapter 11, this volume) are mediators who, by presenting children's utterances as evidence of the social and linguistic control that play affords, enable the children to speak for themselves. Altman and Fong speak effectively for the administrator and teacher (and indirectly for parents). Yet, it is clear that these different authors have different concerns, and it is only through further dialogue that varied concerns can lead to improved practices.

Dialogue, then, has been shown to be essential not just for children's social play but also among adults who make decisions about the course of early childhood education. That is, the language used in dialogue is both a *topic,* something that adults study as an "object" in itself to learn about children, and a powerful *resource,* something that both children and adults use to influence others' actions (Cook-Gumperz, 1981). Dialogues among the many voices that contribute to the development of practice are a chief resource for taking further action.

The topic of play weaves an underlying theme of power throughout this book. But because children generally have so little power, the child-like activity of play is seen as endangered. And perhaps by extension those who advocate play are also vulnerable. If we are to act on the recommendations and implications of this volume, dialogue among the more and less powerful voices in it is critical. Dialogue that leads to reflection and action is collaborative, and collaboration is a democratic process, one in which participants try to share equally in the power needed to improve educational practices (Erickson, 1989). Those whose voices are least often transformed into print—such as those of children, teachers, and administrators—need to be heard as forcefully as the voices of policy makers and researchers (Genishi & Dyson, 1989). For these voices point most tellingly to what practices are and what they might become.

No one believes that even the most open dialogue will lead to complete agreement among differing groups. In fact, some voices will tell stories that upset listeners, for example, Altman and Fong's story about concerned parents who see their children playing too much in school (also see Delpit, 1988, on the variety of parental voices); stories about children whose ways of learning challenge current theories (Dyson, 1990); stories about promising students in extreme poverty, few of whom succeed in school (Taylor & Dorsey-Gaines, 1988); and often unheard stories about teachers without administrative or other support who lack the power to make space in their classrooms for children's choices.

All of these voices need a responsive audience because each is linked to the contexts where children spend their days. It is these contexts that this volume seeks to influence so that they become places where children develop and learn in appropriate and satisfying ways.

Conclusions

In this chapter I have proposed that the stories contained in case studies provide a link and mutual point of reference among voices, a way of establishing dialogues among groups with different styles of expressing themselves: practitioners, administrators, parents, and university researchers. Because they tell stories from life, case studies allow us to see what kinds of contexts support children as they develop and control play. Altman and Fong depict such a setting, and both Dyson and Ervin-Tripp use examples of talk—of playful interaction—to provide direct evidence of how play functions in settings where children learn. As Dyson points out, those interactions help us see how children *contextualize* play and other activities, how they build scaffolds for themselves, as they construct their learning.

Similarly, adults might contextualize—build up, rather than remove, scaffolds—and communicate through case studies of play (as Monighan-Nourot, Scales, Van Hoorn, & Almy, 1987, do) as a link among different groups and between practice and theory, relying on what they know from past experience and on their abilities to imagine new relationships and scenarios. In addition, dialogues incorporating case studies that go beyond child-controlled situations can add to a more comprehensive theory of practice. Such studies would include stories in which play does not occur, stories in which adults have a major role, stories with unexpected events or unhappy or ambiguous endings. An expanded range of stories can create a continuing dialogue whose goal is not always persuasion, but more often understanding others' experiences and points of view. That understanding might lead to the articulation of realistic goals for practice that values play and the contexts that support and enhance it.

References

Ayers, W. (1989). *The good preschool teacher: Six teachers reflect on their lives.* New York: Teachers College Press.

Cocks, J. (1989). *The oppositional imagination: Feminism, critique, and political theory.* New York: Routledge.

Cole, M., Gay, J., Glick, J., & Sharp, D. W. (1971). *The cultural context of learning and thinking.* New York: Basic Books.

Cook-Gumperz, J. (1981). Persuasive talk: The social organization of children's talk. In J. L. Green & C. Wallat (Eds.), *Ethnography and language in social settings* (pp. 25–50). Norwood, NJ: Ablex.

Delpit, L. (1988). The silenced dialogue: Power and pedagogy in educating other people's children. *Harvard Educational Review, 58,* 280–298.

Dyson, A. Haas. (1989). *Multiple worlds of child writers: Friends learning to write.* New York: Teachers College Press.

Dyson, A. Haas. (1990, February). Research currents: Diversity, social responsibility, and the story of literacy development. *Language Arts, 67,* 192–205.

Erickson, F. (1989). Research currents: Learning and collaboration in teaching. *Language Arts, 66,* 430–442.

Fein, G., & Schwartz, P. M. (1982). Developmental theories in early education. In B. Spodek (Ed.), *Handbook of research in early childhood education* (pp. 82–106). New York: Free Press.

Genishi, C., & Dyson, A. Haas. (1989, March). *Making assessment functional: Fighting what comes naturally.* Paper presented at the annual meeting of the American Educational Research Association. San Francisco.

Kelly-Byrne, D. (1989). *A child's play life: An ethnographic study.* New York: Teachers College Press.

Monighan-Nourot, P., Scales, B., Van Hoorn, J., & Almy, M. (1987). *Looking at children's play: A bridge between theory and practice.* New York: Teachers College Press.

Paley, V. G. (1981). *Wally's stories.* Cambridge, MA: Harvard University Press.

Paley, V. G. (1986a). *Mollie is three: Growing up in school.* Chicago: University of Chicago Press.

Paley, V. G. (1986b). On listening to what the children say. In *Teachers and schools: Ideas for action* (pp. 18–27). Cambridge, MA: *Harvard Educational Review.*

Piaget, J. (1937/1954). *The construction of reality in the child.* New York: Basic Books.

Stake, R. (1988). Case study methods in educational research. In R. M. Jaeger (Ed.), *Complementary methods for research in education* (pp. 251–300). Washington, DC: American Educational Research Association.

Taylor, D., & Dorsey-Gaines, C. (1988). *Growing up literate: Learning from inner-city families*. Portsmouth, NH: Heinemann.

Tizard, B., & Hughes, M. (1984). *Young children learning*. Cambridge, MA: Harvard University Press.

Yin, R. K. (1989). *Case study research: Design and methods*. rev. ed. Newbury Park, CA: Sage.

CHAPTER 6

Play in Language Development

SUSAN ERVIN-TRIPP

Among the many changes that we see taking place in preschool children is the rapid growth of language—most apparently, the development of vocabulary, sentence complexity, conversational skill, storytelling, register and style variation, and persuasiveness. If several languages are heard, children become competent bilinguals in preschool. Play can provide an ideal setting for the study of these developments in young children's language. In this chapter we shall address the question of the effects of play on language.

Defining the Problem

The search for the effects of preschool play on language development has two aspects. One is the difference between peers and adults as partners, or facilitators of development. Would children learn language faster by interacting primarily with adult teachers and parents or by playing with other children? The other issue is the effects of play on language, in contrast to other activities, such as organized instruction.

Potential language "teachers" may be adults, peers, or older children. In the case of an older child, the precise age gap between the children is relevant, since a child one year older than the learner is a very different model and play partner than one three years older. The type of activity in which talk takes place changes with age; adults do not engage in the same activities (e.g., sound play) as children. So if partners make a difference, we have to find out if it is their age or their activity that is crucial. Furthermore, the stage of language development matters. The learning needs of the child are different at different stages: In the first few years the need is to get into language; later, it is to expand and elaborate skills.

At the beginning of language, before age 3, the most extreme cases of delay or impairment are found in children in institutions and in twins. Institutionalized children may suffer from lack of organized language stimulation. We know that twins understand each other too well, have less need of explicitness, and develop their own way of communicating. Their knowledge of adult language can be less because their knowledge of their twin language is relatively greater (Bates, 1975).

Conditions of Learning

Let us step back a moment and ask what is necessary for the initial acquisition of a language. This question has been most clearly addressed in second-language learning, where conditions vary even more widely than in first-language acquisition. The notion has developed that for successful language acquisition the following conditions must be met:

1. *Exchanges should be salient and motivating enough for the learner to pay attention.*
2. *Language "input" should be comprehensible but only slightly in advance of the learner's own knowledge in either form or ideas.* These conditions ensure that the learner hears language forms (words, phrases, sentences), while at the same time understanding the context and inferring the meanings of the forms or the structures underlying them. In this way, the learner can match new forms to these meanings. If either the language heard or the ideas expressed are too difficult, the learner might just tune out, might not understand the meaning or the syntax, or might not be able to retain enough to make use of the models for changing his or her own system.
3. *The learner should be able to engage in one-on-one exchanges.* These transactions allow the learner to practice producing new forms in natural contexts, while permitting the partner to see what is understood by the learner, so that the *"input" is delicately tuned* to the learner's knowledge and interests.

Learning from Siblings

Dunn and Kendrick (1982) have noted that 1-year-old children spend as much time playing with siblings as with their mothers in English and Canadian families. Slightly older siblings or verbally skilled friends might be ideal partners for learning, because they can play at the level of the learner, gain attention, and provide meanings and forms closely tuned to the child's level. A study by Patricia Zukow (1989) demonstrated the effectiveness of sibling partners for learners. In Mexican families siblings often take on care-giving roles. Zukow did a fine-grained analysis of interaction between Mexican mothers and their infants, and between siblings and infants. The siblings had a greater effect on the level of performance of the infants than did the mothers. When the babies did not understand, the mothers' remedy was to explain verbally, but the siblings were more likely to demonstrate, gesture, and show, resulting in better comprehension. The siblings pointed out the younger children's mistakes and showed the right way to do what was discussed. In this way, they provided the necessary form–meaning match.

Andersen and Kekelis' (1986) study of blind children with older siblings found more language facilitation from the older siblings than from the mothers. Parents in their study had a stereotyped way of talking with the blind infants. They spent a lot of time being teachers and testers, directing, labeling and requesting labels, rather than describing events around the children and engaging the children as participants in what was happening. The siblings, while they used many strategies like the parents', increasingly diverged in interactional style. They were less accommodating of the children, they "modeled formulae and general linguistic strategies for topic initiation and maintenance, for group inclusion and for conflict resolution" (Andersen & Kekelis, 1986, p. 147). Most important, they wanted to set up joint play and struggled to get the blind child to understand how to play, and so they set more challenges, made more communicative demands, joked more, and prepared the blind children for normal interaction.

Judy Dunn (1989) found that when relations were warm and affectionate, the older child of a sibling pair engaged the younger child as a pretend-play partner. The younger child in such a pair learns to negotiate rules and roles and to offer suggestions to the older child. Pretend-play is not part of many busy mothers' repertoires, but it is a rich source of important language practice in different styles and vocabulary. For "older" learners, those of 4 and up, it provides a chance to practice a range of speech acts, styles, and registers. Siblings in these skilled age cohorts incorporate the younger learners in their play and initiate the learners into this skill.

In sum, these studies imply that siblings can in fact be a valuable source of experience in language, even for beginners, but definitely so for children of 4 or more. We know relatively little about the differences that surely affect these family processes. Older sisters, for instance, may be more likely to involve younger siblings in role play than are older brothers, since girls role play more than boys. There are wide cultural and subcultural differences in the extent to which adults engage young children in talk at all (Ochs & Schieffelin, 1984; Schieffelin & Ochs, 1986); in some groups if there is to be practice or child participation in talk outside of school, the dyad must be with child care-givers, play-mates, or siblings.

Age of Learner

The facilitating role of peer interaction in the preschool is likely to change its properties because the aspects of language undergoing growth change with age. At ages 1 and 2, children are busy developing the rhythms and sounds of language. Their peer play gives them practice in sound play, which helps tune their prosodic and phonetic articulation to what they hear. Adults are often bored and even irritated by sound play. At age 2, children are developing rudimentary syntax from conversational exchanges during play. Between ages 3 and 4, children develop conversational and strategic skills in negotiating object play with each other, so that by age 4 their talk is surprisingly mature from the standpoint of the rudiments of conversation; at ages 4 and 5 we see a much wider range in styles and ability to adopt other roles (such as daddy, teacher, or doctor), which normally children could not practice with adults.

While we know that new vocabulary often comes from travel and from experience gained outside the peer group, at least by age 3½ the peer group can bring considerable stimulation to language learning. By then children have had more diverse experiences, verbalize experience more, and take more initiative in play. For these reasons, children can become effective sources of stimulation and instruction to age peers, like the older sibling with the infant. The fact that it is peers and not just adults who are the sources of children's language knowledge is readily evident in the facts of language change, in the spread of new vocabulary, and in detailed phonological features; the sound systems used by children increasingly reflect their friendship networks throughout the school years (Eckert, 1989).

Peer Influence on Language Learning

It is folk wisdom that children learn second languages more readily from other children than they do in formal instruction. One can see how such "instruction" takes place by observing the natural interaction between learners and peer models. The learning of a second language is not basically different from first-language learning in this type of natural context, so it is a good source of clues about peer input.

The data below come from home tape recordings of peer play of English-speaking children ages 4 to 11 who had been placed in French medium schools near Geneva, Switzerland (Ervin-Tripp, 1986). A typical recording situation consisted of an English or American child, a French-speaking friend, a sibling of either or both, and sometimes a parent in the vicinity. I made repeated recordings; the activities of the children included jump-rope, card games, table soccer, dress-up, and role play. In addition to this material, I used tapes of kindergarten and first-grade Chinese and Hispanic immigrant data collected by Lily Wong-Fillmore.

In these studies it was possible to identify instances in which children added to the vocabulary, syntax, and conversational formulas that they knew. The interactional processes that brought such changes about are described below.

Imitation

When the activities were repetitive, or there were social routines where imitation was possible, the beginning efforts often relied on copying a partner. I found such imitation in the soccer game, where the same situation occurred over and over, and in play phone conversations where children were obligated to greet, make opening moves, and terminate. The easiest way to make these moves was to imitate the formulas used by others. It is important to note, however, that this is a tactic that can be used successfully only when the expected formulas are identical, not complementary: "Hi . . . Hi . . . Bye . . . Bye." In many languages, a child may not be able to greet an adult in the same way the adult greets the child, so that learning to use even simple routines cannot be based entirely on imitation of the addressee. However, in a group context like a nursery school, peers in parallel situations are always available to imitate.

Talk About Context

Young children's play with objects can include talk about the objects that the participants are playing with. If you are playing with an infant who has a ball, and you say, "Throw the ball," the child may throw it because that is what one usually does with balls. The conjunction of the typical activity with an object, and talking about that activity, helps the child match the words and meaning. There must be that kind of redundancy or predictability for language to be learned. Child play embeds talk into actions with the objects that are being referred to, ensuring that language is usually understandable because it is redundant with the context. Immigrant workers doing manual labor that is demonstrated while it is described have the same advantage.

For contrast, think of tuning into a television program in Chinese or Japanese if you do not know these languages. It would be very hard to learn meanings because you do not know what the people are talking about at each moment.

Children engaged in joint action, imitating each other's actions and talk about the actions, can learn language because the meaning of the talk is obvious. This learning was obvious in the data we gathered on soccer games.

Contextual Inference

In nursery school, children learn the structure of many games and regular play forms, just as at home they have learned household routines and can guess the meaning of new words and phrases from their situation within a routine, as in the following second-language example. The children were playing a game with repetitive turn cycles. At the end of each cycle the alternate child got to start the next cycle. The French-speaking child said to the American: "Tu commences," as she set out the materials for the next round. The American child looked puzzled at the new word, but began the round. At the end, she did the same, saying "Tu commences" to her partner. We do not know what she thought this meant; perhaps she thought it meant "It's your turn" rather than "You begin." But it is not unusual for the first uses of forms to have relatively situated, local meanings. Unlike talk about context, the meaning is inferred; the beginning of a round is not a visible referent but a concept or a position in a structure. As children learn increasingly complicated pragmatic, situated patterns, they are ready to acquire language about these patterns.

Predictable Talk Schemata

Certain speech activities have internal structure. We could say they have predictable routines. A good example of predictable routines is the framework of phone conversations. One of my children showed attention to this framework when, at about 18 months, she picked up the phone and said "Hi. Fine. Bye." She had the bare bones of the responses in the phone schema: Greeting-introductory exchange—farewell.

A fuller example appears in two 5-year-old immigrant children. By age 5, phone conversations have five steps: greeting, introductory exchange, core, pre-parting, and farewell.

> A: Hello, what ya doin?   [greeting, intro. ex.]
> B: Got two people here.   [intro. ex.]
> A: Fine. My mommy told me to go to school.   [core]
> B: Me too.
> A: Okay, bye. I'll call you back tomorrow.   [pre-part]
> B: Okay, bye.   [farewell]

In this conversation, A, the more competent speaker, produced both a greeting and introductory move on the first turn, as well as initiating the core topic about school, the farewell, and pre-parting move. In each of A's turns, she makes two moves. In each, if she replies, she also initiates. B's moves are all one-move replies, reflecting prior experience with this genre and skill that is still rudimentary but beyond mere imitation.

Correction

Children correct each other if they make errors in the predictable routines or in game talk. An indirect form of correction, common among children, who are often less didactic than adults, is to demonstrate the correct mode, without saying the other is wrong. In a play telephone conversation between an English- and a Spanish-speaking kindergartener, the Spanish speaker said, "Hello, come to my house, please." She was corrected and told, "No, you've got to say 'what are you doing'?" In this case, the learner had not correctly performed the routine for children's introductory moves following the greeting, and was explicitly taught. Children correct role play performance, as, for example, a child who told another, "You can't say 'honey'; I'm the mommy." In role play, address forms are crucial to correct enactment and would be noticeable. The location for such explicit language correction is most often in verbal routines like phone conversations, in role play, or in games requiring a specific wording of moves.

Permutation and Combination

Recombining is an important feature of learning from dialogue. Each child makes use of the material provided by the partner. We see this vividly in the sound play of 2- and 3-year-olds, who can get a lot of mileage from making rhythmic and phonological changes on each other's sound material. Unfortunately, this nonsense play often disgusts serious adults, who can rapidly tire of hearing it.

A more advanced form appears in Lily Wong-Fillmore's (1976) study of how immigrant kindergarten children took a few elementary conversational components and permuted and recombined them, as in the following example (months of exposure to English are indicated in parentheses):

(2 months) How-you-do-dese?
(5 months) How-do-you-do-dese + noun or prepositional phrase
How-do-you + verb phrase
How-did-you + verb phrase
(7 months) How-do + clause
How-does + clause
How-did + clause

We can see such pushing of resources in children's argument structure. Lein and Brenneis (1978), in elicited arguments, showed vividly how alterations of rhythm, emphasis, and values can keep turn cycles going in arguments. There is a good example in an argument in English between Chinese-speaking 5-year-olds who were newcomers to English:

B: My father, bigger your father.
C: You father big big big big big.
B: My father, uh, bigger you father.
C: My father, my father like that! [stands, reaches high]
B: My father stronger your father.
C: My father like that! [arms wide]
B: Don't talk for—I hit you!

Though American teachers often stop arguments on such occasions, children can be highly motivated in arguments to push their language resources to elaboration. Sprott (1990) has shown that justifications occur in children's arguments as early as age 3.

Language Features Learned

Sounds

The youngest children learn about the sounds of language by practicing rhythms and rhymes in sound play, a typical peer activity at age

2. Later, they practice style shifts in pronunciation and in the prosodic features of language during doll play and role play. Children talk in high pitch when they are playing babies and in low pitch when they are playing daddy or doctor. Claudia Mitchell-Kernan (1979) has reported observing Afro-American children who spoke in high pitch when playing whites and in low pitch when playing blacks. These vocal differences appear very early. Children's differentiation of speech to dolls or babies appears by age 2 (Sachs, 1984; Sachs & Devin, 1976).

Vocabulary

In role play, it is especially obvious that children learn vocabulary and set phrases. It has been known for a long time that this aspect of language is the most sensitive to variations in experience, to travel, and to schooling.

A 4-year-old playing nurse said to another, "I'm going to give you a temperature." The nurse put something in the patient's mouth, so she appeared to give rather than to take; perhaps the child assumed the name for a thermometer was "temperature." The child's first use of the term is an approximation, which moves the child into a greater readiness to notice the word at the next visit to the doctor's office. We could say that play has prepared the child for future learning and lowered the future threshold for vocabulary heard in play.

If one child brings a word from outside and uses it in play, it is now available to the others who share the play. Peers thus become a resource for new learning, because their experiences are diverse enough to provide them with material to enrich each other. We know that this transfer of vocabulary takes place, because we see it in children's role play. Children playing doctor learn medical terms from each other just as adult patients have been observed picking up medical terms from doctors.

Social Markers

Part of the need for specialized vocabulary comes from the desire to play a role correctly, to sound like a doctor or nurse. Children are very sensitive to these role or register features. They notice that teachers mark boundaries with "OK" as in "OK, it's time for our math lesson." Andersen (1986) has observed that children use "well" as a discourse marker (Schiffrin, 1986) in role playing adults rather than children. She has numerous examples of the fine-tuning of speech to role, such as the doctor's "Let's take a look at your throat now," rather than "I'll take a look at your throat now," and the following child–father exchange (Andersen, 1990):

[*high voice*] Father, father, come right here now. Baby threw up.
[*deep voice*] Oh, damn it.

The pitch, intonation, vocabulary, syntactic, and discourse marker variations come from the need to represent social categories in the child's version of the social system. It is only in role play that many of these representations are practiced.

The role play we have observed often displays the stereotypes in the oral culture shared by children, rather than directly mimics the realistic life of the family. Children maintain traditions about how to play certain roles; for example, a child whose mother is a doctor still called role-played females "nurse" and males "doctor." Daddies go to work, mommies don't, despite the child's own life. Andersen found that even in a university nursery school, fathers ordered mothers about, mothers were more polite to fathers than fathers were to mothers, and children were more polite to fathers than to mothers. Children learn social markers from each other, like the "OK" or "now" of teachers, and the bossiness and imperatives of daddies, which may occur in dramatic play regardless of the home model presented by the children's fathers.

We know that children learn both vocabulary and social markers in their play with other children. We are beginning to discover, in our studies of children's syntax, that the learning of syntax also occurs in social contexts of use.

Syntactic Elaboration

In a recent project, Aura Bocaz and I (Ervin-Tripp & Bocaz, 1989) examined the development of temporal conjunctions like "when," "while," "before," and "after." These conjunctions are syntactically important because they reveal the development of complex sentences. We found the earliest examples of temporal clauses did not appear in narratives, as was assumed, but in children's joint planning for play and in their directives to each other.

Examples of children's "planning" speech that is oriented toward the future are

—I'm going to make a garbage can when I'm all through with the train.
—When I grow up and you grow up, we're going to be the bosses.

Lots of children's talk during play involves directions about what to do, disputes over toys, claims to space and goods, and requests for permission to use goods. In these exchanges, we found many conjunctions, as in these examples:

—You listen while I read.
—Can I have your worm when you get finished?

We found that the highest frequency of this kind of speech is in peer talk, because the greatest amount of joint planning occurs in peer talk.

Another example is the causal conjunction "because." Many people assume that the early use of causality has to do with physical explanations, but instead we found in our texts that children are more interested in what we call justifying. They are trying to persuade someone else to comply with a request, or explain why they are not complying. Children use these justifications to support requests and plans as well as their explanations of the world. Causal and purposive justification, at least in our data, seems to be rooted in social interaction and social motives (Kyratzis, Guo, & Ervin-Tripp, 1990).

In our laboratory, Richard Sprott examined young children's arguments and found that arguments are the locus for development of a rich use of justifications, often with causal clauses (because . . .). Arguments about the world push the youngest children to examine evidence, and as they mature and begin to argue about goals, their disagreements lead them to make plans explicit and to support their purposes in a way that will be persuasive (Sprott, 1990).

An important feature of the syntax of the sentence is verb expansion with auxiliaries. Auxiliaries first develop at around 30 months of age. They considerably enlarge the potential of verbs, making possible elliptical replies, tag questions, and the kinds of inversion English requires in questions.

Like causals, the modal auxiliaries like "can" and "will" and catenatives like "gonna" and "hafta" are learned first for interactive, social uses. In some children, the earliest examples of "can" are in permission requests. In Julie Gerhardt's studies of modal auxiliaries in children's play, it was apparent that the children used them to make delicate social contrasts and to indicate their intentions to their conversational partners (Gee & Savasir, 1985).

"Gonna" was used by 3-year-olds in planning future activity, as in "I'm gonna make a worm," and in adversarial contexts like "No, I'm gonna be the mommy." In contrast, when children in joint play with a partner had face engagement and were enacting immediate events, they were more likely to use "will."

When children were doing doll play, in which they sometimes played director and sometimes enacted the role of doll vocally, they might as director say, "The baby is gonna have a bath," but while enacting a role they might say, "Hi, Baby, will you carry me?" The children shifted frequently, using choice of auxiliary to reveal their perspective on the action.

This kind of shifting indicates a developing awareness of the larger units of organization in discourse. It is possible to see this skill only when children are involved in peer play, because when children talk to adults, the adults commonly dominate the organization, timing, content of talk, framing of what is to be done, and definition of the situation.

Strategic Language

The social skills involved in carrying on an argument, helping other children resolve disputes so play can continue, nurturing each other, and persuading other children to collaborate involve strategic deployment of language (Corsaro, 1985). By examining language in a variety of contexts, with adults and children, we have seen that children shift their language resources according to addressee (Ervin-Tripp & Guo, in press), as well as shifting a wide range of features of conversational structure (McTear, 1985).

Peer interaction may aid in the loss of egocentrism, necessary for the development of conversational abilities. By age 5, children begin to consider the point of view of the addressee (Ervin-Tripp & Gordon, 1986). Differences in children's skill in understanding the perspective of other speakers may, for example, be fundamental to later discourse where there is less situational support, such as reading, as Ioanna Dimitracopoulou (in press) has shown in pilot research.

If children interact only with adults, or only in controlled didactic contexts, they are constantly in a subordinate situation with respect to both knowledge and power. Children in such conditions of subordination have no chance to practice the language of organization, negotiation, instruction, and nurturance, which constitutes an important component of their "linguistic capital."

Summary

I have indicated in this chapter that play gives opportunities for children to learn language from each other and to practice what they have learned elsewhere. This process of learning affects all levels of language: prosody and sounds, vocabulary, syntax, the verb system, social markers and stylistic features, and organized routines. The process of learning through interaction with other children probably is similar in first language to observations in second-language contexts: Children imitate their models, receive corrections, copy predictable routines, figure out meanings from context, and then permute and recombine what they have learned.

The opportunity to practice new forms is particularly available in play, because (as we have observed) in peer contexts children are required to negotiate what they want, to argue for their positions, and to explain plans and games. In role play they can enact a far wider range of verbal styles and genres than are available to them in adult–child contexts. In play they have the chance to acquire and practice strategic language used in social relations where adults or more powerful partners do not control them.

References

Andersen, E. S. (1986). Register variation among Anglo-American children. In B. B. Schieffelin & E. Ochs (Eds.), *Language socialization across cultures* (pp. 152–161). Cambridge: Cambridge University Press.

Andersen, E. S. (1990). *Speaking with style: Sociolinguistic development in children*. London: Croom Helm.

Andersen, E. S., & Kekelis, L. (1986). The role of sibling input in the language socialization of younger blind children. In J. Connor-Linton, C. Hall, & M. McGinnes (Eds.), *Southern California occasional papers in linguistics 11: Social and cognitive perspectives on language* (pp. 141–156). Los Angeles: University of Southern California Press.

Bates, E. (1975). Peer relations and the acquisition of language. In M. Lewis & L. A. Rosenblum (Eds.), *Friendship and peer relations*. New York: Wiley.

Corsaro, W. (1985). *Friendship and peer culture in the early years*. Norwood, NJ: Ablex.

Dimitracopoulou, I. (in press). *Conversational competence and social development*. Cambridge: Cambridge University Press.

Dunn, J. (1989). Siblings and the development of social understanding in early childhood. In P. G. Zukow (Ed.), *Sibling interaction across cultures: Theoretical and methodological issues* (pp. 106–116). New York: Springer-Verlag.

Dunn, J., & Kendrick, C. (1982). *Siblings: Love, envy, and understanding*. Cambridge, MA: Harvard University Press.

Eckert, P. (1989). *Jocks and burnouts: Social categories and identity in the high school*. New York: Teachers College Press.

Ervin-Tripp, S. M. (1986). Activity structure as scaffolding for children's second language learning. In J. Cook-Gumperz, W. Corsaro, & J. Streeck (Eds.), *Children's worlds and children's language* (pp. 327–348). Berlin: Mouton.

Ervin-Tripp, S. M., & Bocaz, A. (1989). *Quickly, before a witch gets me: Children's temporal conjunctions within speech acts* (Technical Report No. 61). Berkeley: University of California, Institute of Cognitive Studies.

Ervin-Tripp, S. M., & Gordon, D. P. (1986). The development of children's requests. In R. L. Schiefelbusch (Ed.), *Communicative competence: Assessment and intervention* (pp. 61–96). San Diego, CA: College Hill Press.

Ervin-Tripp, S. M., & Guo, J. (1990). Politeness and persuasion in children's control acts. *Journal of Pragmatics, 14,* 307–331.

Gee, J., & Savasir, I. (1985). On the use of *will* and *gonna:* Towards a description of activity-types for child language. *Discourse Processes, 8,* 143–176.

Kyratzis, A., Guo, J., & Ervin-Tripp, S. (1990). Pragmatic conventions influencing children's use of causal constructions in natural discourse. *Proceedings of the Berkeley Linguistic Society.* Berkeley, CA: Department of Linguistics.

Lein, L., & Brenneis, D. (1978). Children's disputes in three speech communities. *Language in Society, 7,* 299–324.

McTear, M. (1985). *Children's conversation.* Oxford: Blackwell.

Mitchell-Kernan, C. (1979, March). *Social and linguistic knowledge in the role-playing of Afro-American children.* Paper presented at a symposium on "Communicative competence: Language use and role-play" at the Biennial Conference of the Society for Research in Child Development, San Francisco.

Ochs, E., & Schieffelin, B. B. (1984). Language acquisition and socialization: Three developmental stories and their implications. In R. Shweder & R. LeVine (Eds.), *Culture theory: Essays on mind, self and emotion* (pp. 276–320). Cambridge: Cambridge University Press.

Sachs, J. (1984). Children's play and communicative development. In R. L. Schiefelbusch & J. Pickar (Eds.), *The acquisition of communicative competence* (pp. 109–140). Baltimore: University Park Press.

Sachs, J., & Devin, J. (1976). Young children's use of age-appropriate speech styles in social interaction and role playing. *Journal of Child Language, 3,* 81–98.

Schieffelin, B. B., & Ochs, E. (Eds.). (1986). *Language socialization across cultures.* Cambridge: Cambridge University Press.

Schiffrin, D. (1986). *Discourse markers.* Cambridge: Cambridge University Press.

Sprott, R. (1990, July). *Cognitive and social effects on children's use of justifications.* Paper presented at the conference of the International Pragmatic Association, Barcelona, Spain.

Wong-Fillmore, L. (1976). *The second time around: Cognitive and social strategies in second language acquisition.* Unpublished doctoral dissertation, Stanford University, Stanford, CA.

Zukow, P. G. (1989). Siblings as effective socializing agents: Evidence from Central Mexico. In P. G. Zukow (Ed.), *Sibling interaction across cultures: Theoretical and methodological issues* (pp. 95–105). New York: Springer-Verlag.

CHAPTER 7

The Roots of Literacy Development
Play, Pictures, and Peers

ANNE HAAS DYSON

"Bombs away!" shouts 5-year-old Chiel, in the midst of a World War II sea battle. Brandon, a classmate, is intrigued and joins in the play, adding more sound effects: "Lalalalalalalala." Chiel responds by setting the current scene and narrating the action: "There's still a second ship—a blue ship. And the first spared—the lasers! Oh oh. It destroyed my black ship. But it won't get to my blue ship."

Chiel's dramatic adventure unfolded as he sat during journal time, composing with line and color, sound effects and spoken words. His loud voice captured Brandon's attention, and he too entered into Chiel's imagined world. The wild lines of Chiel's final composition suggested the great excitement that had produced it.

Chiel's adventure with picture and peer is not the sort of image that has inspired most literacy curricula for young children. Rather, the guiding vision more often seems to be that of literacy as a solitary, quiet, and colorless activity: A child sits alone, silently writing letters. And, since young children are not viewed as "ready" to compose essays or stories

This chapter is a major revision of an article first published as "Research Currents: The Space/Time Travels of Story Writers," in *Language Arts,* 1989 vol. 66, pp. 330–340. The research project upon which it is based is described fully in Dyson (1989). Support for this work was provided in part by a seed grant from the Spencer Foundation, distributed by the School of Education, University of California-Berkeley, and by the Office of Educational Research and Improvement/Department of Education (OERI/ED) through the Center for the Study of Writing. However, the opinions expressed herein do not necessarily reflect the position or policy of the OERI/ED, and no official endorsement by the OERI/ED should be inferred.

conventionally, the children repeatedly form a single letter in orderly—
or not so orderly—rows (thereby violating the principle, explained to me
by a 5-year-old, that "if you want it to be [say] anything, you have to
mix'em up"). If pictures are involved, they are perhaps pictures of objects that begin with the sound of "the letter of the week."

And yet, as Chiel suggests, the developmental precursors to literacy,
and writing in particular, are not to be found in children's lonely, passive
behavior with worksheets, nor even exclusively in literacy behaviors
themselves. The products of skillful adult authors hint of their earlier
symbolic and social roots. Consider, for example, the directives issued
by one author, Truman Capote (1956), in *A Christmas Memory;* while
greatly different in tone from Chiel's work, it is not so different in raw
material:

> *Imagine* a morning in late November. A coming of winter morning more
> than twenty years ago. Consider the kitchen of a spreading old house in a
> country town. A great black stove is its main feature; but there is also a big
> round table and a fireplace with two rocking chairs placed in front of it. Just
> today the fireplace commenced its seasonal roar. (p. 1; emphasis added)

Truman Capote may have been physically alone when he wrote this
piece, but in his mind we, his readers, were there, just as we are there in
the quoted passage. Indeed, Capote invites us to create a world with
him: "Imagine," he says, addressing us directly. And then Capote shows
us around, pointing out colors, shapes, and sounds. This imagined world
is of a particular time and place, a present constructed from memories of
the past. And, while the memories are Capote's, our own memories, our
own experiences, allow us to paint for ourselves the scene Capote describes. "The reader's mind is the author's box of paints" (Burt, cited in
Britton, 1970, p. 116).

As Chiel and Capote suggest, for extended texts, and stories especially, authors use the stuff of children's constructive play: Young artists
build with color, shape, and sound, just as do adult authors (Tannen,
1987). And too, the essence of the story-composing act of adults is contained in children's dramatic play; young players, too, collaboratively
construct pretend worlds of other times and places, and they do so by
transforming past experiences, both actual and vicarious, into shared
imagined ones—"Let's pretend there was a battle" or, to change the
mood to one more in keeping with Capote's bittersweet book, "Let's pretend there was a party and somebody came."

It was the Russian psychologist Vygotsky (1978) who located the
prehistory of written language in children's drawing and playing.

Through drawing, children graphically represent their experiences, using lines and curves to name their world ("This is a cake"). Through play, they create imaginary situations and govern their own behavior according to rules inspired by the "real" world. The children baking the cake for the (pretend) party must act like people baking a cake, and, if past experiences give each player different rules for cake baking ("No, not like that"), those rules must be negotiated so that the present social play can continue. As in story writing, then, story players resolve tensions between the real and the imaginary, between self and others; and also as in story writing, picture painters must find lines and shapes to capture their multisensory experiences.

There are, though, developmental challenges to be met, as story players and drawers become more accomplished in the medium of written language. In writing, lines and shapes are not related in direct ways to their meanings—the lines and curves of the word *cake* are not chosen to represent the physical characteristics of cake, but are arbitrarily related to the sound of the word. As Vygotsky (1978, p. 115) explained, "the written language of children develops in this fashion, shifting from drawings of things to drawing of words." Moreover, to extend Vygotsky, if children are to collaboratively enact an imagined world in writing, they must draw, not only words, but voices, the voices of actors, of observers or narrators, and of stage directors who negotiate with the anticipated voices of their ultimate collaborators, their readers; for those readers must accept the premises of the play if it is to go on. In a timeless and ongoing social world, these voices together construct an imagined—a visualized, heard, felt—world. That is, authors shape an imaginary world, often set in time past, but which induces in their readers an anticipatory stance toward that world—their readers are drawn into the sounds and images evoked by the printed words, wondering what will happen next (Rader, 1982): "Imagine . . ."

To illustrate the roots of literacy in constructive and dramatic play, in this chapter I examine the behaviors of young school children (5- to 8-year-olds) learning to create scenes and dramas in written words. Because they are so intensely involved in this learning, the children illustrate well how their earlier experiences as drawers and players provide both resources and tensions for them.

In documenting the children's efforts, this chapter is reflective of the growing interest in young children's written language development, an area of study sometimes referred to with Marie Clay's (1966) term "emergent literacy." Most broadly, emergent literacy researchers have examined how children are socialized into their families' ways with print (Heath, 1983). They have observed young children's (particularly 3- to

6-year-olds') ways of reading—albeit unconventional reading—everything from toothpaste tubes to storybooks (Goelman, Oberg, & Smith, 1984). And they have studied as well children's early writing, which may look like "scribbling" to the uninformed (Farr, 1985). As a part of this latter work, researchers have analyzed young children's ways of figuring out how the written language encoding system works—how children discover that they can draw words, the sounds that come from their mouths (Dyson, 1983; Ferreiro & Teberosky, 1982; Read, 1986).

However, the current project is broader than most studies of emergent writing, as it focuses, not only on young children's writing, but also on the relationships among writing and earlier controlled ways of forming imagined worlds. It differs too in its concern with relationships among children themselves, a concern that grows from an interest in settings outside the home, where children, gathered together in groups, weave their lives together, influencing the course of each other's development.

Specifically, I asked: How do children transform meanings formulated in colorful drawings, often accompanied by lively talk, into the flat, black and white surface of written text? How do they formulate pretend stories about their real experiences? And, most broadly, given a setting in which peer talk and the relationships fostered by such talk are valued, how do children use written stories as part of their social lives? To put these questions in a different way, how do children come to negotiate among multiple space/time worlds when they write: among the differing symbolic worlds of pictures, sounds, and written words; and among the imaginary world (often set in the distant past), their ongoing social worlds, and the wider experienced "real" world? How, in the midst of all these realms, do they "find a place to stand" (Polanyi, 1982, p. 169)?

The data upon which the chapter is based came from a longitudinal study in an urban magnet school. (The project is detailed fully in Dyson, 1989). One teacher, Margaret, taught all the children language arts, and they all—kindergarteners through third graders—had journals in which they drew and wrote, and, in the kindergarten, dictated. As they worked in their journals, the children talked with (and occasionally shouted at) each other about their activity and also about other happenings in and out of school.

I closely observed journal time in Margaret's classroom over a two-year period. With the assistance of Carol Heller and Mary Gardner, I took handwritten observation notes and collected 144 hours of audiotaped data and 346 written products. While I came to know all the children, I focused on eight of them, four kindergarteners (Jesse, Ruben, Regina, and Maggie) whom I followed through first grade, and four first graders (Jake, Manuel, Mitzi, and Sonia) whom I followed through second grade.

The project resulted in eight detailed case histories of these young artists. Initially, as will be illustrated, the children's writing did not contain the color and drama of their drawing and playing, nor did it seem as central to their social lives. But, gradually, the children learned to "draw" and "play" together within and through the written words. As their written symbolic worlds became more connected with their drawn and spoken symbolic worlds and their social worlds, they left "footprints" in their written stories that suggested their negotiation among these varied realms. These footprints were often shifts of tense and/or points of view.

As the children's ways of writing changed, so too did my own understanding of literacy development. In the following sections, I use excerpts from the children's case histories to illustrate the developmental challenges the children faced and also the growth of the theoretical perspective presented here—this metaphor of multiple worlds—for capturing the developmental drama I observed. I then consider the implications of this perspective for early childhood language and literacy curricula.

The Discovery of Multiple Worlds

Moving Among Children's Symbolic Worlds

When I first began visiting Margaret's room, I did not have this broad perspective—this notion of multiple worlds. I was initially interested in how writing came to have a symbolic niche in children's artistic lives—that is, in how the liveliness of their drawing and talking came to exist within their writing. So, I examined the set of "composing events" compiled for each child. For each composing event—each time the child was observed composing a journal entry—I had the child's drawn picture, an audiotape of the child's talk to self and others during journal time, and the completed written text. I focused only on talk that seemed "task involved"—directly relevant to the world the child was constructing (see Figure 7.1.).

The children's journals reinforced the distinction between drawing and any accompanying talking, on the one hand, and written text, on the other: Their journals had lined paper for writing, blank for drawing. I began, then, by comparing how children built worlds of actors, actions,

FIGURE 7.1.   The Children's Talk: References to Multiple Worlds

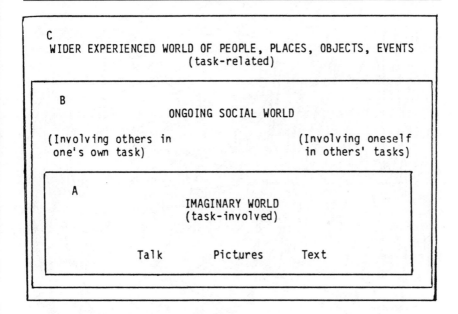

and objects through drawing and talk with how they created worlds through written text.

In kindergarten and early first grade, the children's written products were often controlled by their pictures—their written texts had little independent existence. Indeed the written texts often seemed afterthoughts. In that sense, writing was not very embedded in their social and intellectual lives. The majority (67%) of the kindergarteners' texts could be called "Art Notes"—they pointed to the pictures ("This little girl is jumping . . .") with deictic expressions ("This . . .") and/or progressive verbs ("is jumping"). Yet, increasingly, the children's talk and their texts reflected the tensions that can exist when children move among the overlapping symbolic worlds of pictures, talk, and text.

For example, Jesse, a kindergartener, acted out an elaborate narrative as he drew the piece in Figure 7.2. While he was drawing a picture, he was clearly engaged in dramatic play as well (for a discussion of children's dramatic play while drawing, see Gardner, Wolf, & Smith, 1982). Listen to Jesse as he draws and dramatizes.

ERRRRRRRRRRRRRRRRRRRRRRRRRRRRRRRRRRRRRRRRRRRRR [the sound of a motorcycle being driven]. And he falls off, and he hurts himself, and he

FIGURE 7.2.   Jesse's Motorcycle Guy

gets back up. [And so the motorcycle racer continued on the winding track.]

When asked to dictate a story about his picture, Jesse was confronted with symbolic tensions, tensions that resulted from the different space/time qualities of pictures, on the one hand, and narrative talk, on the other. His pictorial image existed in the present, but the talk and dramatic gestures that had accompanied his drawing were now past. Jesse's dictated text reflects these tensions:

This is a motorcycle guy [a present tense description of his picture]. And then the motorcycle guy won [a record, in past tense, of the told and dramatized action].

As author of this text, Jesse seems unsure of where to stand, of what stance to take. First he becomes a commentator on his picture (he presents an Art Note); then he is an observer of a past tense world.

Regina provides an example of a child confronting symbolic tensions in a different way. Unlike Jesse, Regina tended to construct scenes—images of one moment in time—rather than dramas when she drew. As a first grader, Regina drew a little girl who was holding up her dress because "she fell into the mud puddle" and "had some stuff on her shoes, and she doesn't want her dress to get all dirty—that stuff on her stockings." To accompany her picture (see Figure 7.3), she wrote an Art Note:

> This is a girl She has something on her leg's but she doesn't know that it was on her but she will know it.

When Regina reread her text, she became quite concerned: "It [the text] can't say that," she explained. The girl could not be unaware of the mud on her legs "because she's going like that [holding up her dress]." Regina was trying to resolve within her text the space/time dimensions of her picture, on the one hand, and language, on the other. Her picture existed in the present, in a frozen moment in time and space, while her language

FIGURE 7.3.   Regina's Girl with Dirty Stockings

was free to move through time. Regina, therefore, adjusted her written language so that it coordinated with her picture: Her new entry read that the girl "*know now* that it was on her legs" (rather than "doesn't know") and that "she will not *like* it" (rather than "will know it"). (For a fuller discussion of the transitions and tensions between picture making and story composing, see Dyson, 1986.)

Viewing Child Artists Within Their Social World

Over time the observed children, as authors, became less involved with their pictures. In fact, only 7 percent of the second graders' texts were Art Notes. This greater involvement with the text worlds themselves seemed to be supported in part by the children's progressively greater involvement as authors with the ongoing social world in the classroom, a world that was forming in part through the children's talk during journal time. Indeed, I could no longer focus only on "task-involved" talk, which each child engaged in about his or her own imaginary world—the children were talking a great deal about the content of *each other's* worlds.

Initially, this talk about each other's imaginary worlds occurred primarily during drawing. Talk during writing tended to be focused on spelling, a process that took great effort for most children. In time, though, the children's social talk began to focus more on the content of each other's writing. In fact, the children's very struggle with encoding helped that text world become more accessible to their peers. One child might overhear another reread his or her text; and although the rereading peer was focused on remembering and encoding a message, the listening child might react to the sense of the read message. Thus, the children's imaginary written worlds were increasingly embedded within their ongoing social world (see Figure 7.1, Part B).

Indeed, the children began to take themselves and often their peers into their texts. And then they wrestled with the border between their imaginary worlds, on the one hand, and their ongoing social world on the other. These struggles too left little footprints in their texts—shifts of tense and of person or stance.

Jake's case history provides a good illustration. As a first grader, Jake told wild narrative adventures for the benefit of his amused friends while drawing. The majority of his texts, however, were not narratives (i.e., they did not involve at least two chronologically ordered actions). Rather, Jake's texts stayed within his picture frame. For example, Jake told an elaborate narrative as he drew the picture in Figure 7.4. But after completing his picture, Jake produced a non-narrative text. While

FIGURE 7.4.   Jake's Flying Jets

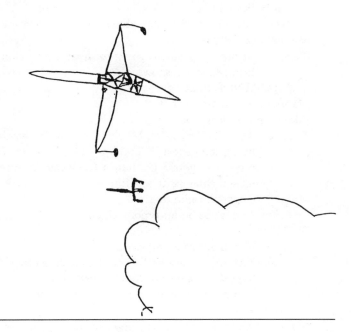

writing, he struggled with spelling and punctuation; during that struggle, he periodically referred to his picture to help him plan and remember his text. The following in his completed entry:

> I saw a jet flying over the desert. And the little jet almost got away. But the little jet is trying to get away.

But the jet couldn't get away. Like Jesse's and Regina's, Jake's figure—his jet—was stuck in his picture frame.

In the second grade, Jake's texts changed notably. He began to lean for support not on his pictures, but on interactive play with his friends, especially Manuel. And then he brought that social play into his texts and thus began to move through time—not without some vacillation, but moving nonetheless. In the following illustration, Jake is playing with Manuel as he composes an action-packed space adventure.

Jake begins writing—he has not yet drawn his picture:

Jake: (to Manuel) I'm deadly. I am deadly. I'm gonna put your name in this story and you are gonna be dead too. I'm gonna make sure you get blown to pieces. (laughs)

Manuel: Blown to pieces. (softly and a bit awed)

Jake: Yes, sir. You won't be able to see your mommy ever again.

Manuel playfully retaliates:

Manuel: In my story you're going to meet a magician who's going to turn *you* into a snowman.

Jake: Well, actually, guess wha—

Manuel: And melt you flat.

Jake seems to back down:

Jake: Actually, um, I I'm, I—we're gonna, I'm writing about um us flying the fastest jet in the world. . . . None of us—both of us are—isn't gonna get blown to pieces because it's the fastest jet—it can outrun any bullet.

Manuel: Oh wow! I like that.

Jake: And it's as bullet-proof as it can get.

But later:

Jake: Watch out Manuel! (writes *blow up*)

Manuel: Just at the very end when they're [the other children] just so happy, it's almost—they're just so happy and they read the entire story and they loved it, I get blown up.

Jake: Yeah.

Manuel: And they cry and cry and cry and cry—it's so dramatic.

When he finishes his story, Jake reads it to Manuel, grinning with Manuel's every grimace:

Jake: Once there was a boy that is named Manuel. Manuel is going to fly the fastest jet and I am going to fly the jet too. But Manuel's headquarters is going to blow up But I am OK. But I don't know about Manuel but I am going to find Manuel. . . . But I think I see him. He is in the jet. Manuel are you OK? Yes I am OK. you are being attacked. I will shoot the bad guys out of the universe. OK yes shoot them now. The end.

In his text, Jake does move through time, something an Art Note doesn't allow. He begins as a past tense observer and then becomes a present time actor. His text is movie-like—not stable but dynamic as he brings his imaginary and social worlds close together. Many of Jake's peers used dialogue in their early extended narratives; dialogue allows authors to move through time, without necessarily moving through space.

Moreover, while Jake and Manuel are clearly engaged in social play as they write, Manuel's comments suggest his awareness that story constructing, unlike much of children's social play, will be reconstructed by others, their readers, in future times and places. Through their written words, children will play with others without talking or acting at all.

Studying Child Authors' Reflections on Their Experienced Worlds

There is one more world to add to our vision of the multiple worlds of readers and writers. Frequently, the children's comments on each other's work led to talk that was task-related—talk about the wider experienced world of people, places, events, and things (see Figure 7.1, Part C). The children's imaginary worlds were thus increasingly embedded within yet another world. This embedding too could lead to clashes, as the children wrestled with how true experiences and personal opinions figured into their "made-up" worlds. For example, Mitzi confronted that dilemma in the following excerpted event, from her first-grade data set.

> Mitzi has used "Snoopy stickers" to create a picture of the cartoon character Snoopy and a small bear at the beach. She then writes:
> > Once there was a bear. And there was Snoopy too. They were
> She stops and comments:
> *Mitzi:* OK, there'll be a little tiny sister.
> Sonia overhears her:
> *Sonia:* They were sisters?
> *Mitzi:* Yeah.
> *Sonia:* Snoopy isn't a girl.
> *Mitzi:* I know. Sister AND brother.
> Mitzi then completes her text:
> > They were sister and brother. And they were at the beach, Snoopy is a boy and the bear was the girl. The End.

In her text, Mitzi temporarily changes her role as writer. She abandons her observational perch by the imaginary world set in the indefinite past to make a "real" world observation about Snoopy. She was motivated to do that by the reaction she received in her ongoing social world. As peers did in all case histories, Sonia focused Mitzi's attention on her text and implicitly pointed out that texts were not simply representations or comments on her pictures or her feelings—her texts were social acts. They could affect how others behaved toward her, as peers passed judgment on her texts' accuracy—and her own competence. In the ongoing social world, readers—peers—judge the imaginary world as they reflect on their own experienced worlds.

Analyzing Children's Negotiation Among Multiple Worlds

In order to put all these worlds together, I present a final example of Mitzi at work at the end of her second-grade year. Mitzi wrote a deceptively simple text about cats. Her text, unlike her Snoopy piece, presented a unified—a stable—world, but she, as author, moved among worlds in an impressively sophisticated fashion, for her imaginary text was embedded within her ongoing social and her experienced world.

> On this day, Mitzi wants to write about cats. The topic of her imaginary world seems to serve her in her ongoing social world, for her friend Jenni consistently writes about cats. Days earlier, Mitzi wrote the title for the entry. So she knows that the story has to have something to do with "The Surprise Party."
>
> *Mitzi:* Jenni, what can I write about? Um, I'm thinking about cats. It's gonna be a surprise party about cats. What should I write about? You're good, you're good at that. . . . [i.e., writing about cats] (pause) I know! A bird that'll go and kill a cat!
>
> *Yahmya:* A vulture?
>
> *Mitzi:* No! They're my made-up cats. Once I made up some cats. . . . And there were some birds. Birds! And they eat'em too.
>
> *Yahmya:* They eat CATS?
>
> *Mitzi:* Mm mmm. [Yes]
>
> Mitzi seems to justify her story in her ongoing social world by separating her imaginary world from her experienced real one ("They're my made-up cats"). But when Mitzi finally begins writing, she writes about cats that eat birds. After writing her piece, Mitzi begins drawing a tree and soon realizes that she needs "dead birds down here" under her tree.
>
> *Jenni:* Cats?
>
> *Mitzi:* Yeah—listen:
> "Once there was a bunch of cats. Then all of a sudden there came a flock of birds. This was a BIG surprise to the cats. At once the cats started to kill them." [Mitzi has actually written "At once they started to kill them." Perhaps Jenni's confusion

about who is eating whom led to the change, a change Mitzi
later makes in the text itself.]
Jenni suggests a strategy for avoiding a picture full of dead birds:
Jenni: You can put some flying away up here.
Mitzi pauses and then has yet another thought:
Mitzi: No, I know what I'm going to do.
Mitzi then adds "and eat them" to the last line of her text, eliminating
the need for dead birds. She draws one bird; it's crying as it hovers near
the tree. (See Figure 7.5.)

In this event, Mitzi produced a carefully coordinated picture and
text that combined to tell a sensible, imaginary tale to her interested,
inquisitive friends. She was not simply creating a more stable text world,
but she was moving among worlds, using her written world to make connections with her drawn, social, and experienced worlds in deliberate,
controlled ways.

FIGURE 7.5.   Mitzi's Hovering Bird

On Embedding Writing in Children's Lives as Artists and Friends

In recent years, many early childhood and language arts educators have discussed the importance of young children's play *with* written language. Given the opportunity, perhaps at an open-ended drawing and writing center stocked with markers and paper, children will engage in exploratory play, experimenting with the visual features of written language or the details of the encoding system (Clay, 1975; Dyson, 1983; Genishi & Dyson, 1984). Given similarly equipped dramatic play areas, children may incorporate print into their social play, as they read and write grocery lists, construct signs for the fire station and grocery store, or jot down urgent phone messages for husbands or wives (Schickedanz, 1986).

This sort of play with print is clearly valuable. Yet, as Margaret's children suggest, if we are to understand how children come to create imaginary written worlds—how they come to play together *inside* the writing—we must look not simply to play with print, but to imaginative play itself. As Vygotsky (1978) explained, "imagination in adolescents and adults is play without action" (p. 93) and, in imaginative writing, it is play through the medium of written language. Understanding the roots in children's play of this aspect of literacy—this capacity to construct "possible worlds" through print—Bruner (1986) provides yet another reason for resisting simplistic visions of literacy and literacy learning, particularly visions that locate literacy's roots in children's distinctly unimaginative copying of lifeless letter forms, connected to and signifying nothing.

When children engage in constructive play with paints or markers, they use line, shape, and color to capture, to transform, to think about some aspect of experience; eventually, imaginary worlds come to life on their papers, worlds of time and space, and of actors, objects, and actions (Smith, 1983). Through social and dramatic play, children also come to collaboratively construct worlds, which they mark as separate from their perceived real worlds, even as they work to transform those constructed worlds in sensible (or playfully nonsensical) ways (Franklin, 1983). Of course, the raw material for children's play is not only real but also vicarious experiences, as the characters and plots from books, television, and films find a place in the play.

Beginning in the early years, teachers can help infuse print with the liveliness of other symbolic forms and of children's social relationships. Talking with teachers and peers about their dictated and authored texts provides children with information on the meanings others find in their work and thus with opportunities to become aware of artistic tensions (Smith, 1983). Drama allows children to treat their own and others' written texts as scripts and thus to actively manipulate time and space. As Paley (1981, 1986) has illustrated, even 3-, 4-, and 5-year-olds can collaboratively transform themes of their dramatic play into dictated texts and back again to play—given, of course, an observant teacher who can help children make the needed transformations. Paley, herself such a teacher, notes how interested her kindergarteners became in story dictating—when it was linked to story playing:

> [I]t had always seemed enough just to write the children's words. Obviously it was not; the words did not sufficiently represent the action, which needed to be shared. For this alone, the children would give up play time, as it was a true extension of play. (1981, p. 12)

As illustrated by Margaret's children, just as drawing, social talk, and dramatic play help infuse writing with meaning, their interweaving with writing poses developmental challenges, since, eventually, drawing and drama themselves must be differentiated from written language. Gradually, children become aware of the tensions among varied symbolic media and among different social beings as well. Worlds first discovered through talk and pictures do not so easily fit on a page. Current feelings and past experiences must be transformed if they are to find expression within imaginary worlds. And, to add to the challenge, those imaginary worlds, often set in the distant past, are the author's means for interacting with future (and for these young authors, with their present, sitting-right-beside-them) readers.

From these productive tensions emerge new ways of using these support systems. For example, during the years from 6 to 8, children may begin to sequence drawings to capture narrative movement, incorporate talk as dialogue in written texts, or transform friends into characters in their written worlds. Teachers help too, as they talk with children about their processes and products and about those of professional authors as well. (See Teberski, 1987, for a thoughtful discussion of one primary-grade teacher's strategies for helping children write fiction.)

To move from the study of Margaret's children to the broader area of emergent literacy research, this view of children as constructing written language knowledge, rather than passively absorbing it, has enormous potential for helping early childhood educators plan and evaluate the literacy experiences offered children in centers and schools. Part of the power of this perspective is its conception of written language, not only as an object of knowledge or a kind of skill, but also as a social tool that children can use to connect with important others, including their friends. Thus, the development of literacy depends on the nature of the social relationships within which that literacy is embedded, and much talk among children—not much silence from children—is viewed as critical.

But this emergent literacy perspective is not without potential problems. Without knowledgeable advocates, it can be used to support less, not more, play in the curricula. The aspects of early literacy research often stressed in the literature do not necessarily challenge the essence of literacy programs for young children. As illustrated by the often cited report *Becoming a Nation of Readers* (Anderson, Hiebert, Scott, & Wilkinson, 1984), much attention has been given to parents' reading to preschoolers and *what* children learn from this experience. Much attention has also been given to the nature of young children's alphabetic invented spelling, that is, how they sound out words when they spell and thus practice "phonics" (another *what*—and, in fact, a very developmentally sophisticated child behavior [Dyson, 1983; Ferreiro & Teberosky, 1982]). Much of this research has taken place in middle class homes, where there tend to be more of the kinds of literacy experiences that are valued—expected—by the school (Heath, 1983).

Despite the obvious value of reading to children and the skill suggested by invented spelling, if the emphasis is primarily on what some children come to school already knowing about print, there is the danger that this research could be used to reinforce more structured literacy activities, particularly in kindergarten. After all, the argument goes, "children" are coming more "ready" than ever before. But other children—also competent, if in different ways, and full of possibility—are being judged at ever younger ages as not quite measuring up to expectations (Charlesworth, 1989). The challenge for early childhood educators, then, is to take advantage of children's capacity for exploring and creating with and through varied symbolic media, including written language, without contributing to the trend toward less playful, more structured academic programs for young children.

To this end, the research emphasis might best be on understanding the *process* of becoming literate, the sorts of symbolic and social supports that nurture this process, and how this process plays itself out in a variety of settings in our diverse society. The educational emphasis, then, might best be on providing young children with the sorts of supports required for literacy growth, so that we may help children to build on the variety of kinds of knowledge and know-how they bring with them to centers and classrooms. Included in these supports are not only time and materials for exploring books and paper and pencils, but also a talk-filled and playful social world in which literacy—and children's capacity for naming, expressing, and collaboratively imagining ways of living—can grow.

If children, including Chiel, are to experience intellectual, emotional, and social satisfaction through writing and reading imaginative worlds, just as they do through drawing and playing them, they must not see written texts as things set apart from their own lives. Through the developmental resources and tensions provided by peers, pictures, and play, children may come to understand that the meaning embedded in written words exists because those words form worlds embedded in people's lives. As readers and, as stressed here, as writers, they can enter into imaginative worlds; moreover, they can invite their friends in as well. And from inside those worlds of possibilities, they can explore the outside world of actions, characters, and feelings, and, in the process, can solidify their own ongoing relationships, their shared social world. It is through the evolution of a practical understanding of this power—this capacity of authors for action in multiple worlds—that Chiel's playful adventures and his excited, colorful graphic swirls will come to exist one day within the deceptively bland pages of written text.

References

Anderson, R. C., Hiebert, E. H., Scott, J. A., & Wilkinson, I. A. G. (1984). *Becoming a nation of readers: The report of the Commission on Reading.* Washington, DC: The National Institute of Education.

Britton, J. (1970). *Language and learning.* Harmondsworth, Middlesex, England: Penguin Press.

Bruner, J. S. (1986). *Actual minds, possible worlds.* Cambridge, MA: Harvard University Press.

Capote, T. (1956). *A Christmas memory.* New York: Random House.

Charlesworth, R. (1989). "Behind" before they start? Deciding how to deal with the risk of kindergarten "failure." *Young Children, 44*(3), 5–13.

Clay, M. (1966). *Emergent reading behavior.* Unpublished doctoral dissertation, University of Auckland.

Clay, M. (1975). *What did I write?* Auckland, New Zealand: Heinemann.

Dyson, A. Haas. (1983). The role of oral language in early writing processes. *Research in the Teaching of English, 17,* 379–409.

Dyson, A. Haas. (1986). Transitions and tensions: Interrelationships between the drawing, talking, and dictating of young children. *Research in the Teaching of English, 20,* 379–409.

Dyson, A. Haas. (1989). *Multiple worlds of child writers: Friends learning to write.* New York: Teachers College Press.

Farr, M. (Ed.). (1985). *Advances in writing research: Vol. 1. Children's early writing development*. Norwood, NJ: Ablex.

Ferreiro, E., & A. Teberosky. (1982). *Literacy before schooling*. Portsmouth, NH: Heinemann.

Franklin, M. B. (1983). Play as the creation of imaginary situations: The role of language. In S. Wapner & B. Kaplan (Eds.), *Towards a holistic developmental psychology* (pp. 197–220). Hillsdale, NJ: Erlbaum.

Gardner, H., Wolf, D., & Smith, A. (1982). Max and Molly: Individual differences in early artistic symbolization. In H. Gardner (Ed.), *Art, mind, and brain: A cognitive approach to creativity* (pp. 110–127). New York: Basic Books.

Genishi, C., & Dyson, A. Haas. (1984). *Language assessment in the early years*. Norwood, NJ: Ablex.

Goelman, H., Oberg, A., & Smith, F. (Eds.). (1984). *Awakening to literacy*. Portsmouth, NH: Heinemann.

Heath, S. B. (1983). *Ways with words: Language, life, and work in communities and classrooms*. New York: Cambridge University Press.

Paley, V. G. (1981). *Wally's stories*. Cambridge, MA: Harvard University Press.

Paley, V. G. (1986). *Mollie is three: Growing up in school*. Chicago: University of Chicago Press.

Polanyi, L. (1982). Literary complexity in everyday storytelling. In D. Tannen (Ed.), *Spoken and written language: Exploring orality and literacy* (pp. 155–170). Norwood, NJ: Ablex.

Rader, M. (1982). Context in written language: The case of imaginative fiction. In D. Tannen (Ed.), *Spoken and written language: Exploring orality and literacy* (pp. 185–198). Norwood, NJ: Ablex.

Read, C. (1986). *Children's creative spelling*. London: Routledge & Kegan Paul.

Schickedanz, J. A. (1986). *More than the ABCs: The early stages of reading and writing*. Washington, DC: National Association for the Education of Young Children.

Smith, M. L., & Shepard, L. A. (1988). Kindergarten readiness and retention: A qualitative study of teachers' beliefs and practices. *American Educational Research Journal, 25*, 307–333.

Smith, N. R. (1983). *Experience and art*. New York: Teachers College Press.

Tannen, D. (1987). The orality of literature and the literacy of conversation. In J. Langer (Ed.), *Language, literacy, and culture: Issues of society and schooling* (pp. 67–88). Norwood, NJ: Ablex.

Teberski, S. (1987). From fake to fiction: Young children learn about writing fiction. *Language Arts, 64*, 586–596.

Vygotsky, L. S. (1978). *Mind in society: The development of higher psychological processes* (M. Cole, V. John-Steiner, S. Scribner, & E. Souberman, Eds. & Trans.). Cambridge, MA: Harvard University Press.

CHAPTER 8

Perspectives from the Field

MARIAN K. ALTMAN
WENDY FONG

As the principal (Altman) and a kindergarten teacher (Fong) at a California primary school, we have experienced first hand the concerns and issues that led to the report of the California Task Force on School Readiness (see Chapter 3). For some time our school has been trying, often against considerable odds, to preserve a place for play and self-directed cognitive activity in its curriculum.

We have long been aware of the researchers and professors in education and psychology at work in the nearby university. We knew that research in early education and child development done there and elsewhere supported many of the recommendations for change made by the California task force. Accordingly, we welcomed the invitation to participate in the Symposium on Play and the Social Context of Development in Early Care and Education. It provided a chance to understand the profound changes in education that are happening, on the one hand, and the effects of the changing social structure on our students, on the other.

The following sketches, written after the conference, attempt to present realistic pictures of principal and teacher at work in a particular school. The school is not unlike many other primary schools in the diversity and complexity of the problems it confronts, the number of solutions it must find, and the questions that remain unanswered.

The Principal's View

Some days are so filled with the unexpected, with the need to make instant decisions, that little time is left for reflection. This day was, in that respect, an exception.

The Hour Before School

It was a typical early hour in my office, a quiet hour before staff, children, and parents came. A deliberate hour in a California primary school. But the principal's mail would be no different in other places: Would the principal please respond to schedule a new dental education program; meet with the parent advisory committee to discuss the elimination/reduction of kindergarten instructional assistants; prepare documentation to support the Board of Education's goal of 1.5 years' academic growth for one year's schooling for all children receiving Compensatory Education Services; be interested in a presentation to help prepare children for the spring Comprehensive Test of Basic Skills (CTBS); verify the order for science and social studies texts—". . . did I mean to order so few books for first, second, and third graders and none for kindergarteners?" queried the clerk.

A note from a parent sounded somewhat exasperated that her daughter was told by the third-grade teacher, "You can't have free choice until you finish your work." Since her daughter never could finish the assignments, the child never got free play and now didn't want to come to school. "Please talk to the teacher," pleaded this parent.

Another letter requested a meeting with me "and others" to find out why the first-grade academic program was still so weak in her son's class in spite of previous conversations on the subject. Yes, her son loved school, was reading well, and had lots of information, but he hated to spend after-school time writing and spelling. His spelling was so "bad" that only he could read his stories, he resisted writing on lined paper, and he kept wanting to do the same math algorithms over and over again. What was I going to do about her complaints? Why did she have to teach her son at home the very things she learned in school? After all, he was going to be in second grade soon. He was almost 7 years old and all he ever did in school was play!

From my experience, I knew that the "whole language" approach (see Chapters 6 and 7) works. I thought about the viewpoints of the parents. How does one respond to a constituency with so many different values among them? How do you explain the routines, procedures, and constancy needed to define limits when children are often left to write their own rules?

Next was the phone call saying that Hal's father had been arrested in a drug bust, with Hal witnessing everything. "His teacher better make him behave himself. Hal's here listening to me," said his mother. Hal is 8, sullen, belligerent in class, and a two-fisted itchy ball of explosives outdoors. I recalled the teacher's recent analysis, "Hal will make it. He can read well." Is that all it takes? More to ponder.

On the Play Yard

Thinking about Hal, I walked into the hub-bub of the outer office and onto the play yard—a microcosm of California's child population reflected in the multi-ethnic faces of 360 primary-school children. The children played on a yard designed for them, and would enter room environments designed for them, guided by teachers and staff who took the time to care. The teachers, a diverse group in age and training, were understanding of play as a child's reality and the vehicle for literacy. But what did the teachers need to face today's children? And tomorrow's? And what did a principal have to know for today's teachers? And tomorrow's?

This campus is burgeoning with children from dawn to dusk, children whose formal schooling is sandwiched between child care arrangements both simple and complex, public and private, on and off campus. And many of the children live in stressful situations that the school must not overlook.

The Story of Jimmy

Jimmy is part of that scene. He came to us as a repeating first grader who clearly challenged all ideas: some of the children's and many of the adults'. I placed Jimmy in a first-second combination class and put his progress under close scrutiny. Jimmy lives in Northtown about 30 miles away from this city with his mother and younger sibling. Jimmy's mother is a meter reader. Each morning Jimmy and his sibling leave home to be dropped at a sitter's place near the school so his mother can be at work by 6:30. At 7:30 they are left at the extended day care on school campus so the sitter can get to work by 8:00. At the end of the school session, the procedure is reversed. The children go to extended day care, where they are picked up by yet another sitter and eventually by their mother to return to Northtown. Jimmy's mother is a very responsible parent. She leaves us with four phone numbers because she knows how hard it is to reach her when she is on her route. She calls these numbers for messages from the school. The children are healthy so there is usually no message. But I had many messages from Jimmy's teacher about his brash behavior, low self-esteem, neatly done homework, and eagerness to learn. I left a message for his mother to call me. When we finally made our rendezvous, I heard about a little boy who had formerly gone to his neighborhood school but knew his mother was far away all day. He had spent two years brooding and not learning. So she transferred her children to our school. Now he and his mother get to talk and visit on the long drives to and from Northtown. So what if he had to get up an hour earlier! She told me of Jimmy's fierce loyalty to his little brother, how well he handled home chores, his many organizational skills, his love of singing and of his teacher. And how he hated to be in first grade again.

And so I made a bargain with Jimmy's mother: If he could "catch up" I would move him into his proper grade the following year. I didn't even know what "catch up" meant, but it was the phrase his teacher used when I passed the suggestion to her. It was agreed that Jimmy would not be told about this bold decision until school was out, but his mother did tell him that if he could behave better in school he would have a wonderful surprise at the end of the school term. What inner fortitude for this 7-year-old to wait for the unknown surprise! Jimmy's behavior was a roller coaster for the rest of the year. The last morning of school Jimmy came running to me across the yard as I went to seek him out. "My mother told me the surprise," he said as he grabbed me around the waist in a giant hug. "Thank you. I promise I'll 'catch up' over the summer." I guess Jimmy knew what it meant. That was the important thing. Double promoting him is a big risk.

The point is that we have to take risks now that may not have presented themselves before. When we speak of educating the whole child, that child carries baggage of a society in flux. That child is family, neighborhood, and culture all in transformation when he or she crosses the threshold of the school. I think about the responsibility for raising America's children that falls more and more heavily on our public schools. I think about my sphere of influence. I think about the lack of money.

Insufficient Funds

There is always the funding. It is never enough. Priorities? A child will be 6 years old only once. Can we settle for second quality paints or pencils? Maybe this year we could use the state textbook kindergarten apportionment to buy manipulative math items. Maybe this year we can replace the 15-year-old wooden puzzles. The 30-year-old easels will go on forever. The 10-year-old easels need replacing. Could this be a class discussion item for third graders? Why do the teachers' wish lists grow smaller with their teaching longevity? Have they "given up"? Become more inventive? Gotten too harried to follow the catalogs? Could this be a discussion item for staff meetings? Will we always have to depend on PTA fund raisers as we lurch from crisis to crisis? Will primary school teachers keep subsidizing the schools from personal purses?

I think about staff development. I read and value the latest research about children, language, and literacy. The school district values curriculum. The state is loyal to its frameworks. Are we in balance? I hope not! I want our staff development to stay tipped toward the children, to keep a vision of the "perfect school," where the teachers and I work together in a rhythmic flow from kindergarten through third grade without tests, lists, deadlines, territories, and the burden of "outside agendas." Now the children read their journals to me and each other, write love notes to the office, sing songs, and grow flowers. The California Assessment Program (CAP) scores are published in the *Oakland Tribune*! The State Superintendent of Schools writes, "Congratulations! Your school met the statewide performance goal and is in the highest performance category. I hope you continue the good work and continue meeting goals." I think of my question to the staff, "What is it like to be a student in this school?" I think about the ratio of students to adults in our primary school and the struggle to find volunteers, and I marvel at the little miracles that teachers create every day.

What is it like to teach here? As the principal, I see it as part of my job to free the teachers from the overburden of institutional trivia and guide them to experiences that maximize teacher-child and child-child learning, self-esteem, and dignity. I think about all the requirements. In the fall, I meet with each teacher to review written goals for every student assigned to his or her class. It is a big chunk of time, but then I know we have reviewed each student carefully. And that exercise leads teachers to talk to each other about students. How necessary that is when the school considers that the students belong to us all. We have the weekly assemblies, when we all participate in songs, stories, play, presentations, concerts, patriotic exercises, and affirmations of our success. A monthly writing sample from each student affirms by June that learning has been significant, and I require report cards to be read by me before distribution to ensure that messages sent will be useful to the receiver. Basically, I require a structure.

Within that structure, I require diversity, reflection, and play to lead the children to opportunity, choices, discussion, and language. The teachers have to have the freedom to experiment with the many different approaches it takes to reach and teach all our students. After all, we have 14 languages spoken here and a four-year strand of three Chinese bicultural classes. And try ideas we must. We talked of videotaping our children learning and of the time, expense, and value. Can researchers help us use the new technology to look at our classrooms, define our specific problems, and see our way to new solutions?

A School at Work and Play

In my mind's eye, I see the school again. The third grades are filled with literature, writing, art, music, self-governance, and lots of social interaction; the second graders are busy besting each other verbally, working on murals, stories, and creating clay and cardboard cities; the first graders are at the easels, blocks, books, and calendars, some are planting a garden, others are examining sugar crystals. Some of our classes are multi-age grouped, but an observer probably could not tell the difference. The kindergarteners are full of chatter and activity. The doors are standing ajar. I walk into the Chinese bicultural kindergarten.

The Teacher's View

A brief but typical period in my classroom shows what goes on in children's play. It also shows some of the rewards that have accrued to me as I have observed the children through the year.

An Interval of Play

I looked up suddenly from writing down the last line of a child's dictated story, to notice that the principal had walked into our classroom. I wondered if there was another problem to solve. I glanced around the room to assess the activity of each child.

Five children in the dramatic play corner were in the midst of an argument about whose turn it was to be the mother, father, sister, brother, and baby for the day. We call the corner our "dollhouse" (mispronounced consistently by some as "doghouse"), but over time it has changed from house, to supermarket, to Chinese deli, to restaurant, to store, and even to bus.

Another two children were discussing how to change the game on the Apple computer, an activity popular enough to warrant a check-off list for those who have had a turn. My instructional assistant was now being approached by the "artists" who needed assistance with mixing new colors of paint for their easel paintings. Marie and Rachel were busy deciding what to add to the one painting they were working on together.

Meanwhile, a group of boys were zooming their lego planes and flying buses around the room. Inevitably, I received complaints about how the planes were flying too low over the skyscrapers in the block center, causing some major problems for the builders.

A quiet, desperate voice interrupted me, pleading for a piece of that shiny, copper-colored paper just like the one Tina has, so that a crown can be made. "No, I'm sorry, I don't know how to make a crown. Maybe Tina can show you how."

Next, I found Ming's face right in front of mine, saying in a demanding tone of voice, "I want another little book. I am writing another little book." Each word in his sentence was punctuated as his sentences were uttered haltingly. What progress, I thought to myself. Ming spoke very little English when he entered kindergarten and he had had such difficulty making eye contact with any person addressing him or with those to whom he spoke. I quickly handed him another little blank book. "How do we ask for things in a polite way?" I asked with a smile. "Please may I have another book?" Ming smiled back. He walked off happily to illustrate his second book before returning to ask for help with writing the text for his illustrations. I glanced over at the children who were responding to the principal's inquiries about their project.

As a teacher, I am faced daily with the task of encouraging maximum growth and development within each child in my classroom. From a professional perspective, I know that this progress needs to be individually evaluated. I also face the challenge of meeting standards imposed by the school district via curriculum requirements, standardized tests, and teaching standards subtlely conveyed by the administration; and meeting expectations of the children's parents and the children's next teacher. To discover through the use of play in the curriculum an effective way of dealing with stresses coming from multiple sources has been both exciting and lifesaving for me: exciting, because it allows me to be creative and flexible in the types of learning situations I offer my students; lifesaving, because my professional career may have long ago expired had I been relegated to rigid teaching programs that focus on the product and not the process. Play programs offer experience that the child individualizes for him or herself. They can result not only in satisfactory standardized test performance scores but also in immeasurable increases in achievement and development that extend far beyond the school district's current test requirements. These are, of course, the achievements that I get most excited about.

Learning and Development in Activity Time

The scene described above is typical of our daily activity time. In it we see children busy talking to each other, children walking around for various reasons, children deeply involved with what they call their "work."

Activity time occurs once or twice a day, depending on our schedule, and usually lasts for about 50 minutes. Our favorite time of day allows children to make choices independently within a structure defined by the schedule, materials available, and student-made and teacher-imposed guidelines for behavior. This freedom of choice within a safe environment is met with various reactions, especially at the beginning of the school year. Some children are ready for such independence and quickly make the necessary decisions and take the steps for immersing themselves into whatever activity they choose. Others have difficulty making their choice or choices and sometimes ask to have the decisions made for them. Regardless of the children's initial response, progress in this learning process is observable over time. Seth, who was always the last person to leave the rug after everyone else had chosen their activity, soon learned that nothing happened during activity time unless he made it happen.

Activity time provides a multitude of learning experiences individualized for each child. The little girl who asked for a piece of shiny, copper-colored paper for making a crown, proceeded to gather the materials she needed after observing another child's work and determining for herself exactly what she needed for her project. When she consulted her friend Tina for instructions on how to make a crown, that provided an opportunity for Tina to rethink the construction process and give instructions clearly. The conversation between the two children allowed for meaningful oral language practice.

The emphatic speaker learned to read and comprehend books in English while he was learning to express himself clearly in English. He was fascinated by the idea that he too could be an author. Activity time creates an optimal situation for oral language development. The children find many opportunities to learn new vocabulary in their conversations with others about their work. Furthermore, they have a genuine need for communicating with their peers and adults about their interests and projects. There is a constant exchange of ideas, and time is available for developing these ideas.

Since the children are given the freedom to make their own choices, some repeat the same activities for many days. I recall how Toby sat and read the Sesame Street Dictionary day after day, chuckling to himself, not wanting to get involved with the other children or other activities. I almost wished that he hadn't yet learned to read so that he couldn't escape so easily into his own world. However, I soon discovered that Toby's behavior reflected his deepest need. His mother, a young lawyer, had died shortly before he entered kindergarten. Toby needed to "play" in his own way. Throughout the school year, he slowly became more interested in others and other activities. I can imagine how he would have responded if he had been pressured to complete worksheets or color pictures when he entered kindergarten, already a reader and creative storyteller, but one who experienced extreme difficulty controlling a pencil.

Another child, Fanny, chose to build with blocks every day for about two weeks. She began simply with building structures and later decided to use blocks to designate boundaries for different rooms in "her house." Her project culminated with floor plan drawings, which she used to replicate her building projects. I was impressed with the way she had reenacted her father's work as a builder. Unlike filling in blanks or dittoed worksheets, the activities available and the repeated experiences allow the children to increasingly develop their ideas. Watching a child model with clay, paint, or build with blocks day after day, one can witness a growth process—a development of ideas, improved skills, deepened interests, and a discovery of new ways to look at the familiar. Jerry started out with very few ideas as to what he could do with blocks, but his constructions became increasingly sophisticated over time. His projects toward the end of the school year included mazes with a variety of secret hiding places, and, of course, traps for the enemies.

Seeking Parental Support

Most parents have been tremendously supportive of such humanistic goals and of learning through play. However, some parents observing the play just described may feel that their child is learning nothing because he or she is "not reading yet" or because the teacher is not standing in front of the class "teaching." This is where we can ask, "Does learning only follow teaching?" Many parents are very concerned about their child's ability to achieve. Here is where I have incorporated teaching the parents about how children learn as part of my professional duty. I do this via Back-to-School evening with parents at the beginning of the school year, explaining my approach to teaching and enlisting them as allies in the process. I also share my ideas with parents during their individual conferences or phone calls in the evening. As a professional, I need to believe that I possess a unique body of knowledge that enables me to make assessments about a child's learning potential and to create educational experiences that foster the development of healthy attitudes and learning skills. A parent's insistence on a change in the curriculum is less threatening if I know that the decisions I have made are based on research and have resulted in greater observed learning and development in my own classroom experience. Of course, once the parents are made believers, my work is lightened because they will be enforcing the same principles at home, thereby speeding the growth process in many instances.

Advocating for the Children

As I contemplate the children's participation in the CTBS, I realize that some will have difficulty despite our having practiced such test-taking skills as coloring in bubbles. Some of them know the information required in the test, but when it is in a different context, or asked in a slightly different way, some children will "fail." It is difficult to understand why we should give children such an inaccurate message as "You don't know what you should know; you are a failure," when it can have a great negative impact on their self-esteem, often affecting their attitude toward school and learning in general. Furthermore, some individuals have struggled all year learning to follow directions, developing self-control, increasing their English vocabulary, learning how to make choices independently, learning to work with others, learning what it feels like to do something well—planning and implementing projects that they often come up with completely on their own. How can we monitor such successes that set the foundation for future learning?

Perhaps only by the end of kindergarten is Johnny ready to practice the alphabet, write his name, count things, and so on. Do we applaud him, or do we convey the message that he has failed because he is "behind"? Who is so bold as to set the standards or the time-line for a child's development and maturity? Why should we label children "delayed" in kindergarten when they are at the beginning of their growth process? We pat ourselves on the back when the state school superintendent congratulates us for meeting the statewide performance goal for the California Assessment Program, but how much more should we commend ourselves when children leave us as caring individuals who can make decisions and judgments independently, who work hard to carry out their own ideas, who can work cooperatively in a group, who can express themselves with conviction because they have experienced and internalized the information that has been presented to them or that they have discovered for themselves?

While the task of education grows increasingly more complex and the challenge is overwhelming at times, I continue to find satisfaction in my teaching.

Part III

PLAY,
COGNITIVE DEVELOPMENT,
AND THE SOCIAL WORLD

CHAPTER 9

Play, Cognitive Development, and the Social World

The Research Perspective

AGELIKI NICOLOPOULOU

This chapter will attempt to provide an overview of the psychological research on play and cognitive development by sketching out the predominant theoretical frameworks that have informed it. An overview of this sort is necessary to help uncover the perspectives that have directed research on play; to evaluate the strength and weaknesses of the research; and, even more important, to consider what directions might be useful to follow in future investigations. In particular, I will suggest how some of the unexplored possibilities inherent in existing perspectives could be developed to contribute to a more powerful program of research that can address the concerns of both researchers and practitioners. In addition, this overview will help to situate in their larger context the issues addressed by the next three chapters.

The relationship between play and cognitive development has dominated psychological research on play over the last three decades. Two major theoretical frameworks have played a predominant role in shaping and organizing this research. For a long period the dominant influence was that of Piaget, whose approach to play formed an integral part of his larger theory of cognitive development. Though the Piagetian research program is far from exhausted, there is an increasingly widespread sense of its limitations, and Piaget's developmental theory has drawn a growing range of criticism. In particular, it has been argued that the Piagetian framework pays insufficient attention to the social and cultural elements in cognitive development. Research on play that pays systematic attention to these factors has been gaining steadily in recent years; and, while this research has drawn on several sources, the framework that increasingly informs and unifies it has been Vygotsky's sociocultural theory of mental development.

The position taken in this chapter is that Vygotsky's theoretical framework offers, at the very least, a useful complement to the Piagetian approach and is likely to be increasingly significant in shaping research on play. The approach advocated here will draw heavily on the Vygotskian perspective; and I will therefore attempt to clarify how Vygotsky's understanding of play as a social activity is connected to his broader concern for the sociocultural bases of cognition.

Piaget on Play

A resurgence of psychological research on play in the 1970s was stimulated in large measure by Piaget's seminal work, *Play, Dreams and Imitation in Childhood* (1945/1962). Piaget's treatment of play places it squarely in the context of cognitive processes and cognitive development. For Piaget, the play element in mental life is characterized by a particular orientation toward behavior, which can find greater or lesser expression in a range of activities. This orientation is defined by the more or less exclusive predominance in mental activity of what Piaget terms the tendency toward "assimilation."

For Piaget, every act of intelligence is characterized by an equilibrium between two polar tendencies: assimilation and accommodation. In assimilation, the subject incorporates events, objects, or situations into existing ways of thinking, which constitute organized mental structures; in accommodation, the existing mental structures reorganize to incorporate new aspects of the external environment. During an act of *intelligence,* the subject adapts to the requirements of external reality, while at the same time maintaining his or her mental structure intact. *Play,* however, is characterized by the primacy of assimilation over accommodation: That is, the subject assimilates events, objects, and so on, to the ego and its existing mental structures.

Piaget sketched the broad outlines of the evolution of children's play in the first seven years of life by identifying three successive systems: practice play, symbolic play, and play with rules. Practice play is the first to appear and is dominant during the first 18 months of life. It involves the repetition of well-established sequences of actions and manipulations, not for practical or instrumental purposes, but for the mere pleasure derived from the mastery of motor activities. But around one year of age, these practice exercises become less numerous and diminish in importance. Over time, they seem to be transformed in one or more of the following ways: (1) The child passes from mere repetition to fortuitous and then to *purposive* combinations of actions and manipulations; as soon as that happens, the child sets definite goals for himself or herself, and the "practice games" are transformed into constructions. (2) Mere practice games may become symbolic, or at least are "coupled with symbolism," so that the constructions or the sequences of actions that children perform become *symbolic*. (3) Games can become *collective* and acquire *rules*, and thus evolve into "games with rules." This third transformation is the last to be achieved.

Symbolic play appears during the second year of life with the onset of representation and language. According to Piaget, "pretend play" is initially a solitary symbolic activity involving the use of idiosyncratic symbols; sociodramatic play using collective symbols does not appear until the latter part of the third year of life. In the Piagetian model, early pretense play involves the following elements, whose combination changes over time: (1) decontextualized behavior (e.g., performing a familiar behavior such as sleeping, eating, or drinking "in the void"); (2) shifts from self- to other-references (e.g., instead of putting herself to sleep, making the bear go to sleep); (3) use of substitute objects (e.g., a block stands for a doll); and (4) sequential combinations (e.g., instead of imitating a single action, the child constructs a whole scene in make-believe).

With the development of symbolic play, according to Piaget, the child goes more and more beyond the simple satisfaction of physically manipulating reality. Increasingly, he or she can symbolically assimilate the external reality to the ego, in the process indulging in symbolic distortions and transpositions. Thus, symbolic play is used to achieve fantasy satisfactions through compensation, wish fulfillment, liquidation of conflicts, and so on. It declines around the age of four as the child becomes progressively able to subordinate the ego to reality.

The third type of play, which Piaget examines very briefly in *Play, Dreams, and Imitation,* is play with rules, which, according to him, marks the transition to the play activity of the socialized individual. This type of play, he argues, rarely occurs before the period of 4 to 7 years and belongs preeminently to the period from 7 to 11 years. Piaget emphasizes that rules presuppose the interaction of at least two individuals, and that rules function to regulate and integrate the social group. (The larger argument on which Piaget is drawing here is that of Durkheim; see *Moral Education,* 1925/1973.) As regards rules themselves, Piaget distinguishes two categories: those that are handed down from above, and those that are constructed spontaneously. The contrast between these two types of rule-governed action is explored most fully in Piaget's truly seminal work on these themes, *The Moral Judgment of the Child* (1932/1965) (a centerpiece of which is an extensive analysis of children's understanding of playing the game of marbles).

In *Play, Dreams and Imitation* Piaget focuses on spontaneous games with rules based on temporary agreement. He sees these spontaneous games as representing the outcome of the socialization either of mere practice games or, sometimes, of symbolic games. Still, Piaget's account of the psychological significance of games with rules stresses the continuity of their functions with those of previous forms of play. He sees in games with rules a subtle equilibrium between assimilation to the ego—the principle of all play—and social life.

In sum, Piaget asserts that the development of play progresses from purely individual processes and idiosyncratic private symbols to social play and collective symbolism. It derives from the child's mental structure, so that it can only be explained by that structure. With the advent of the capacity for representation, assimilation for assimilation's sake becomes not only distorting, but also a source of deliberate make-believe. Thus, pretense play enables the child to relive his or her past experiences for the ego's satisfaction rather than for the ego's subordination to reality.

Piagetian Research on Play

Numerous psychological studies on play have used the Piagetian model as a springboard and have attempted to put several of his specific claims to rigorous experimental test, while also gathering more systematic observations. The bulk of the research has focused on pretense play, an area that has dominated the play literature over the last decades. Some of the questions that have received attention include determining the onset and waning of pretense play, as well as charting the sequence of pretense forms in relation to cognitive maturity and language acquisition. Several of the factors identified by Piaget have been investigated particularly thoroughly: the move toward increasingly decontextualized behavior, the change from self- to other-reference, and the growing ability to substitute objects and use them for representation (for extensive reviews see Fein, 1981; Fein & Rivkin, 1986; Rubin, 1980; and Rubin, Fein, & Vandenberg, 1983).

Although these studies have greatly enriched our understanding of aspects of children's play that Piaget had only sketched out, they have also had some serious and persistent drawbacks. At first, these studies exclusively used the laboratory as the proper setting to study play, and advanced solitary pretense play as the proper object of analysis. These limitations have been overcome only slowly and partially. The researchers have rarely returned to critically evaluate their findings by applying them to observations from naturalistic settings—the home, the playground, and so on. As a result, researchers became detached from the original object of study, so that observations from laboratory settings have not effectively enriched our understanding of children's spontaneous play—a sentiment felt strongly among teachers and other practitioners. In fact, the research studies seem to have isolated for careful observation behaviors that, although present during play, do not by themselves amount to play.

Aside from the methodological problems of this research, there is also a weakness in the underlying conceptual approach. Some of this weakness comes from Piaget himself, but it has been exacerbated by his followers.

Play, Dreams and Imitation in Childhood, although written by Piaget more than a decade after *The Moral Judgment of the Child* and related early works, accords with those works in method and intellectual concerns. Piaget's analysis of the second stage of play is marked by an emphasis on fantasy, and on the emotional element in psychological activity and development, which has no real counterpart in his later work. His analysis of the third stage retains some traces of his early concern (due partly to his critical engagement with Durkheim) with situating individual development in a social context. But, as Piaget states clearly in the introduction, his central goal in *Play, Dreams and Imitation* is to identify the symbolic function as an *individual* mechanism. Furthermore, he wants to show that the existence of this mechanism is a *prerequisite* for any communication among individuals, and therefore for the constitution or acquisition of collective meanings. It is significant then that, once Piaget has identified the third stage, he gives collective meanings only cursory attention. In his later work, the social and emotional concerns essentially disappear; and Piagetian research has largely followed the master in this respect. The absence of a sociocultural dimension in Piagetian research on play has been a major factor in creating a space for the influence of Vygotsky, for whom this dimension is central.

The Vygotskian Alternative

The second major influence that has shaped the course of psychological research on play can be attributed to the Soviet psychologist L. S. Vygotsky. His approach seems to be emerging as a viable alternative to Piaget's comprehensive cognitive theory, one that informs and unifies researchers' concerns about the social formation of mind.

The influence of Vygotsky's theory on play research is, however, much more complex and diffuse than the Piagetian influence. This is due partly to the nature of Vygotsky's writings and partly to the kind of influence he has had on those who have identified with his central message. Although his writings are full of intuitions and illuminations, they are often sketchy and at times incomplete. His major work on play available in English is restricted to a single article that was, in fact, delivered as a lecture and contains only the broad strokes of an alternative approach to play (Vygotsky, 1933/1966). Thus, Vygotsky—unlike Piaget—does not offer a systematic and carefully documented program of research; rather he offers a set of orienting concepts that, if accepted, foster a new way of viewing the psychological terrain.

For Vygotsky, genuine play begins around three years of age with pretense play, which he does not distinguish from sociodramatic play. For him, play is always a *social* symbolic activity: It typically involves more than one child; and the themes, stories, or roles that play episodes enact express the children's understanding and appropriation of the sociocultural materials of their society. Thus, even when a young child plays alone, Vygotsky still considers this type of play to be, in an important way, social because the themes or episodes of play express sociocultural elements. Furthermore, Vygotsky considers this type of solitary play to be a later development than play involving more than one participant.

Vygotsky's emphasis on the essentially social character of play accords with the main thrust of his larger psychological theory, which gives a key role to culture, and to its transmission through social interaction and communication, in the formation of mind. A central notion in his theory of cognitive development is that of the "zone of proximal development," which he defines as the difference between a child's "*actual* developmental level as determined by independent problem solving" and the level of "*potential* development as determined through problem solving under adult guidance or in collaboration with more capable peers" (Vygotsky, 1978, p. 86). In his use of this notion, which attempts to capture the process by which the social world guides and stimulates the child's development, Vygotsky in effect justifies theoretically the special role that society assigns to teachers. Among other things, this role involves the systematic transmission to children of the accumulated cultural resources, including linguistic and other symbolic systems, cognitive frameworks, and concrete knowledge. These resources guide children's interpretations of the world and help them systematize the diverse physical and social phenomena they encounter (for further discussion see Vygotsky, 1978, 1986; Wertsch, 1985).

Therefore, the teacher's influence, not only at the moment of interaction but in structuring the learning environment, can be crucial because, when appropriately applied, it can shape and direct the child's cognition by providing the mediating and enabling frameworks from the adult culture. (Chapter 10 in this part of the book, though focusing on parents rather than teachers, is relevant here since it provides a nice illustration of how shared meanings between adults and children are negotiated. The establishment of a context of shared meanings is an important precondition for the successful further transmission of culturally elaborated symbolic systems, meanings, and norms.)

The actualization of the "zone of proximal development" thus depends on social interaction within a shared cultural framework. This interaction can consist, in particular, of both instruction and other forms of joint activity; and Vygotsky further comments that a child benefits most from such interaction when it is geared appropriately to his or her level of *potential* development, thereby advancing his or her actual development. As Rogoff and Wertsch (1984) inform us,

> Vygotsky criticized the view of instruction that is based on an assumption that "instruction must be oriented toward stages that have already been completed." He argues instead that *"instruction is good only when it proceeds ahead of development. It then awakens and rouses to life those functions which are in a stage of maturing, which lie in the zone of proximal development.* It is in this way that instruction plays an extremely important role in development." (p. 3)

This is the larger theoretical context within which Vygotsky situates his analysis of play. Vygotsky sees play as contributing significantly to cognitive development—rather than simply reflecting it—and he treats play as an essentially social activity.

This does not mean simply that Vygotsky takes up where Piaget leaves off, and that Vygotsky's analysis of social play can be added on straightforwardly to Piaget's analysis of presocial play, because Vygotsky's position—in effect—calls into question Piaget's developmental scheme of play and imitation as a whole. If Vygotsky is correct, Piaget's analysis of the earlier stages of play would also have to be reconsidered, since what Piaget calls "symbolic play" is already social; what Piaget sees as idiosyncratic symbols are really made up of sociocultural elements, and the ways they are put together are culturally patterned. (Chapters 11 and 12 in this book take up this issue.)

In characterizing play, Vygotsky stresses the presence of two essential and interrelated components: (1) an imaginary situation, and (2) rules implicit in the imaginary situation. An *imaginary situation* is a defining characteristic, not only of pretense play, but also of games with rules—though in the latter case the imaginary situation may be present in concealed form. For instance, the (highly abstract) game of chess is structured by an imaginary world peopled by specific actors—king, queen, knights, and so on—who can move only in specified and rule-governed ways. The system of rules serves, in fact, to constitute the play situation itself; in turn, these rules and the actions based on them derive their meaning from the play situation. Equally, the presence of *rules* is a defining characteristic, not only of "games with rules" in the specific sense, but also of pretense play—though here the rules may be implicit. These implicit rules become apparent if, for example, we consider the restrictions placed on children's behavior by virtue of the roles they adopt. When a child pretends to be a "mother" or "father," the child cannot adopt any behavior he or she wishes, but must try to grasp and follow the rules of maternal or paternal behavior as understood and perceived by him or her and the other children. An important cognitive effort is involved here: "What passes unnoticed by the child in real life becomes a rule of behavior in play" (Vygotsky, 1933/1966, p. 9). In short, pretense play and games with rules are two poles in a single continuum, and Vygotsky sees the long-term development of play as a gradual movement between them: from an explicit imaginary situation with covert rules (i.e., pretense play) to an implicit imaginary situation with explicit rules (i.e., games with rules).

In the early years of the child's life, "play is the source of development and creates the zone of proximal development" (Vygotsky, 1933/1966, p. 16). By providing an imaginative opportunity for the self-empowering internalization of social rules, play contributes to the development of a capacity for "the creation of voluntary intentions and the formation of real-life plans and volitional motives—all appear in play and make it the highest level of preschool development" (p. 16).

> In play a child is always above his average age, above his daily behavior; in play, it is as though he were a head taller than himself. As in the focus of a magnifying glass, play contains all developmental tendencies in a condensed form; in play, it is as though the child were trying to jump above the level of his normal behavior. (p. 16)

Thus, play provides an opportunity to expand one's world; and Vygotsky therefore sees the cognitive-developmental benefits of play in the preschool-age child as, in important respects, a prototype of the teaching and learning that occur during successful education in later years.

Vygotsky's Influence on Play Research

Vygotsky's most important influence has been on those researchers who emphasize the social formation of mind and of play activity. Psychological research informed by this perspective has demonstrated conclusively that play is, from its origins, an essentially social activity—primarily involving, at first, interaction between caretakers and infants and, later on, carried out among siblings or groups of children. Play and games are initially learned by young ones in a social context under the supportive guidance of caretakers (or even older cooperative siblings), who at first act out both roles until infants start to assume the role of active participants. There is some evidence that these games play an important part in the emergence of the early communicative role of language, the development of turn taking, the learning of conversational conventions, and the acquisition of other social skills (see, e.g., Bruner, 1975, 1977; Cohen, 1987; Garvey, 1977; Kaye, 1982; Ratner & Bruner, 1978; Ross & Kay, 1980; Sachs, 1980).

Furthermore, recent research has provided evidence that caretakers' support and shaping extend beyond infancy to the pretense activity of young children. A few studies have gone on to document in detail how the shaping of social role playing takes place; these have usefully focused not only on the role of caretakers but also on that of peers (Dunn & Dale, 1984; Miller & Garvey, 1984). Unfortunately, this important line of research has been limited to a single type of role playing, that of the mother-baby role.

The focus of this research, however, has been narrow in two ways. First, it has attempted to trace the effects of the social world by focusing only on the context of direct face-to-face interaction. And second, the emphasis in the analysis of these interactions has been, with few exceptions, almost entirely on the linguistic means by which shared meanings among the participants are achieved. The combination of these two factors has limited the research to a search for direct and unmediated effects that can be captured during the time that the research is taking place. But, as Vygotsky himself stresses, the effects of the social world are often indirect, mediated, and diffuse; capturing them requires an interpretive framework wider than the actual interaction, and one that takes into account more than the discourse between the participants during the interaction.

For all these reasons, furthermore, the focus of the research has been exclusively on the transmission of cognitive, linguistic, or social skills rather than on the sociocultural matrix within which the interaction occurs, and from which the meanings, images, and roles enacted during the interaction are drawn. Thus, ironically, although the lack of a sociocultural dimension in Piaget's theory created the space for Vygotsky's influence, the research generated so far has not been extended in any systematic way to the wider sociocultural elements that define and inform the play context. In the next section, I will briefly outline some ideas for research that bear on these general issues.

Some Possibilities for Future Research

The review of the two main theoretical influences that have informed the psychological research on play reveals that researchers have gradually moved away from a conception that views play only as an individual psychological process to one that regards it as a social activity. The researchers, however, have not gone far enough in exploring the sociocultural matrix within which play occurs, as well as the cultural meanings enacted through play.

A related weakness that has characterized this psychological research is its tendency to adopt basically reductionist and utilitarian conceptions of play, usually in combination—even though seeds of an alternative scheme can be found in Vygotsky's insistence on the importance of the imaginary situation. As teachers familiar with play research have often noted, play is almost never studied on its own terms as a vehicle of the expressive imagination of children. Either it is treated simply as a reflection of some other well-established psychological function, such as cognition, language, or communication (see Franklin, 1983, for a similar argument); or it is studied only in terms of its causal role in the appearance of some other nonplay activity. While both approaches can be useful, and at times appropriate, the point is that they do not exhaust the phenomenon of play. They often bypass play and fail to capture its most characteristic contours because the researchers are interested in translating it into more established psychological functions. Play should also be studied on its own terms as one expression of imaginative activity that draws and reflects back on the interrelated domains of emotional, intellectual, and social life.

Many of the resources for doing this can be drawn from the underdeveloped possibilities within the Piagetian and Vygotskian perspectives themselves—particularly if these are traced back to their Durkheimian and Freudian sources. (These connections became clear to me through reading Weintraub, 1974.) Combining these insights, we can view play from a holistic perspective that captures it as a genuinely social activity—which means not only an interactive activity but also a cultural and imaginative one. The behavior of the participants at play is guided by a set of rules, whether implicit or explicit, whether negotiated at that moment or handed down by previous generations. Guided by the rules of the play, the participants step out of "real" life into a temporary sphere of activity that proceeds within its own boundaries of time and space.

Such an enriched conception of play opens up new possibilities and directions. First, it is a conception congenial and familiar to practitioners because it clearly reminds them of the play episodes that they observe in their settings. Due to this convergence of definition, researchers and practitioners can work together: While the researchers might attempt to describe and understand play, the practitioners might attempt to direct and shape it, providing interesting phenomena for the researchers to observe. Second, it recaptures the insights of early childhood educators in the 1950s, who had noticed the shaping role of culture in play, although they did not make it an explicit theme of investigation (see Biber, 1984). And third, it allows us to join forces with the rich and extensive field of ethnographic studies of play by sociologists and anthropologists (e.g., Fine, 1985; Schwartzman, 1978, 1980).

One of the areas of research to which this holistic perspective points is exploring the relation between play and the broader cultural context. Two of the chapters offered in this part of the book partly address this issue.

One of the themes explored in the chapter by Reifel and Yeatman is how the introduction of an overall curriculum theme in the classroom comes to affect children's play. Their account provides a faithful and rich picture of the classroom. They focus on a single child making an elaborate block structure, and they follow the different physical and symbolic transformations of the structure as other children appear on the scene, and how their dialogues with the protagonist affect his building and symbolic activity. Each child has constructed his or her own interpretation of the curriculum theme, and they dovetail in different ways with the creative imagination of the central block builder.

The research described in my own chapter also addresses the question of cultural context and shared symbolic meanings, but from a different angle. Children were given a set of abstract geometrical materials with which to work independently of one another, and we witnessed their shared cultural meanings as they spontaneously combined the pieces in similar ways and made similar (though varied) patterns and scenes with them. Even the youngest children showed a common aesthetic sensitivity of preferred combinations of colors and spatial harmony among the pieces, which was further enriched as older children were able to achieve more elaborate spatial combinations and express symbolic themes drawn from their cultural environment.

One can go even further than the research outlined by these two chapters in exploring the relation of sociocultural context and play. For instance, a careful ethnographic analysis of children's play could focus on the themes and topics elaborated by them in the spirit initiated by Vivian Paley (e.g., 1981, 1986; see also Corsaro, 1985). Collaboration with a teacher would yield much richer data than any researcher could obtain alone, because of the privileged position of the teacher in the children's world. Such an analysis, extended over a period of time, could reveal whether and how children come to share a common repertoire of themes. When the group achieves such a common repertoire, the researcher could also explore how variations and new themes get introduced. For instance, are the same children always responsible for new themes, or do responsibility and initiative shift? How do the themes relate to the children's background and their home cultures? Another topic for exploration is whether there are variations in the types of make-believe worlds created through play. Do some groups show a greater tendency toward realism while others show a greater predilection for the fantastic? In addition, the relation of the play themes to popular culture should be explored carefully.

This perspective thus introduces the notion that play themes embody sociocultural meanings of the larger society and in this sense contribute to the identity and character of the group. Thus, a program of research that addresses the sociocultural content of play might also examine one of the defining characteristics of "deep" play as analyzed by Geertz (1973): that is, the involvement of emotions for cognitive ends. Instead of merely noting the surface meanings of children's play acts, such an analysis would attempt to uncover the deeper sociocultural meanings that contribute to the cohesion and identity of the group, thus helping us understand the emotional appeal of cultural forms adopted in play. As noted above, Piaget and Vygotsky were conscious of the emotional component in play, although neither of them carried this line of analysis very far. But the researchers influenced by these thinkers, rather than developing their sketchy suggestions, have tended to ignore this aspect completely; teachers, on the other hand, have been fully aware of its presence, but have not always considered whether it might have educational value. Only when we arrive at such a rich understanding of play and the cultural forms it embodies will we be able to better direct and further enrich it.

References

Biber, B. (1984). *Early education and psychological development*. New Haven: Yale University Press.

Bruner, J. S. (1975). The ontogenesis of speech acts. *Journal of Child Language, 2,* 1–19.

Bruner, J. S. (1977). Early social interaction and language acquisition. In H. R. Schaffer (Ed.), *Studies in mother-infant interaction*. London: Academic Press.

Cohen, D. (1987). *The development of play*. New York: New York University Press.

Corsaro, W. (1985). *Friendship and peer culture in the early years*. Norwood, NJ: Ablex.

Dunn, J., & Dale, N. (1984). I a dady: 2-year-olds' collaboration in joint pretend with sibling and with mother. In I. Bretherton (Ed.), *Symbolic play: The development of social understanding* (pp. 131–158). New York: Academic Press.

Durkheim, E. (1973). *Moral education*. New York: Free Press. (Original work published 1925).

Fein, G. G. (1981). Pretend play: An integrative review. *Child Development, 52,* 1095–1118.

Fein, G. G., & Rivkin, M. (Eds.). (1986). *The young child at play: Reviews of research* (Vol. 4). Washington, DC: National Association for the Education of Young Children.

Fine, G. A. (Ed.). (1985). *Meaningful play, playful meaning*. Champaign, IL: Human Kinetics.

Franklin, M. B. (1983). Play as the creation of imaginary situations: The role of language. In S. Wapner & B. Kaplan (Eds.), *Toward a holistic developmental psychology* (pp. 197–220). Hillsdale, NJ: Erlbaum.

Garvey, C. (1977). *Play*. Cambridge, MA: Harvard University Press.

Geertz. C. (1973). *The interpretation of cultures*. New York: Basic Books.

Kaye, K. (1982). *The mental and social life of babies*. Chicago: University of Chicago Press.

Miller, P., & Garvey, C. (1984). Mother-baby role play: Its origin in social support. In I. Bretherton (Ed.), *Symbolic play: The development of social understanding* (pp. 101–130). New York: Academic Press.

Paley, V. G. (1981). *Wally's stories*. Cambridge, MA: Harvard University Press.

Paley, V. G. (1986). *Boys and girls: Superheroes in the doll corner*. Chicago: University of Chicago Press.

Piaget, J. (1962). *Play, dreams and imitation in childhood* (C. Gattegno & F. M. Hodgeson, Trans.). New York: Norton. (Original work published 1945)

Piaget, J. (1965). *The moral judgment of the child*. New York: Free Press. (Original work published 1932).

Ratner, N., & Bruner, J. S. (1978). Games, social exchange, and the acquisition of language. *Journal of Child Language, 5,* 391–402.

Rogoff, B., & Wertsch, J. V. (1984). Editors' notes. In B. Rogoff & J. V. Wertsch (Eds.), *Children's learning in the "zone of proximal development".* New Directions for Child Development, No. 23. San Francisco: Jossey-Bass.

Ross, H. S., & Kay, D. A. (1980). The origins of social games. In K. H. Rubin (Ed.), *Children's play* (pp. 17–31). San Francisco: Jossey-Bass.

Rubin, K. H. (1980). Fantasy play: Its role in the development of social skills and social cognition. In K. H. Rubin (Ed.), *Children's play* (pp. 69–84). San Francisco: Jossey-Bass.

Rubin, K. H., Fein, G. G. & Vandenberg, B. (1983). Play. In P. H. Mussen & E. M. Hetherington (Eds.), *Handbook of child psychology: Vol. 4. Socialization, personality, and social development* (pp. 693–774). New York: Wiley.

Sachs, J. (1980). The role of adult-child play in language development. In K. H. Rubin (Ed.), *Children's play* (pp. 33–48). San Francisco: Jossey-Bass.

Schwartzman, H. B. (1978). *Transformations: The anthropology of children's play.* New York: Plenum.

Schwartzman, H. B. (Ed.). (1980). *Play and culture: 1978 proceedings of the anthropological study of play.* West Point, NY: Leisure Press.

Vygotsky, L. S. (1966). Play and its role in the mental development of the child. *Soviet Psychology, 12,* 6–18. (A stenographic record of a lecture given in 1933).

Vygotsky, L. S. (1978). *Mind in society: The development of higher psychological processes* (M. Cole, V. John-Steiner, S. Scribner, & E. Souberman, Eds. & Trans.). Cambridge, MA: Harvard University Press.

Vygotsky, L. S. (1986). *Thought and language.* Cambridge, MA: MIT Press.

Weintraub, J. (1974). *Some reflections on Durkheim's concept of human nature: Preliminary expectoration* [sic]. Unpublished manuscript, University of California, Berkeley.

Wertsch, J. V. (1985). *The social formation of mind: A Vygotskian approach.* Cambridge, MA: Harvard University Press.

CHAPTER 10

The Social Organization
of Early Number Development

GEOFFREY B. SAXE
MARYL GEARHART
STEVEN R. GUBERMAN

Research in cognitive development is generally motivated by the concern to understand the nature of developmental shifts in children's conceptual understandings and logical operations. To pursue this research interest, investigators have often studied children removed from the everyday social contexts in which they use their conceptual skills, and have interviewed and observed children as they solved problems without the support and collaboration of others. While divorcing the investigation of children's conceptual development from the social contexts in which it occurs permits the researcher greater access to the child's reasoning processes, it removes from observation the ways in which the development of children's reasoning is supported and informed by interactions with others.

The writings of Vygotsky (1962, 1978) and elaborations of his works (e.g., Wertsch, 1979) address the social network of meanings, activities, and historical achievements within which the individual operates and learns. Using such constructs as the zone of proximal development, Vygotsky argues that an analysis of the social organization of a child's problem-solving efforts is essential to an understanding of cognitive development and its cultural origins. Vygotsky's approach has provided us

This chapter originally appeared in B. Rogoff & J. V. Wertsch (Eds.), *Children's Learning in the "Zone of Proximal Development"* (pp. 19–29), New Directions for Child Development, no. 23. Copyright © 1984 by Jossey-Bass, Inc., San Francisco. It is reprinted here with permission of the publisher. The research was supported by grants from the National Institute of Education (NIE–G–0119), the Spencer Foundation, and the Research Committee of UCLA (No. 3862).

with a framework for investigating the social roots of one domain of cognitive development, children's numerical cognition.

Number development is a particularly fruitful domain for the investigation of developmental relations between culture and cognition. Number systems are evolving cultural constructions. This is apparent both in the wide cultural diversity of number systems (Saxe & Posner, 1982) and in the remarkable history of our own number system and procedures for calculation (Menninger, 1969). In focusing on aspects of the social organization of children's early number development, we gain access to a process whereby an evolving cultural construction—the number system—is communicated to children, who transform and incorporate it into the fabric of their own cognitive activities. In our research, we have been examining that process by observing how mothers teach their children to solve a counting problem.

Our analysis of adult–child interactions is set within a general model of cognitive development. It is our view that children's novel cognitive constructions result from the dynamic interplay between their elaboration of problem-solving goals and coherent means to achieve those goals. As children identify new goals, they attempt to elaborate novel cognitive means, including conceptual structures, symbolic vehicles, and problem-solving strategies, in order to achieve those goals. These cognitive constructions in turn provide a new framework within which individuals attempt to identify new goals. The aim of our research on mother–child interactions is to explore whether and how mothers participate in children's elaboration of problem-solving goals and problem-solving means.

Research Plan

In order to study the social organization of goals during mother–child teaching interactions about number, we videotaped mothers and their 2½- to 5-year-old children as the mothers attempted to teach the children a number reproduction game. We also interviewed children individually to obtain a characterization of children's unassisted performances on the number reproduction and other related tasks. For the interaction session, we instructed mothers that the goal of the number reproduction game was to get the same number of pennies (from an available set of 15) as there were Cookie Monsters (pictures of the puppet from the *Sesame Street* television show) on the model board, and we encouraged mothers to organize the interaction in whatever way they felt would encourage learning and understanding in their child. We asked the mothers to keep the pennies five to six feet away from the model and to have their children bring the pennies back in a cup. These instructions were designed to discourage the mothers from organizing local task-completion strategies, such as pairing pennies with cookie monsters one by one, strategies that radically simplify the goal of numerical reproduction. Mothers helped their children to complete the task four times for model set sizes of 3, 4, 9, and 10, in that order. We thus varied task difficulty according to the number of Cookie Monster pictures in the model.

To understand the goal structure that emerges during the adult–child teaching interactions, we found it necessary to develop a method of study in which we produced a coordinated set of analyses of three aspects of the numerical activity. The method entailed an analysis of the goal structure of the activity as it was understood by the mother (or practiced in "culture"), a developmental analysis of the goal structure that children imposed on the activity, and an analysis of how the adult participated in the child's construction of the goals in the activity. In the discussion that follows, we show that each of these analyses is a necessary complement of the others, and that together they lead to new insights about how children's developing numerical understandings are jointly rooted in their own constructive activities and in their social interactions with others.

Analysis of the Goal Structure
of the Number Reproduction Task

To understand the functional requirements of any task—the work that the subject needs to accomplish in order to solve the task—an analysis of the goal structure that leads to task solution is necessary. The counting game that we ask mothers to teach to their children is similar to many everyday counting activities. To reproduce a given quantity of objects, as our task requires, an individual must accomplish a hierarchy of goals and subgoals. The superordinate goal is to produce an accurate numerical copy. In order to accomplish this, the subject must first accomplish a subgoal: to produce an accurate estimate of the model. One means of accomplishing this subgoal is by counting the model. In order to count, further subgoals must be elaborated and accomplished, such as applying the sequence of number words in one-to-one correspondence with the target elements. Once the goals pertaining to the model have been achieved, a similar set of subgoals must be constructed to obtain an accurate number of objects from the available set. Finally, the individual can choose to check his or her accuracy by either recounting the sets or establishing a one-to-one correspondence between the two sets.

Although the description of the goal structure just presented corresponds to the procedures that we as adults would use to produce a solution to the numerical reproduction task, it does not correspond to the organization of the child's activity as he or she proceeds to solve the task. In order to understand how adults can influence and elaborate children's goals, it is first necessary to understand children's goals during their solution of the task.

A Developmental Analysis of Children's Goals

An analysis of children's unassisted performances on the numerical reproduction task reveals that younger children do not simply make errors in their solution of the task, but that they conceptualize the task quite differently than adults do. Table 10.1 contains a summary description of developmental shifts in children's unassisted performance on the numerical reproduction task and what we infer to be general features of children's goals associated with these behaviors (see Saxe 1977, 1979).

Young children (Level 1) who are presented with the task often act as if they have two distinct and fluctuating goals during this activity. One goal is to get some or all the elements in the available set. If, during their activity, these children are asked whether counting the model would help them, some (Level 1A) seem to construct another goal: to produce a count of one set or of both sets continuously as if they were one. Slightly more advanced children (Level 1B) focus on producing separate counts

TABLE 10.1.   Developmental Analysis of Children's Goals
            on Numerical Reproduction Task

Level	Child's Behavior	Inferred Goals
1A	Child brings all of available set. "Would counting help?" Child counts only own copy.	Single array goals
1B	Same as 1A, but child counts model and copy and produces no subsequent modifications.	Single array goals
2A	Child equalizes model and copy through successive counts, additions, and subtractions.	Double array goals
2B	Systematic reproduction using counting.	Double array goals

of the sets but do not use the information obtained to relate the copy to the model. It is important to note that when children at Levels 1A or 1B identify counting as a goal of the activity, they seem to do so only with regard to the production of a count of a single array. Thus, if they produce two counts (Level 1B), they treat their counts separately, and they do not compare the values produced. Moreover, children at these levels often do not treat the last number word of their count as having a cardinal value. For instance, if a child at either sublevel counts a set and is then asked how many items are in the set, he or she is likely either to recount the set or to offer the last several number words of the count as a reply.

At Level 2, children's goals seem to shift. Now, children exhibit double array goals: They produce separate and distinct numerical representations of the model and copy, which they compare. Nonetheless, their solution strategy at Level 2A remains different from that of adults. Children at Level 2A count the model and available set without a clearly articulated overall plan for the task. Then, through a process of recounts and successive additions and subtractions, they attempt to equalize the model and their copy. At Level 2B, children produce systematic counts and an accurate reproduction of the model.

A Framework for Understanding the Emergent Goal Structure of the Activity During Mother–Child Interaction

The actual goal structure of the activity as it emerged over the course of mother–child interactions was analyzed by constructing coding schemes that were guided both by a logical analysis of the goal structure of the number reproduction activity as communicated to the mothers and by developmental analysis of the child's shifting goals.

We suspected that adults interweave their instruction with children's ongoing problem-solving activities by adjusting the goal structure of tasks to the children's level of functioning. For instance, in presenting the number reproduction task to children, mothers can define or help their children to accomplish goals at any one of many levels of task structure. Table 10.2 contains the hierarchical description of the goals and subgoals of the task. Mothers can offer directives during the interaction at any of these levels.

At the most general goal structure levels, the mother presents the goal structure of the entire task without specifying any of the subgoals (directives 1 and 2). At each of these levels of description, the mother provides a double array goal—the child must produce and compare nu-

TABLE 10.2.   A Hierarchical Ordering of Maternal Directives
for the Numerical Reproduction Task

Maternal Directive	*Example*
Directives Pertaining to the Goal Structure of the Entire Task	
1. Mother provides the superordinate goal of the entire task.	"Get just the same number of pennies as Cookie Monsters."
2. Mother provides the superordinate goal of the entire task after a representation of the model has been accomplished.	"Get just the same number of pennies as Cookie Monsters."
Directives Linking a Representation of the Model with a Production of a Copy	
3. Mother directs the child to obtain a specified number from the available set.	"Go get nine pennies for the Cookie Monsters."
Directives to Produce a Representation of the Model	
4. Mother directs child to produce a representation of the model without specifying how to do so.	"How many Cookie Monsters are there?"
5. Mother directs child to produce a representation of the model and specifies a procedure whereby this can be accomplished.	"Count the Cookie Monsters."
6–10. Mother provides increasing assistance on some aspect of the child's counting activity with each successive level.	Mother counts as child points to each Cookie Monster.
Directives Providing a Representation of the Model	
11. Mother provides a cardinal representation of the model for the child.	"There are three Cookie Monsters."

merical representations of the model and the copy. At the next level (directive 3), the mother guides the child to a specific subgoal by directing him or her to get a specific number of pennies from the available set. This form of directive is transitional between a double array and a single array goal specification of the task in that the mother directs her child to produce a specific representation of the available set of pennies (single array goal), but she does so in the context of achieving a representation of the model set. The remaining directives entail increasing specificity of how to achieve a numerical representation of the model set, each referring to a single array goal or to some aspect of a single array goal. For instance, at the fourth level, the mother asks the child for a numerical representation of the model without providing information on how to accomplish this. At the fifth level, the mother specifies not only the subgoal concerning the need for a representation but also the further subgoal concerning the need to count to achieve the representation. The remaining levels each represent more specific directives concerning how to achieve an accurate count.

Analyses of the Interactions

On the basis of the children's unassisted performances, we divided them into two groups, a low-ability group and a high-ability group. We inferred that these groups would tend to apply single and double array goals, respectively, to the reproduction tasks during the interactions. We then conducted a number of analyses on the interaction using the scheme presented in Table 10.2 to determine whether and in what way mothers adjusted the organization of the task to the children's understanding of the task's goal structure.

Task Introductions

First, we asked whether mothers introduced the task differently to children of different ability levels of numerical competence. For this analysis, we examined introductions only to set sizes 3 and 9, since many mothers organized set sizes 4 and 10 as problems of addition to set sizes 3 and 9, not as independent trials.

We found that mothers were making adjustments appropriate to the ability levels of their children. The mothers of low-ability children introduced the task differently from the mothers of high-ability children. Most mothers of low-ability children began with a single array subgoal request (e.g., a Level 4 "How many Cookie Monsters are there?" or a Level 5 "Count the Cookie Monsters"). A few mothers of low-ability children formulated a superordinate double array goal, but they used it only as a context for a more specific single array subgoal request. Here is an example of such a strategy:

Example 1. Low-Ability Child; Set Size: 3
Mother: Are you ready to learn a game? (Mother leans over to look in child's face. Mother gives cup to child.) Okay [What] we're going to do is we're going to count the Cookie Monsters. Okay? (Mother pushes set size 3 Cookie Monster boards to-

> ward child while pointing to each monster.) And, then I want
> you to go over to the pile of pennies over there and put the
> same number of pennies in the cup . . . so all the Cookie
> Monsters have one. (Superordinate as context)
>
> *Child:* Okay.
> *Mother:* Okay? So, should we count the Cookie Monsters? (Level 5
> directive)

A few mothers of low-ability subjects immediately transformed the
entire goal structure of the task and presented a simplified goal structure
(not coded within the level analysis); for example, "I want you to get a
cookie [a penny] and put it in the cup to give it to the Cookie Monster."
Such a simplification redefined the task from a numerical one to one that
involved non-numerical correspondences. Thus, the task structure presented to these children entailed neither double nor single array goals.
Instead, the goal entailed merely getting elements of a set. We find these
adjustments all the more significant in light of our attempts, in our initial
instructions to the mothers, to prevent such radical simplifications.

No mother of a high-ability child immediately simplified the goal
structure of the task, nor did any of these mothers specify the means for
achieving a representation of the model, that is, counting (Level 5). The
typical introduction for mothers of high-ability children was, "How
many Cookie Monsters are there?" (Level 4), a request intended to help
focus the child on the need to achieve a numerical representation of a
single array (the model set of Cookie Monsters) without specifying the
means for doing so. Some mothers of high-ability children specified just
the superordinate goal (e.g., "You have to get the same number of pennies as there are Cookie Monsters and put them in the cup" [Level 1]).
In contrast, mothers of low-ability children never specified just a superordinate goal.

Mothers tended to introduce set size 9 numerical reproductions differently from set size 3. Some mothers in both high- and low-ability
groups adapted their task introductions to set size 9 by increasing their
assistance and initiating the task with a more subordinate directive. In
addition, we found another form of adaptation for the mothers of high-
ability children. The trial for set size 9 was always preceded by trials for
set sizes 3 and 4. Some of the mothers of high-ability children made use
of these previous interactions by introducing the task with a request that
the child merely "Do this one now"—an "empty" task marker that displayed the mother's belief that after two trials her child now shared with
her an understanding of the task goals. No mother of a low-ability child
introduced the task with only a marker of this nature.

Formulations of Superordinate Goals

The preceding analysis indicates that mothers of high-ability and low-ability children differed in the degree to which they specified the task structure in their introductions. Mothers of low-ability children tended to structure the subgoals for their children to a much greater extent than did mothers of high-ability children. In a related analysis, we examined whether mothers formulated the superordinate goal of numerical reproduction (Level 1 or Level 2 in Table 10.2) at any point in the model phase (when the child was to determine the number of Cookie Monsters) or in the initiation of the available set phase (when the child went to get the same number of pennies).

In set size 3, most mothers of both low-ability and high-ability children formulated the superordinate task goal at some point before the child gathered pennies from the available set. In set size 9, however, most mothers of low-ability subjects did not formulate the superordinate goal, while most mothers of high-ability subjects were still likely to formulate the superordinate goal. It is likely that, by set size 9, the mothers of low-ability subjects had learned from repeated task trials that the superordinate double array goal was not understood by their children and thus that formulation of it was not useful in supporting their children's task activity.

Median Assistance Levels

In order to obtain an index of the extent to which the mothers themselves structured the subgoals of the task for their children, we next calculated a median score for each mother's goal directives in the model phase for each set size. Consistent with the analyses of task introductions and superordinate goal formulations, we found that mothers of high-ability children gave their children less assistance in constructing the subgoals of the task than did mothers of low-ability children. We also found that task complexity influenced the teaching strategies of mothers of both high-ability and low-ability children. As task complexity increased, both groups of mothers shifted to more subordinate goal directives. Examples 2 and 3 illustrate the way in which the mother of a high-ability child adjusts the goal structure of the task as a function of the model's set size. In this case, the adjustment occurs in the task introduction.

Example 2. High-Ability Child; Set Size 3; Median Assistance: 3.0
Mother: Look at this board. Now, can you tell me how many Cookie Monsters are on there? (Level 4 directive)

    Child: Yep. One, two, three. (Child touches each Cookie Monster.)

    Mother: Okay. Now, the trick is this. We have to—you have to get the same amount of pennies and put them in the cup that are on here. (Mother points to cup and touches board. Child goes to penny pile.) (Level 2 directive)

Example 3. High-Ability Child; Set Size: 9; Median Assistance: .5

    Mother: Close your eyes. (Mother gets set size 9 board. Child opens eyes and gasps.) Wow! Now, can you count? (Level 5 directive)

    Child: One, two, three, four, five, six, seven, eight, nine. (Child touches each Cookie Monster in turn.)

    Mother: Okay, How many Cookie Monsters are there? (Uptake on last numeral)

    Child: Nine. (Child "sings," sweeping hand around board.)

    Mother: Now we have to put the same amount in the cup that are here. (Level 2 directive)

Mother's Shifts in Goal Directives Within Set Size

Not only do mothers adjust their organization of the task as a function of the child's ability level and task difficulty, but the social organization of the task is dynamic and shifts during an interaction as a function of whether the child achieves an accurate count. We found that mothers generally shifted to a goal directive subordinate to their previous one after the child produced an inaccurate count, and that mothers generally shifted to a superordinate goal directive after the child produced an accurate count. These trends occurred regardless of task difficulty and the child's ability level. Example 4 illustrates a shift to a subordinate goal following an incorrect count (Level 4 to Level 10 assistance) and a shift to a more superordinate goal following an accurate count (Level 10 to Level 3 assistance).

Example 4. High-Ability Child; Set Size: 9; Median Assistance: 4.0

    Mother: Here's one that's much harder. (Mother puts out set size 9 board.) How many Cookie Monsters do we have here? (Level 4 directive)

    Child: One, two, three, four, five, six, seven, eight, nine, ten. (After two, the child's pointing gestures either omit or double count Cookie Monsters.)

    Mother: Let me help you count them, okay? (Mother and child count and point in unison until five, whereupon child mistakenly says seven.) Forgot, you forgot about five. (Mother and child count and point in unison from five to nine.) (Level 10 assistance) Golly, that's a lot. Can you count nine pennies and put them in the cup? (Level 3 directive)

Mothers' Uptake on Children's Accurate Counts

The use of the last number word of the count to represent the quantity in the model array presents special difficulty for children, and the analysis of developmental shifts in this understanding has received considerable attention in the research literature on children's early cognitive development (Gelman & Gallistel, 1978; Gelman & Meck, 1983; Schaeffer, Eggleston, & Scott, 1974). To assess how mothers signal the special utility of the last number word, we focused on what mothers said following the child's first accurate count as a function of the child's ability level. For instance, once the child completed a count, some mothers repeated the number word; others asked the child how many there were. We found that mothers of low-ability children provided an uptake on the last number word of the child's count more often than did mothers of high-ability children. In addition, the frequency of mothers' uptakes tended to increase with task difficulty for high-ability children.

Summary and Conclusions

In this chapter, we have provided coordinated analyses of three aspects of the social context of children's developing conceptual understandings: an analysis of children's developing operations within a knowledge domain, a functional analysis of the cultural task context in which these operations are deployed, and an analysis of the way in which other people can bridge and adapt the cultural definition of the task to the child's developing operations. We believe that the insights gained from this type of analytic approach are critical in understanding the way in which young children come to make the historical achievements of culture a part of their own problem-solving activities.

At the beginning of this chapter, we argued that very young children who engage in the number reproduction activity often impose the goal of producing a count of a single array (Levels 1A and 1B) on the nominal task and that their means of accomplishing the count are typically not well developed. The results for our low-ability subjects indicate that their mothers provided assistance appropriate to their developing numerical operations. For instance, these mothers were more likely to initiate the task with specific directives, such as, "Count the Cookie Monsters." Moreover, as the greater median assistance levels reveal, these mothers often assisted their children's model set counts by modeling or directing very low-level subgoals, such as the repetition of number words in the correct sequence or the assignment of number words in one-to-one correspondence with objects (Levels 6 through 11). In their uptakes to accurate counts, these mothers also attempted to highlight to their children that the last number word recited could be used as a summary description (cardinal representation) of the entire array. Not surprisingly, these mothers were less likely than the mothers of high-ability children to formulate only the overall double array goal structure of the task, and they were less likely than the mothers of high-ability children to formulate it. Thus, the mothers themselves more often took responsibility for relating the numerical value of the model to that of the copy. We interpret these mother–child interactions as a context for the low-ability child to generate a system of understanding and symbolization commensurate with the child's definition of the goal structure of the task: the representation of single arrays by means of our conventional numeration system.

Older preschool children begin to construe the task as having a double array goal structure. They attempt to produce numerical representations of the model using the means that they have developed to achieve single array goals. This generally entails counting the model and the available set and then, by a trial-and-error process, equalizing them through a succession of counts, additions and subtractions, and recounts (Level 2A). Gradually, these older children structure increasingly systematic solution strategies so that they organize their counting to achieve a precise copy (Level 2B). The results for high-ability children revealed that mothers provided directives that supported the children's construction of these systematic solution strategies. Mothers of high-ability children were more likely to introduce the task at superordinate goal levels, and they were more likely to formulate the goal structure of the entire task when using large set sizes. These mothers provided less assistance in the model phase, and they were less likely than mothers of low-ability children to provide uptake on the last number word of their children's counts. Thus, they were more likely to relinquish responsibility to the child for relating the numerical value of the model to that of the copy.

In addition to these group differences, we found that all mothers continually adjusted the goal structure of the task during the activity itself. So, while children of low ability succeeded less often than did children of high ability, the mothers of low-ability children, like those of high-ability children, tended to shift to more superordinate goal directives when the children succeeded. Similarly, when children of both ability levels had difficulty, mothers shifted to more subordinate goal levels.

The analyses that we have presented in this chapter indicate that the goal structure of numerical activities as they occur in social interactions is an emergent phenomenon: Located neither in the head of the mother nor in that of the child, this goal structure is negotiated in the interaction itself. Thus, the emergent goal structure simultaneously involves the child's understandings and the historical achievements of the culture as communicated by the mother. We argued that children construct means to achieve these socially negotiated goals. For a young child, this can entail the imitation of the number string in the same sequence as the mother articulates it. For an older child, it can entail discovering the importance of systematically counting both the model and the copy. As children generate coherent means to achieve these socially negotiated goals, they create for themselves a system of representation that reflects achievements that have been generated in our culture's social history.

References

Gelman, R., & Gallistel, R. (1978). *The child's understanding of number.* Cambridge, MA: Harvard University Press.

Gelman, R., & Meck, E. (1983). Preschoolers' counting: Principles before skill or skill before principles? *Cognition, 13,* 343–359.

Menninger, K. (1969). *Number words and number symbols.* Cambridge, MA: MIT Press.

Saxe, G. B. (1977). A developmental analysis of notational counting. *Child Development, 48,* 1512–1520.

Saxe, G. B. (1979). Developmental relations between notational counting and number conservation. *Child Development, 50,* 180–187.

Saxe, G. B., & Posner, J. (1982). The development of numerical cognition: Cross-cultural perspectives. In H. P. Ginsburg (Ed.), *The development of mathematical thinking.* New York: Academic Press.

Schaeffer, B., Eggleston, V. H., & Scott, J. L. (1974). Number development in young children. *Cognitive Psychology, 6,* 357–379.

Vygotsky, L. S. (1962). *Thought and language.* Cambridge, MA: MIT Press.

Vygotsky, L. S. (1978). *Mind in society: The development of higher psychological processes,* (M. Cole, V. John-Steiner, S. Scribner, & E. Souberman, Eds. & Trans.). Cambridge, MA: Harvard University Press.

Wertsch, J. V. (1979). From social interaction to higher psychological processes: A clarification and application of Vygotsky's theory. *Human Development, 22,* 1–22.

CHAPTER 11

Action, Talk, and Thought
in Block Play

STUART REIFEL
JUNE YEATMAN

How can we describe what occurs in block play, especially block play as a representational activity in which children's constructions stand for aspects of their world? A solid literature on block construction, going back at least as far as Froebel (1887) and the early kindergarten movement, proclaims the many educational benefits of block play. A range of assertions about its value has kept block play as a part of most early childhood classrooms, but there has been little research to document what occurs in the process of block play and how children might benefit from it.

When this chapter's first author began his research on blocks, all we had were Francis Guanella's (1934), Paul Vereecken's (1961), and Harriet Johnson's (1984) classic descriptions of the developmental progression in the forms children produce in their block play, and some fascinating analytic and clinical interpretations of the meaning of constructions for preadolescents. In all of this earlier research, an observer recognized the child's labels for block constructions, then went on to analyze other features of block play. It seemed possible to conclude that children use blocks representationally, although we had little data on the form, content, or development of those representations.

Block Play as Representation

In *Play, Dreams and Imitation* Piaget (1945/1962) wrote about children's "brick" (i.e., block) representations of houses and other objects:

Using interlocking bricks and rods she built a big house, a stable and a woodshed, surrounded by a garden, with paths and avenues. Her dolls continually walked about and held conversations but she also took care that the material constructions should be exact and true to life. (p. 137)

Piaget related such observations to the foundations of the "semiotic function," or theory of signs and symbols. He noted that play representations reflect the child's differentiation of the signifier (the block construction) and the signified (the house, woodshed, path, etc.). In his discussion of Piaget's work, Mounoud (1976) built on this distinction in an important way. He argued that Piaget had studied "psychological development from the subject's point of view (that is, structure or operations) and not from the object's point of view (that is, representations or translations of the object as content)" (p. 177). Piaget's work told us more about the child's egocentric organization of experience (the child's play view of "true to life") than about the objective experience (i.e., a real-world referent) being organized by the child. This seems to be an important distinction to make, especially in terms of the young child's learning and the curriculum that is to support that learning. What experiences (in the world and in the classroom) contribute to the child's "egocentric organization of experience"? What experiences help transform that egocentric organization into "objective experience" that has social or shared meaning? Are there patterns in block play that researchers and teachers can recognize and educationally enhance? What constitutes a so-called "real-world referent" that a child could come to transform?

Early researchers noted that real-world experiences provide ideas for block representation (Bailey, 1933; Guanella, 1934). They saw that blocks can represent unspecified objects, such as houses, roads, and trains, and that by at least the primary grades, groups of children can use blocks to represent locations they have visited. However, no systematic collection of evidence to document the contribution of referential experience to block representation or of developmental changes in the representational use of blocks preceded the first author's research concerning the structural and spatial forms that mark the development of those transformations. One study generated a measure of structural complexity for representational constructions (Reifel & Greenfield, 1982). We demonstrated that construction becomes more structurally complex with increasing age, even when children have similar understanding of a referent. For example, a 4-year-old is more likely to construct a house that is less complex than a 7-year-old's; the younger child simply designates parts of the house verbally, while the older child depicts them structurally.

Construction and Pretense

While the forms of block construction are interesting and fairly easy for classroom teachers to identify (Reifel, 1984a, 1984b), the pretense associated with block play is more difficult to understand. Much of the research that has been done has dealt with this difficulty by working with individual children, usually outside the classroom. With the growing literature on pretense and dramatic play, it seemed desirable to look at representational block construction in the classroom. Our question has been, "What contributes to the pretense of block play that can be associated with these structures?" Where do children get their ideas, and how do those ideas for play take shape? This appears to be one way of understanding more about the development of the relationship between "real-world objects" and the child's structuring of developing experience, or, to put it another way, the developing relationship between signifier and signified.

These questions are important in terms of the curriculum, in that they reflect the linkage between developmental norms (as seen from the research on play) and the persons, materials, time, space, and ideas that children encounter in the classroom. While teachers can (and should) learn to recognize the norms of play, it is from daily encounters in individual classrooms that children learn (and play with) new ideas. It is this situated learning, this interface between play and the rest of the curriculum, that interests us.

Play and the Curriculum

From some points of view it is undesirable to separate curriculum and play; some see play as the curriculum for the early childhood years. We think that it is necessary and desirable to see play as a significant part of the school day for young children. It is important to acknowledge the other parts of the curriculum that can complement play, the books read at story time, field trips, the bird nests placed on a science table. Children's play is enhanced when the child's environment is carefully planned for rich learning opportunities.

We need to learn more about the unique, classroom-specific features of play that let children enhance those understandings that adults intend to promote in the classroom. We strongly believe that children, individually or socially, will create play irrespective of the environment in which they find themselves, but that the environment (materials, ideas, other persons) and how it is used (arranged spatially and manipulated over time) make distinctive contributions to each play situation. These contributions can, but may not, be reflected in play-related talk and construction. That is why we are interested in the course of ideas as they are presented for children in the classroom and are translated into actions and talk as children play; these ideas, as enacted and talked about by children, become the curriculum in practice in the classroom.

Context and Procedures

We audiotaped a group of 4- and 5-year-olds as they worked, talked, and played in a classroom provided with ample materials and a generous, atypical adult–child ratio of 1:4. The head teacher in this classroom was the second investigator. A graduate student and a student teacher assisted her daily, while eight undergraduate students rotated through the classroom on a weekly basis.

Our subjects were enrolled in a half-day university laboratory program that met four times a week. The eight boys and eight girls were from middle class white families. The majority of the class had spent the previous school year together in the same program but with different teachers. All were accustomed to interacting with peers and adults in a group setting.

We collected data for seven consecutive school days, during the regularly scheduled one-hour interval designated for indoor play. At this time the children chose from among a number of activities, including painting at an easel with tempera paint and building with wooden unit blocks on a large (10' × 10') rug. We placed a cassette tape recorder in one of these two "target areas" and audiotaped the children as they interacted with materials, peers, and adults. Sessions varied in duration from 25 to 55 minutes, for a total of 4½ hours of tape.

A Session in the Block Center

We focus here on the first of four recording sessions that took place in the block center. The curriculum theme was "Pets." The center contained animal puppets, plastic animals, and small construction toys in addition to the usual unit blocks. The children also brought in materials from the nearby dramatic play area, set up as a "pet store" with dress-up clothes, stuffed animals, play money, and food containers. Additional theme-related materials were available throughout the room, and the daily routine included activities that focused on pets. Group time (which preceded the indoor play period) included songs, fingerplays, creative dramatics, stories, and discussions concerning animal behavior, types of pets, and their proper care. A rabbit, hermit crabs, hamsters, and a small aquarium were available in the classroom for observation and interactions. Pets from home (a bird, a cat) had visited the class as well. Art materials (cotton balls, paper plates, string, tape, and the like) were put to use on a regular basis; theme-related products (masks, animal ears) were generated by the children, as were non-related items such as rainbows, swords, "slimers," and other nonpet creations. Children's creations, regardless of their connection to the stated weekly theme, met with enthusiastic response from the adults in the classroom.

Throughout the play period, the 16 children in the group moved freely around the room. Seven boys and five girls chose to spend time in the block center. We will summarize the session prior to looking at it in more detail.

Anthony entered the area as the recording session began. His play at this point centered around a "pig" for whom he built a pen and a cornfield. Bill arrived soon after and constructed a bridge. Cathy entered with her "kitty cat," followed by Dani, who sat down in the teacher's lap. Later Frank played "Ghost Busters" and "hurricane" while Evan and Anthony focused on "Mighty Bird," building a "delicate cage," and collecting "money, money, money." Gayla approached the teacher with "Clifford the Big Red Dog" and was encouraged to build a house for him. Hannah joined Gayla, while Ian and Jack joined in the play of Anthony, Evan, and Frank. Meanwhile, Karen stopped by to inform the teacher of her plans to make a "cat mask" at the art table. Larry was the last child to enter the block center; he played silently throughout his time in the area. Eventually play ended as the teacher initiated clean-up procedures.

Throughout the play period summarized here, most of the children carried on conversations with the teacher and with each other. Their words provide us with clues concerning the process of creating play. As we examine the audiotape transcript more closely, the influence of materials, ideas, and people on the children's play becomes apparent.

Children Construct Their Ideas

Early in the play session, the following exchange took place:

Anthony: I take some corn. Hey, look he's eating corn.
Teacher: Hm hm hm hm hm (laughing).
Bill: I'm gonna build a bridge.

Teacher: All right.
Anthony: After I'm finished with this, I'll build a cornfield so I can feed 'em.
Teacher: Good idea, Anthony. (Anthony hums and builds with blocks.)

What influences do we see shaping the play of Anthony and Bill? It is obvious that the two made different use of both the curriculum theme ("pets") and the materials. Anthony utilized the theme of animals and animal care as a framework from which his play developed. His dramatic play with a small stuffed animal pig and his construction of a pen enclosure and cornfield contrast sharply with Bill's arch bridge building. Anthony incorporated the theme and related materials, while Bill ignored the theme completely, choosing to utilize one type of curriculum material (the wooden unit blocks) to carry out an idea that he had brought with him to the play situation.

Both Anthony and Bill directed their utterances to the teacher, rather than each other, seemingly intent on their own constructions—a classic instance of "parallel play." Despite this fact, we see that Anthony and Bill influenced each other's talk and actions. Bill did not comment on his plans to build a bridge until Anthony had pointed out his own actions with the "pig"; Anthony expressed his intention to create a cornfield following Bill's announcement. The two seemed to serve as "triggers" for each other's play shaping, even though at this point they were not engaged in a direct peer interaction.

With his first utterance, spoken as he picked up a small cylinder block, Anthony transformed the block (now an ear of corn) and himself (he *is* the pig, for a brief moment). He immediately shifted his transformation from self to a toy pig ("Hey, look *he's* eating corn" [emphasis added]). We sense a congruency between Anthony's actions and his talk. We also see that simple classroom materials—a wooden block, a toy pig—served as pivots for Anthony. These pivots were objects through which Anthony could express meaning (Vygotsky, 1978), allowing him to play out at least part of what he knows about pig behavior and care. Bill's actions and talk reflect a different type of congruency. He announced a plan as he gathered materials (double unit blocks and roof boards), responding to the blocks as objects for construction, and operating with ideas outside the realm of the curriculum theme. Bill's mode triggered a change in Anthony's play; following Bill's single utterance Anthony moved beyond building a pen to planning the creation of a cornfield. Bill continued his planned construction play.

Peers Influence Ideas

Anthony's awareness of and responses to his peers' actions and talk are also demonstrated in a later segment of the transcript:

> *Teacher:* You're taking your kitty cat for a walk. I bet your kitty cat likes being outside.
>
> *Anthony:* What's her name, what's her name?
>
> *Cathy:* I cannot make, I cannot make a name.
>
> *Teacher:* You cannot make a name for your kitty cat?
>
> *Anthony:* My name is "Oink-Oink," this is—guy's name is "Oinker," I'm building him a house.
>
> *Bill:* I'm building my thing blue thing . . .
>
> *Anthony:* I bought it from the pet store.
>
> *Teacher:* You bought it from the pet store? And Bill is working on his bridge.
>
> *Anthony:* How about Wilbur?
>
> *Teacher:* Wilbur is a good name for a pig.
>
> *Anthony:* Yeah, yeah, do you know the movie?
>
> *Teacher:* I do know the movie.
>
> *Bill:* (inaudible)
>
> *Teacher:* That's a name from *Charlotte's Web*.

Cathy entered the block center from the "pet store," dressed in a striped skirt and pulling a toy "kitty cat" behind her on a yarn leash. She was fully immersed in the curriculum, and the teacher sought to nurture that involvement through comments about her "pet," made within the framework of "pretend that these stuffed animals are our pets." Anthony followed the teacher's lead with an inquiry that was fully within that same framework. But Cathy refused to be drawn into this mode of action and talk. Her blunt denial was addressed not to Anthony but to the teacher. Cathy carried out her pretense solely through actions with classroom materials. Talk had no part in her play at this point.

Anthony handled Cathy's disinterested rejection philosophically, transferring his interest in pet names from her cat to his own pig. His talk indicated that he remained within pretense, while subtly shifting his roles from pig itself, to narrating/dramatizing with the toy pig, to pet owner. As Anthony focused on the pig-naming process ("Oink-Oink" became "Oinker" became "Wilbur"), his talk shifted out of pretense to a conversation with the teacher.

While connected to the theme of pets, this portion of the conversation was at the same time clearly removed from the actions Anthony carried out with the blocks and toy pig. Verbally, Anthony focused on the task of naming pets. Simultaneously, he carried out physical actions with the blocks, forming an arched enclosure "pigpen" (or "house") configuration. He manipulated Oink-Oink/Oinker/Wilbur upon and around the construction as well. On the other hand, the single utterance that Bill managed to inject into the flow of talk was a straightforward comment about his own action directed toward all and sundry, or perhaps to no one in particular.

Like the action–talk shifts that occurred during this segment, the influences shaping the play were, at this point, many. The pet theme remained in operation for some. Anthony's comment concerning his pig's origins (i.e., the pet store) reflected this, as did his desire to name the animals. Cathy's play actions of leading her "kitty" around on a "leash" were also indicative of the curriculum theme. The mass media, in the form of literature and film, proved to be a moving force behind Anthony's play. His talk about "the movie" reflected his familiarity with the animated film version of E. B. White's classic book, *Charlotte's Web.*

Interactions with peers prompted shifts in play actions and talk as well. Bill switched from construction to talking about silent manipulation of the blocks, to talking about his creation directly following Anthony's comment about his own construction play; only after Anthony failed to engage Cathy in a "pet naming" script did he shift out of pretense, to initiate a conversation with the teacher concerning Wilbur and *Charlotte's Web.*

Individuals Differ in Their Play

As we examine a third segment, we begin to see a contrast between the play of Anthony and the play of Bill:

Bill: I, I made a bridge.
Teacher: You did make a bridge, Bill.
Anthony: Bill, how 'bout you go buy a pet from the pet store, like I did. Oh, that was a Pound Purry she had, that was a Pound Purry.
Teacher: A Pound Purry?
Anthony: Yes, Karen was walkin' by with . . . that cat.
Teacher: You thought . . .
Anthony: That's a Pound Purry.
Teacher: Do you mean, Cathy?
Anthony: Yeah, Cathy. She was in my first school.

Bill preferred to remain in the domain of play actions, creating an arched block edifice unrelated to the curriculum theme of pets. His construction was accompanied by an occasional foray into talk, usually in the form of reports or descriptions of his creations, and inevitably directed toward the teacher rather than his peers. For Bill, peers, mass media, and the curriculum theme failed to be of much significance. He appeared to shape his play in response to his own ideas and experiences, in combination with the curriculum materials provided and some encouragement from the teacher, who generally responded positively to his overtures though she did not initiate any interactions with him, as she did, for instance, with Cathy.

Anthony's play, in contrast to that of Bill, seemed to take shape in response to all of the factors that Bill apparently ignored. Anthony invested time and energy in attempting to hook up with peers; these attempts failed just as often as they succeeded (e.g., Bill ignored his suggestion to buy a pet). The mass media, in the form of the Pound Purry, entered as an influential factor on Anthony's actions and talk. (A Pound Purry is the feline counterpart to the Pound Puppy, a stuffed animal toy and cartoon character.) Anthony maintained contact with the curriculum theme, both in his suggestion to Bill that he "go buy a pet from the pet store" and in his conversation with the teacher about the Pound Purry.

Anthony's talk at this time consisted of talk about others' play (Bill's and Cathy's) rather than his own; simultaneously he continued in the domain of play action, constructing the pigpen and cornfield about which he had talked earlier.

The play of the two boys differed, both in the way they coordinated talk and action, and in the factors that shaped their talk and action. Anthony engaged in these two activities simultaneously. For Bill, talk and action were mutually exclusive; thus he handled the two activities in a sequential fashion. Anthony accepted and incorporated external input, reaching out constantly to engage both children and adults. Bill operated from within, expressing himself mainly through his construction play, occasionally stopping to verbally touch base with the teacher.

Even the way in which the two boys completed their constructions reflected the differences in their play:

Bill: I want you to see, I need you to see what my bridge looks like.

Teacher: I can see what your bridge looks like, Bill. You have three boards. Two of them are slanted and one is across.

Anthony: Now, I grow my cornfield.

Teacher: OK, Anthony now you can grow your cornfield.
Anthony: Wheaz. sssssssshhhh.

Bill sought out the teacher and engaged in conversation focusing on his actions with the blocks, while Anthony's verbalizations were part of the pretense he continued to create (i.e., his words and sound effects are the corn stalks, growing.)

Adults and Others Contribute Ideas

Anthony and Bill, each in his own way, were competent builders. Though the two boys sought out and included the teacher in their talk, the teacher felt no need to provide suggestions, structure their use of curriculum materials, or aid them in any way. It was otherwise with Cathy and Gayla.

Teacher: Gayla, would you like to do some building?
Gayla: Yeah.
Teacher: You want to sit in my lap for a little bit?
Let's build something for your kitty cat, Cathy.
That's a good idea.
Let's move over and make some room for Cathy so she can build something for her kitty cat.

Here, Cathy had returned to the block corner with her Pound Purry, and Gayla had entered for the first time. The teacher made an obvious and overt effort to involve the two girls in the curriculum theme and to use the classroom materials in a specified way. Cathy and Gayla were receptive to the teacher's suggestions. Cathy responded by constructing a simple block enclosure; she remained in the action domain, refraining from any kind of talk as she built. Gayla's simple verbal response also was followed by action. Gayla's construction, somewhat more elaborate than Cathy's, included a roof. Her only talk following this was "Woof, woof" (clearly pretend play with talk), as Clifford the Big Red Dog inspected his new home.

The play of Cathy and Gayla clearly reflected the influence of the media as well as the curriculum theme. Unlike Anthony and Bill, they seemed to need adult support in becoming engaged with the blocks, though not with the stuffed animals. Like Bill, the two girls remained in the domain of action and spent little time engaged in talk.

As the play session continued, Anthony remained highly involved in pretense play with blocks and stuffed animals.

Anthony: I'm pickin' the corn.
Teacher: OK.
Anthony, why don't you move over here a little bit?
(several children talking)
Anthony: It has lots of mud, there's lots of mud in it.
Teacher: Lots of mud?
Anthony: Pigs *in* the mud. And I gave, and I gave 'em some.

We are uncertain whether Anthony was simply informing the teacher about his play actions, or engaging in a monologue within pretense play. However, his words clearly reflect his possession of knowledge about what pigs do and what pigs eat. Anthony brought this knowledge with him to his play; the curriculum theme and materials allowed him to use the information within his play.

Dynamic Interaction of Ideas, Peers, and Materials

The sections of transcript examined up to this point were bits and pieces of conversations, usually involving only two people. Little peer interaction was to be found; the play, in Parten's (1932) terms, was "parallel," in that each child utilized the same materials side by side, uninvolved with each other's actions and talk. As we move further into the transcript, and as the children moved further into their play, a change occurred. While Bill remained engrossed in bridge construction, Anthony changed his play in response to the entrance of Evan and Frank, Ian and Jack. Traffic became heavy; the level of movement and noise within the area increased. Conversation overlapped, was interrupted, and left incomplete. The task of sifting through the transcript, identifying influences that shaped actions and talk, and deciphering meaning, became more difficult as boundaries between conversations blurred in the creativity of children's play.

Anthony: Where do we put the bird cage? I'm ready for . . . Help, I'm getting the hiccups again (dum, dum, dum).
Gayla: Woof. Woof. Woof.
Teacher: Hello there. How are you, Clifford, the Big Red Dog.
Gayla: Woof.
Teacher: What a neat idea.
Bill: I need some tape.

Teacher: There should be some on the table. I see some by the aprons.

Frank: Hurricane . . .

Anthony: Can I land on it?

Evan: I made it for you and me. Watch out. My cage is delicate.

Anthony: Make way. Make way. Make way. Make way. Make way. Make way. Make way. Here I come to save the day, Mighty Bird is on the way. (chanted)

Evan: Hey.

Anthony: He didn't see where he was going. Here, I come to save the day, Hurricane, come and try to get me.

Evan: Wah.

Anthony: Here I come to save the day, br, rrrrrrr.

Evan: My cage is falling down.

Teacher: Can I tear it for you, Bill.

Frank: Hurry, the Ghost Busters are still in there.

Teacher: Now it's in two pieces, Bill.

Karen: I'm gonna make a cat's mask.

Teacher: Good idea, Karen.

Frank: See . . . Ghost Busters are . . . (sound effect).

Karen: I'm gonna make a cat's mask.

Teacher: Good idea, Karen.

Frank: The ghost Ghost Busters are all in their their car.

Anthony: Here, here (knocking blocks; screaming).

Evan: Don't, Frank.

Frank: Look at this man. Look at this man. Now there's no more money. Here, I'm looking for it.

Anthony: Here I come to save the day. Mighty Bird is on the way.

Frank: You know why? Cuz Ghost Busters are already in the garage.

Anthony: I charged this with my (inaudible). With a golden boid [bird] (blocks falling). Tweety, Tweety, Tweety (inaudible).

The sequence of utterances presented in written form is a poor representation of the play that actually occurred.

Let us focus first on Anthony. No longer a pigman, Anthony now wielded "Mighty Bird" (a strange cross between Mighty Mouse and Tweety Bird). The pigpen and cornfield, previously built for "Wilbur" the pig, were reconstructed and replaced by a larger, taller arched enclosure: a "delicate cage," built by Evan for Anthony. Anthony's "Mighty Bird" (also referred to as "Tweety" and "Golden Bird") seemed bent on demolition, for after swooping around the block corner he eventually crashed into the "cage."

Meanwhile, Frank introduced "Hurricane" and "Ghost Busters"

with these new elements. His apparent concern with danger and destruction continued. Evan and Anthony managed to incorporate the search for wealth into the script as well. An interval of their play consisted of gathering "money" into an enclosure of blocks (formerly the "bird cage") and chortling over their newfound gains.

The play of Anthony, Evan, and Frank, as reflected by the conversations and sounds recorded on the audiotape, was energetic, at times almost frantic. Action and talk were closely linked, both within and outside of pretense. The teacher no longer served as a focus for Anthony's talk. Instead, the three boys had somehow flowed out of parallel play and the need for adult contact, into interactive play with peers. The connections were sometimes tenuous. Evan focused on building, Anthony on "Mighty Bird," Frank on busting ghosts. Yet, the three managed to communicate with each other within play, about play, about action, some of the time within pretense. They were productively bouncing off one another.

Interspersed among the conversations of the three boys were dyadic interactions between the teacher and two other children, Gayla and Karen. Gayla's utterances occurred within the boundaries of pretense play, and the teacher responded in such a way as to support that. Karen, on the other hand, engaged in talk about her future plans for playing, as Bill had done at the beginning of the play session.

Listening to the audiotape at this point, and even further along into the session when the teacher initiated the task of cleaning up, it was difficult to remember that play in the block corner began with only two children engaged in parallel activities. Over the course of 45 minutes, 12 children entered the area. Nine of the children built with blocks or manipulated toy animals. Anthony and Bill remained in the area virtually the entire session, while others (e.g., Dani and Cathy) entered for only brief periods. Construction (and demolition) occurred almost continuously.

Differences in the amount of talk generated by individual children were noticeable and, we think, important. We heard from Anthony frequently. He explained and discussed his play actions. He engaged in pretense through his verbalizations, either alone ("My name is Oink-Oink") or in collaboration with others. He discussed topics seemingly irrelevant to his pretense and constructions (e.g., bad dreams, a neighborhood friend, previous school experiences).

This contrasts with the talking Anthony did in collaboration with Evan and Frank. These three talked together in a manner that moved each boy from parallel construction and pretense into collaborative pretense. Bill's case represents a further contrast. Bill constructed, apparently pretended about his construction, and then talked about what the construction meant to him; his talk was never within pretense. Others did not talk at all as they built. The range of pretense-related action and talk was immense.

Conclusions

The block building action and talk that we have presented reveal complicated relationships. We see a range of action and talk that appear to come together at times and operate separately at times. Anthony built a series of structures, talking about his plans and talking within character, relating to the scenes he had created. Bill played with his constructed bridge, rarely saying anything at all. Cathy contributed verbally to the block construction of others, while never building anything herself. Clearly, talk, while a valuable source of insight into the construction play of some children, is not helpful for understanding the play of others. Both action and talk must be considered when we assess children's play, contrary to the presupposition of many (e.g., Garvey, 1977; Pellegrini, 1986).

What about the ideas that serve as a basis for the representations, the themes that the children generate with their block play? What "real-world" referents contribute to pretense? It seems clear that children "play what they know," as Almy and others remind us (see Chapter 1; Almy, Monighan, Scales, & Van Hoorn, 1985; Monighan-Nourot, Scales, Van Hoorn, & Almy, 1987) and as Schwartzman (1978) showed us more than 10 years ago. But there is much more of a social source for this knowledge than the phrase "play what they know" reveals. The curriculum, including ideas presented in the classroom, classroom materials, and peers, provides varying but recognizable influences on children's action and talk. Information about pets came from the teacher and from the materials (books, pictures, records) she brought to class. Other materials, like blocks, provided potential for construction, and peers suggested ideas to one another. For example, Anthony knew something about pigs, farms, and corn, which he used as the basis for his first construction, and Bill knew something about bridges. Cathy's chatting as she passed by was also an influence. The "real world" that children use as their ideas for play is (or can be) strongly influenced by the curriculum that teachers present. What we see and hear in children's play should be enhanced by all the curricular resources a teacher can muster, including topics for play, materials for play, opportunities for social interaction, and the time in which all these can blend and brew.

The question of time for children to play deserves special attention as part of the curriculum. Children need time to elaborate the ideas they are encountering, to elaborate their thoughts through play. Over the course of this period, Anthony's one block construction changed from a pig farm to a bird cage to a money box, with the changes due to chance intrusions of children who passed by with materials from another play area in the room. Seeing a bird or being given play money was enough to trigger a change in play theme for Anthony. And each play transformation brought an array of talk by him. Even with materials as static as blocks, the flow of pretense and attributed meanings can remain fluid over time, and this time is important for the development of Anthony's and other children's ideas.

  • Within a play theme, a chance social encounter can elicit variations on a theme, as when Cathy walked by with her Pound Purry and Anthony responded with a series of statements about names for pets and his pet pig. Other children can suggest pretend ideas without the intention of doing so. In block play, social influences can shape themes in a way reminiscent of Dyson's descriptions of early writing (Dyson, 1988a, 1988b). These social contacts based on play with objects may serve an important function in making a child's subjective experience more objective. Other children or objects evoke possible new learning for a child to explore through play (Elgas, Klein, Kantor, & Fernie, 1988). The social and material basis for learning and development is apparent (Vygotsky, 1978).

What contributes to pretense with blocks? We can see a range of sources for play ideas, from the classroom (pets), friends, movies (*Charlotte's Web*), television (Tweety Bird, Mighty Mouse), and others. It is especially interesting to note Frank's first comment in our final segment of transcript: "Hurricane. . . ." He says this word while he knocks down a bird cage. Frank has brought the hurricane theme into his play here as well as into tales at circle time. None of the teachers know where he first learned about hurricanes, but they know that he knew all about them in general and specifically. It seems that immediate stimuli, such as toy birds or toy money, will lead some children to play, while other children will pursue an idea over time, even when there is no physical object present to stimulate its appearance. It is worth wondering more about where children get their ideas, and why some ideas remain while others ebb and flow in the course of play. It is as if some children needed one of Vygotsky's pivots (Vygotsky, 1978) to pretend around an object in order to trigger and allow the expression of ideas; others have internalized those preoccupying ideas and need no object in order to express ideas.

Are there rules to this play, rules that we can use to predict what we should see? In one sense, yes. We can see the concrete forms that children construct, and they do give us a measure of the children's motoric and cognitive development (Reifel, 1984b). But in another sense, we believe that the play children generate with blocks can be understood best not only in terms of rules. Children, alone or in groups, can generate an experience, including construction, seemingly irrelevant talk, talk about the play ideas that interest them, and pretense based on those ideas. The contour will vary with every child or group, and the variation may or may not matter. Further research can help us know that. What matters now is that they are allowed to experience ideas that are of interest and that feel good to them, and to explore those ideas to the extent that seems right to them. They give the ideas meaning. They are in control. And we think that is important in early childhood.

References

Almy, M., Monighan, P., Scales, B., & Van Hoorn, J. (1985). Recent research on play: The teacher's perspective. In L. Katz (Ed.), *Current topics in early childhood education* (Vol. 5, pp. 1–25). Norwood, NJ: Ablex.

Bailey, M. W. (1933). A scale of block constructions for young children. *Child Development, 4,* 121–139.

Dyson, A. Haas. (1988a). Appreciating the drawing and dictating of young children. *Young Children, 43* (3), 25–32.

Dyson, A. Haas. (1988b). *Drawing, talking and writing: Rethinking writing development.* Berkeley: University of California, Center for the Study of Writing.

Elgas, P. M., Klein, E., Kantor, R., & Fernie, D. E. (1988). Play and the peer culture: Play styles and object use. *Journal of Research in Childhood Education* 3(2), 142–153.

Froebel, F. (1887). *The education of man* (W. N. Hailman, Trans.). New York: Appleton.

Garvey, C. (1977). *Play.* Cambridge, MA: Harvard University Press.

Guanella, F. M. (1934). Block building activities of young children. *Archives of Psychology, 174,* 1–92.

Johnson, H. M. (1984). The art of block building. In E. S. Hirsch (Ed.), *The block book* (rev. ed., pp. 15–49). Washington, DC: National Association for the Education of Young Children.

Monighan-Nourot, P., Scales, B., Van Hoorn, J., & Almy, M. (1987). *Looking at children's play: A bridge between theory and practice.* New York: Teachers College Press.

Mounoud, P. (1976). The development of systems of representation and treatment in the child. In B. Inhelder & H. H. Chipman (Eds.), *Piaget and his school* (pp. 166–185). New York: Springer-Verlag.

Parten, M. B. (1932). Social participation among preschool children. *Journal of Abnormal Social Psychology 27,* 243–262.

Pellegrini, A. D. (1986). Communicating in and about play: The effect of play centers on preschoolers' explicit language. In G. G. Fein & M. Rivkin (Eds.), *The* young child at play: Reviews of research (Vol. 4; pp. 79–91). Washington, DC: National Association for the Education of Young Children.

Piaget, J. (1962). Play, dreams and imitation in childhood. (C. Gattegno & F. M. Hodgeson, Trans.) New York: Norton. (Original work published 1945).

Reifel, S. (1984a). Symbolic representation at two ages: Block buildings of a story. Discourse Processes, 7, 11–20.

Reifel, S. (1984b). Block construction: Children's developmental landmarks in representation of space. Young Children, 40(1), 61–67.

Reifel, S., & Greenfield, P. M. (1982). Structural development in a symbolic medium: The representational use of block constructions. In G. E. Forman (Ed.), Action and thought: From sensorimotor schemes to symbolic operations (pp. 203–233). New York: Academic Press.

Schwartzman, H. B. (1978). Transformations: The anthropology of children's play. New York: Plenum.

Vereecken, P. (1961). Spatial development: Constructive praxia from birth to the age of seven. Groningen, The Netherlands: Wolters.

Vygotsky, L. S. (1978). Mind in society: The development of higher psychological processes (M. Cole, V. John-Steiner, S. Scribner, & E. Souberman, Eds. & Trans.). Cambridge, MA: Harvard University Press.

CHAPTER 12

Constructive Play

A Window into the Mind of the Preschooler

AGELIKI NICOLOPOULOU

Jessica, a tall, serious 5-year-old, spots her younger friend Jonathan, who is walking aimlessly in the nursery school's yard holding a tiger hand-puppet. "Let's make a house for your tiger," Jessica shouts enthusiastically as she nears him. Jonathan, who often plays with Jessica, likes the idea and they both head toward the block area inside the school.

An entire wall space in their school is filled with wooden blocks of widely differing sizes, and—to the silent horror of the teacher supervising the inside area—they take down almost all the blocks as they busily build a "house" that keeps getting bigger and bigger. For most of the time, the tiger hand-puppet is lying at the side, as they are totally absorbed in their building activity. Jonathan hands the blocks to Jessica, who seems to be the architect of their elaborate structure. By the end, all three—Jessica, Jonathan, and the hand-puppet—have their own private rooms surrounded by extra walls, rooms, bridges, and so on. However, they don't get much of a chance to play in their structure because school is almost over and the teacher urges them to clean up as the rest of the children start gathering around for story time.

For several consecutive days after this initial incident, Jessica and Jonathan come back to the block area and build elaborate and intricate structures. Sometimes it is a "house" for them, sometimes it is for them and their favorite animal, and sometimes it is "just a building." More often than not, it changes character and identity as they build it. Sometimes they use the structure as a stage for their dramatic play, but often their play consists entirely of block building. They enjoy themselves every time, and their involvement continues day after day and for long periods each time. (from my observations as a nursery school teacher, Berkeley, 1982–83)

How well do we understand the play activity of these children, an activity quite common among young children? What holds their attention and interest for such long periods, so that they end up constructing these elaborate and intricate structures day after day? Why do they find this activity interesting and fun, although they often take the structures down as soon as they build them? Are they simply interested in depicting the world, or do spatial and aesthetic properties equally hold their imagination?

Current Research and Interpretations: Defining the Problem

Young children's building activities have attracted the attention of educators and psychologists since the first nursery schools. Early in the century, several studies were conducted to document young children's block play in "progressive" nursery classrooms (e.g., Guanella, 1934; Hulson, 1930; Johnson, 1933; Pratt, 1948). Building blocks were immediately recognized as a symbolic medium for children; psychoanalysts, for example, have used block play as a means to get into the psyche of the young child (e.g., Erikson, 1972; Klein, 1955). On the other hand, cognitive psychologists set out to formulate developmental stages that captured the increasing spatial and constructional complexities of children's constructions with age. Based on these stages, sample construction tasks have been introduced into psychological and educational tests designed to assess the spatial and cognitive development of young children and to measure them against "normal" development (see discussion in Vereecken, 1961).

Although children's constructions were recognized early on as being both spatial and symbolic in character, these aspects have been analyzed as if they were entirely separate and autonomous from each other. With respect to the first aspect, research on constructive play has characterized in detail the different levels of the elaboration of space that children achieve (e.g., Forman & Hill, 1980; Inhelder & Piaget, 1969; Langer, 1980, 1986; Reifel & Greenfield, 1982; Vereecken, 1961). At the first level (from 6 months to 1 year), infants use blocks in nonspatial ways; that is, they handle mainly single objects, and, as far as their handling extends to more than one object, their interest centers on physical relations (e.g., hitting, rolling) rather than on spatial properties emerging from the combination of objects. It is only during the second stage (second year of life) that children make linear arrangements of objects, either vertical or horizontal. Then, in the third stage (beginning around the end of the second year), they begin to elaborate bidirectional or areal arrangements, eventually producing enclosed horizontal spaces. During the fourth stage—at around three years of age—children construct solid tridimensional structures, which soon give way to enclosed tridimensional spaces. Children's constructions may also include further elaborations such as openings in walls, adjacent structures, "stories" or layers of enclosure, bridges, and so on; but once the fundamentals of space are mastered, there is great diversity in development and we can no longer talk of "stages." Furthermore, after children reach a higher stage, they do not discontinue the use of earlier forms (e.g., Forman, Wolf, Scarlett, Shotwell, & Gennari, n.d.; Guanella, 1934). The chief focus of this research, then, is on the dimensionality of constructions and the gradual move from one, to two, and then to three dimensions.

In this literature, a construction is usually defined as symbolic when children claim—whether spontaneously or not—that their construction depicts a thing in the real world (e.g., "house," "boat," "railroad"). Research has shown that the development of such "symbolic"—that is, mimetic or representational—constructions increases remarkably from about 1 to 7 years. In particular, these constructions come to conform more and more to the actual form of the thing represented; this change in form reflects an increased sensitivity to both the object's contour and its details, as well as to the internal relation of the parts to the whole (Guanella, 1934; Johnson, 1933). Exploring this development in more detail, Reifel and Greenfield (1982) demonstrated that as children grow older their symbolic constructions increase in spatial complexity.

Previous research, however, has rarely paid serious attention to the interplay between the spatial and symbolic aspects of constructions. The neglect of these issues by researchers is probably due in part to their rather narrow interpretation of the"symbolic" element in block play, by which they refer only to those constructions that depict or copy objects in the physical world. Given this narrow definition, a large number of children's constructions appear as "simply" spatial in character and are examined purely in terms of their spatial complexity and dimensionality. The question of why children are interested in making these constructions is, curiously enough, rarely addressed directly; but it seems to be assumed that children have an interest in aligning objects and fitting them together which has no connection to the symbolic properties of the constructions.

However, the symbolic element in human activity cannot be reduced to the direct representation of particular objects. Equally symbolic are those constructions that derive meaning from their formal or aesthetic properties, and that elaborate the structural and aesthetic possibilities of the materials used in making them. Wolf and Gardner (1979) have shown that some children—whom they call "patterners"—choose to elaborate the structural and formal elements of the materials (medium) provided to them, while others—"visualizers" or "dramatizers"—depict objects in the world. What this distinction captures, the present study suggests, are two different styles of symbolic activity—or, perhaps, two different aspects of children's symbolic imagination. When children make designs (or abstract patterns), they elaborate aesthetic principles that are realized by utilizing successfully the inherent structure of the medium. In the case of the "dramatizers" the focus is less on formal aesthetic principles, and more on depicting and copying objects in the world. In both cases, what is involved is an attempt to master the internal possibilities of the medium for symbolic ends. Investigations that address the symbolic dimension of both of these forms of activity can help provide a better understanding of what guides and holds children's interest in constructive play.

The Present Study

Theoretical Concerns and Method

Adopting this broader definition of "symbolic," the present study explores the interplay between the spatial and symbolic aspects of children's constructive play, taking into account not only the final constructions but also the processes by which they were constructed. From a developmental point of view, what is particularly interesting is to investigate the relationship between the level of spatial elaboration of the constructions and the nature and degree of symbolic activity they embody.

Tracing this relationship developmentally allows us to raise the question of what kinds of interest motivate children's involvement in constructive play, and of whether the saliency of these interests changes over time. That is, what is it about constructive activity which holds children's interest; what provides an impetus for them to combine and recombine the objects in new and different ways; which combinations do children find satisfactory at different ages, and so on? To what extent are children guided by an interest in spatial elaboration for its own sake, as a number of studies seem to assume? (We will see that, at certain points, children do seem to use objects simply to fill up space in a fairly random way.) To what extent are their constructions motivated by symbolic concerns, both representational/mimetic and aesthetic/expressive? Do these different concerns develop independently, or do they feed into each other? And to what extent is the structure of their motivation uniform or shifting over time? By paying close attention to children's activity during the building process, we can reconstruct and follow their emerging intentions.

A guiding assumption behind this investigation is that the constructions emerge from a complex interaction between the children's intentions, on the one hand, and the inherent structure and possibilities of the medium, on the other. The set of objects children use in their constructions has an implicit structure, which they come to master gradually as they combine and recombine the objects in the attempt either to elaborate aesthetic principles or to depict the world. The extent of their mastery, and of their capacity to achieve spatial elaboration, must constrain the extent to which children can achieve their symbolic intentions. At the same time, the inherent structure of the medium, as children come to grasp it, will itself influence the nature of their constructions and will affect the kinds of symbolic possibilities they come to discover.

Beginning to grasp the interplay between the spatial and symbolic elements in children's constructions, and the way in which this interplay is affected by the structure of the medium, can improve our understanding of what captures the children's interest in this activity and how this interest changes with age. Such understanding can help teachers direct and enrich constructive play more effectively—whether on the playground, in the arts corner, or even at the science table.

Research Design

Such an investigation requires that we be able to pay systematic attention to the inherent structure of the medium and to the ways in which the children master and utilize it. Because the typical wooden blocks that one finds in almost all nursery schools are far too numerous and too structurally open-ended for this purpose, I decided to construct new materials with a well-defined structure. These comprised four sets of 16 objects apiece that were designed to meet the following criteria: (1) the objects were large enough for young children to manipulate easily; (2) they were not so numerous that children would find it difficult to use the whole set; and (3) each set of 16 objects had a structure defined by systematic variations of perceptual properties (shape, color, and size) to which young children are sensitive. In this chapter the presentation of results will be limited to the first two sets, which varied only by shape and color (i.e., all were of roughly similar size). For easy manipulation of all these properties and their combinations, the pieces were made out of colored cardboard by gluing two identical sides together so that each piece did not have a distinct front and back. The pieces were abstract geometrical shapes that resembled puzzle pieces.

Each of the two sets under discussion, therefore, had its own distinct structure. In each case, four shapes and four colors were used. In the *first set*, each shape had a distinctive and uniform color; thus, shape and color coincided. Each shape was thus represented by four identical objects (see Figure 12.1).

In the *second set*, shape and color varied independently, so that each shape was combined with four distinct colors (see Figure 12.2). It should be mentioned that the four colors making up each of the sets were chosen so that they were perceptually pleasing in juxtaposition.

Twenty-four children played with the objects, eight at each of three ages: 3, 4, and 5 years. Each child was invited individually to play in a room adjacent to the grounds of the preschool, where the entire session could be videotaped. Each child was presented with the two sets of materials consecutively in the order described above. The children were asked to "make something" with the pieces and were allowed to play freely with them and make anything they pleased. As the author of this chapter—who was a teacher's aide at the school—observed the children, she encouraged their efforts all along and also tried to maintain the same kind of interaction that they would have had as a pair on the school grounds.

Basically, the author aimed at striking a balance between being nondirective while also maintaining and sustaining the child's interest in the activity. When children did not use all of the objects spontaneously, she urged them to do so. After they had finished playing with the objects, she asked if they had "made something," unless they provided this information spontaneously. The majority of the children did provide this information spontaneously, either announcing in advance that "I'm going to make [this or that]" or announcing afterward that they had "made [this or that]" during the construction process.

The children were left free to play as long as they wished. The end of a session was always signaled by the child: Either the child sat back in his or her chair, drawing his or her hands away from the materials, and looked at the adult contentedly as if saying "here it is"; or the child pushed all the objects toward the adult; or the child told her that he or she was done; and so on.

FIGURE 12.1. First set: Shape and color coincide.

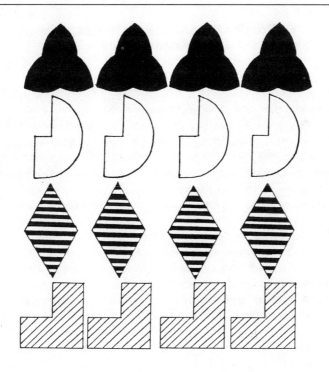

FIGURE 12.2. Second set: Shape and color vary independently.

Children's Spontaneous Constructions:
Process and Product

Three-year-olds

Although the sets of objects were rather novel, even 3-year-olds seemed to regard them as puzzle pieces. They interpreted the task of "making something" as fitting the pieces together and/or aligning them. The majority of the 3-year-olds made several constructions that included a few objects apiece (the most frequent were 2- to 4-object constructions). Only two of the children made single constructions that included all 16 objects. Furthermore, in making their constructions (whether single or multiple), 5 of the 8 children exhausted all 16 objects from the first set of materials, but only 2 children exhausted all of them from the second set. This suggests that 3-year-olds encountered more difficulties when attempting to arrange and order the objects of the second set, where color and shape did not coincide. (This is not simply because they were losing interest after the first set, as some readers might imagine. When presented with the third set, many of the children exhausted all the pieces in their constructions. Thus, it is the characteristics of the different sets, rather than the order of their presentation, that is the crucial variable.)

While most 3-year-olds' constructions used a small number of pieces and were one-dimensional in spatial elaboration, they already manifested aesthetic qualities such as repetition and alternation, symmetry and harmony. When color and shape coincided, the constructions had a clear thematic structure (e.g., the children used identical objects or grouped them into clear oppositions). Furthermore, objects of the same shape were connected by placing them in identical (repetitive) or complementary spatial orientations (Figure 12.3). (The information under each construction gives the child's initials and his or her age in years; months.)

When color and shape varied independently, the patterns children made were mainly symmetrical in character, with a tendency toward spatially closed forms. Two-piece constructions might match pieces of the same color; but, when the constructions included more than two objects, they did not show a clear predominance of any single shape or color. In general, in the complex constructions (i.e., more than two pieces) children seemed to pay more attention to shape than to color (Figure 12.4).

Thus, "patterning" is clearly in evidence. On the other hand, only one child in this age group (JA, 3;04) can reasonably be called a "dramatizer." While making and arranging constructions with both sets of ob-

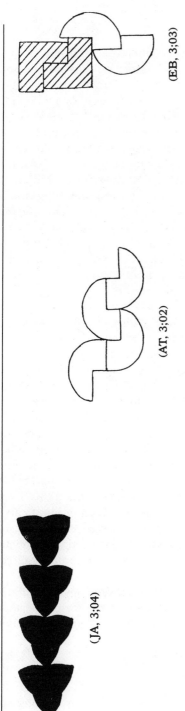

FIGURE 12.3. Constructions by 3-year-olds (first set).

(JA, 3;04)

(AT, 3;02)

(EB, 3;03)

FIGURE 12.4. Constructions by 3-year-olds (second set).

(KK, 3;02)

(EB, 3;03)

(JA, 3;04)

jects, she gave a representational/symbolic label to several single objects (e.g., "flower," "Mary kneeling") and also—more rarely—named some combinations of objects. She was not the only child who used symbolic labels for objects or constructions, but she was the only one who did so with any consistency; naming the objects was a mode that she used persistently with both sets of materials, while the rest of the children provided a representational/symbolic label occasionally at most. About half of the 3-year-olds used a representational/symbolic label at least once for a single object or for one of the constructions they made. Overall, the representational/symbolic labels invoked by this age group were applied overwhelmingly to single pieces rather than to constructions. Furthermore, they seemed to be based largely on the shape of the pieces, which reminded the children of single objects in the world, such as "a flower" or "an umbrella" (and not, for example, on collections of objects or on action scenarios). This symbolic naming did not seem to be very different from naming these pieces as a "square" or a "diamond."

We can conclude that, at this age, the aesthetic and formal properties of the medium capture the children's imagination much more than the representational/mimetic possibilities; the children devote their energies primarily to elaborating the internal structure of sets of objects presented to them. But even so, aesthetic and formal elaboration was almost always limited to single constructions. Only very rarely did we observe a clear thematic or aesthetic relationship between two spatially separate constructions. Even when there was a thematic relation between separate constructions, it was usually not spatially articulated. Children would make a construction and either leave it on the side or push it away before they went on to make a new one. In some cases, while from the observer's point of view the constructions seemed to have a common theme, it was not clear whether the child intended this. In one case, for example, the child was placing together pairs of identical objects; but as soon as he finished with each single construction, he pushed it to the side before he went on to make another construction connecting pairs of identical objects. They were not connected in an overall construction.

In the few cases where a spatial relation between several different constructions was achieved, it was again based on the formal aesthetic properties of repetition, alternation, and symmetry. Figure 12.5 shows an impressive example.

Four-year-olds

Four-year-olds spent more time than 3-year-olds in making constructions, and about half of them used all 16 objects with both sets of

FIGURE 12.5.   Complex construction by a 3-year-old (RR, 3;01), articulating spatial relations between component constructions.

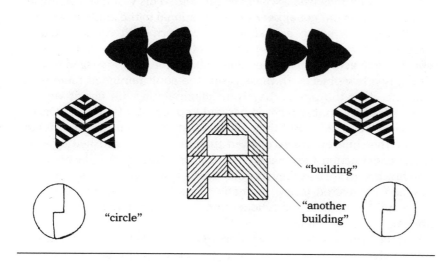

"building"

"circle"   "another building"

materials. They seemed very keen on creating a connected areal space; and about half of them were quite intent on fitting the pieces together well. They also seemed to be more eager to make constructive use of the diversity of shapes and colors provided them. They not only tried to fit together identical shapes, as did the 3-year-olds, but were equally likely to try to fit together objects of different shapes. Whenever 3-year-olds tried to fit together differently shaped objects, they tried very briefly and quickly abandoned them for identical shapes. In contrast, 4-year-olds tried for long periods of time to fit together objects of different shapes; and, when they abandoned one of these efforts, they tried again with different combinations.

Six of the eight 4-year-olds showed a concern to elaborate a connected areal space. Two distinct trends were discerned in the ways that they pursued this goal. One group used all 16 objects, but did not appear to attend carefully to the properties of objects (i.e., shape and color). Rather, they kept adding objects in loose physical contact while working cyclically around a central configuration. The objects merely covered the space, and the children did not spend much time fitting or even aligning them together; they simply kept adding more until all the objects were exhausted. The final construction had no thematic structure. In these respects, there was no clear discernible difference between the two sets of objects. While children did not spontaneously give any indication that their construction was representational, when the adult asked them, "Is this something?" they readily gave it a generic name like "castle," "circle," "Christmas tree," "colors of the sea." This was true even when the construction did not *appear* representational to the adult observer.

The second group also showed a concern with connected areal space, but they tried to leave no speck of space uncovered. They tried repeatedly to achieve this impossible goal, so that they managed to work with only a few objects. In these cases, the adult reminded them more than once that the pieces they were manipulating did not fit well together. They invariably ignored her and kept on with their task. Once a child answered back, "But they have to!" After various unsuccessful attempts, the children finally allowed themselves to be satisfied by some partial construction they were able to form; thus, they indicated they were finished as soon as they had achieved a symmetrical design or when they had discovered a new thematic relation, as in Figure 12.6. This group, unlike the first, rarely identified their constructions as representational.

Among the 4-year-olds, we observe a new reflective and playful attitude, which had only a fleeting appearance among the 3-year-olds. Four-year-olds allow themselves to be carried away by new properties that emerge as they are trying to articulate their initial inclinations. In some cases, this tendency is combined with a new sophistication in their symbolic activity. For example, after the adult asked one child if her construction was something and she answered "Christmas tree," she spontaneously went on and remade her previous amorphous cyclical construction to give it more the shape of a tree. Another 4-year-old arranged the objects of the second set by shape and placed all 4 objects of each shape in a stack. Then, she superposed each stack of identical shapes on top of another stack, making a tall construction. As soon as she was finished, she looked at the stack and said "it's all different colors"; then she went on to separate the objects into four piles, each containing objects of the same color.

Furthermore, these newly emerging properties can have a greater hold on the child's imagination than suggestions from the adult. One child (LA, 4;03) was nearly finished making four distinct constructions that contained identical objects (by shape and color). She was working with the objects of the fourth shape and was fitting two of them together, making a shape that looked like a circle. "I made a circle," she declared immediately and went on to replicate the circle with the remaining two identical objects. She observed carefully the circle she had just made saying, "Let me see, how did I do that?" To replicate the circle, however, she needed first to flip one of the pieces. After a while, the adult tried to

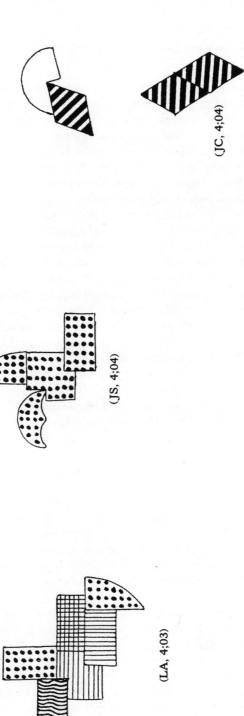

FIGURE 12.6. Nonrepresentational constructions by 4-year-olds.

(LA, 4;03)

(JS, 4;04)

(JC, 4;04)

help her, suggesting "Maybe you can turn one over," and guiding her
and pointing to the piece. The child briefly tried to follow but instead of
flipping one of the objects, she again rotated both pieces and kept trying
to fit them together until she obtained a new shape. Then she declared
to the adult—who was still trying to help her flip one of the objects—
"supposed to be a bridge." Next, she brought some differently shaped
objects and fitted them into the construction she had just made. She
added a blue diamond under it and remarked, "That's the water," then
placed over the diamond an orange corner piece, saying, "In the water,
there are some branches . . . to have some branches, too." Then, she took
both the water and the branches out and, looking at both initial configu-
rations, said, "That could be a . . ."—then, fitting them and arranging
them, she completed her sentence, "That could be a person." The adult
did not appreciate the fluidity of the child's imagination at that moment
and completed the child's utterance by saying, "On top of the bridge."
By then the child had brought together what she previously called the
"circle" and the"bridge"; pointing to the former "bridge" she said, "Here
is arms"; and then, pointing to what she had previously called the
"circle," added, "and here is head" (Figure 12.7).

   In this case, we witness how a reflective attitude leads the child to
observe several new properties emerging from her attempts to spatially
combine the objects, and how she slowly arrives at a symbolic depiction
that seems to her more satisfying.

Five-year-olds

   The constructions of 5-year-olds show a marked advance over those
of younger age groups. They arrive early on during the constructing process at thematic or symbolic themes that they come to express through
their constructions. All of them were able to exhaust all 16 objects given
to them for both sets of objects. Without any reminder from the adult,
they immediately perceived that all 16 pieces did not fit well together as
a space-filling "puzzle," and went on to combine them flexibly. Instead of
merely aligning same sides or fitting complementary pieces, they connected the objects in a flexible way by combining corners or merely placing the objects next to each other, led by the overall graphic properties
of the whole that they were trying to construct. In this way, although the
5-year-olds' constructions were still two-dimensional, the areal space
that the constructions elaborated was not simply connected and filled
space; rather, their designs involved a deliberate combination of filled
and empty spaces. Furthermore, the children could easily perceive in
the objects thematic or symbolic properties that they could use to further

FIGURE 12.7. Fluid representational construction by a 4-year-old (LA, 4;03).

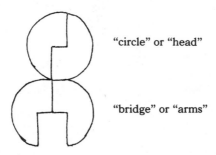

"circle" or "head"

"bridge" or "arms"

organize the objects. Thus, objects of different shapes were extensively placed next to each other; in contrast, when younger children exhausted all the objects, they mainly kept apart differently shaped objects. In this way, the 5-year-olds' constructions show an interplay of same and different objects through continuous and discontinuous space.

It is only with this age group that we can clearly differentiate children into patterners and visualizers/dramatizers, with each group encompassing about half of the children. The patterners, in particular, were able to articulate even the most subtle properties that had been worked into the design of the two object sets. For instance, in each set two shapes were curvilinear while the two others were rectilinear; in each pair one color was light and one dark. One 5-year-old (EF, 5;05) made four exact replica designs, with each design containing, in order, two rectilinear and two curvilinear objects. Another child (AV, 5;01), after making four initial constructions that contained identical objects, announced that she was shifting criteria ("now I'll switch"), and went on to mix curvilinear and rectilinear shapes. In a similar way, after she had made four constructions of identically shaped pieces with the second set of materials, she again announced that she was going to shift; but this time she went on to change the order of the objects in each construction, trying to make sure that all of them had the same internal order by color: Each of the constructions (Figure 12.8) contained a dark and a light color (red and yellow) followed by another dark-light pair (green and turquoise). (In one construction she was unsuccessful; this may have resulted from the difficulty of ordering both shapes and colors properly.)

Among the patterners, the relation between constructions is well articulated: The designs are replicas of each other or repeat the same prin-

FIGURE 12.8. Complex expressive construction by a 5-year-old (AV, 5;01).

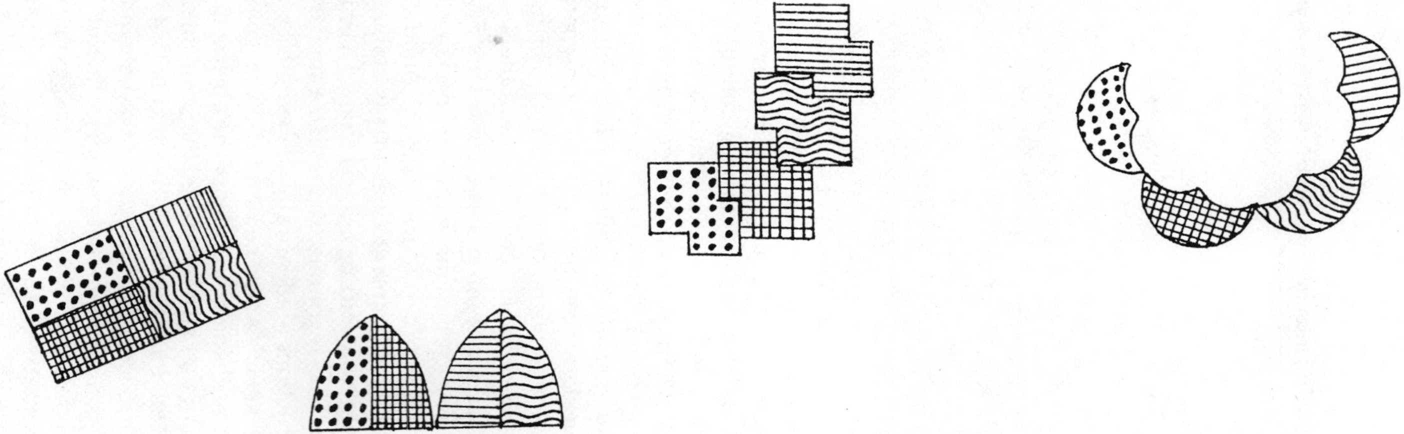

ciple (e.g., the order of colors within a construction, or the order of shapes). Among the visualizers, on the other hand, the different constructions tend to be connected through the representational themes the children are using; and the children attempt to represent, not only discrete objects, but scenes or situations. For instance, one child (JT, 5;05) made two identical sailboats with waves and a building where the sailboats could anchor. Another child (JB, 5;04) made two robbers and two houses for them to rob.

The Interplay of Spatial and Symbolic Capacities

Children from all three age groups undertook the task of "making something" willingly and playfully. They set themselves ambitious goals, even though their success in carrying them out differed considerably. All had a tendency to overreach their capacities occasionally, but all were able to realize their intentions with some degree of satisfaction. On the one hand, since the task was so open-ended, with no clear-cut right or wrong answers, the children clearly enjoyed the opportunity to explore and make discoveries along the way. On the other hand, since the set of materials provided to them had a well-defined structure, it was possible to capture their intentions—whether emerging or preformed—as well as trace any difficulties or hindrances they encountered in carrying them out.

Even 3-year-olds were sensitive to the possibilities offered by the materials provided to them for both spatial elaboration and symbolic expression. They fitted or aligned objects that were identical in shape and color, or combined different objects systematically. Their constructions articulated general aesthetic principles such as symmetry and harmony, repetition and alternation.

Three-year-olds quickly lose interest in their constructions and do not try very hard to articulate relations between them. As children get older, their constructions start gaining greater temporal and spatial stability; and this goes together with a more reflective attitude, which it presumably both reflects and invites. The stability arises either from the successful elaboration of areal space or from the consistency of using the same criteria in organizing objects. As children encounter difficulties carrying out their intentions, they allow their imagination to be captured by new properties that emerge during their efforts to combine the objects. By 5 years of age, the children can immediately attend to both general themes and specific details; and their constructions attest to a flexible coordination of specific and general properties, which allows them to incorporate the entire set of objects.

At each age, we observe a close interplay between the spatial and symbolic aspects of constructive activity, with each presupposing and shaping the other. At first, children focus on one aspect; as they experiment with it, new difficulties and possibilities emerge in the other, which sooner or later capture the children's imagination. It is this gradual, interdependent process of elaboration that allows children to discover both spatial and symbolic properties of object combinations. By 5 years of age, children come to perceive quickly all the relevant properties of the objects, so that spatial and symbolic possibilities are pursued simultaneously. They combine the objects spatially in a flexible way in order to express either representational/mimetic themes or formal aesthetic properties of the medium. In short, spatial elaboration and mimetic or aesthetic expression do not constitute a rigid form-content distinction, with spatial elaboration fulfilling the role of form and symbolic expression that of content. Rather, it is their continuous interplay that guides the children's interest and imagination.

Some Implications for the Classroom

This in-depth analysis of children's play reveals how much "at work" young children are when they playfully combine objects, make interesting designs, make "buildings" and "cities," or even depict scenes from their everyday world. As they elaborate their initial themes and apply them to more objects, they discover new possibilities, which, in turn, they use to organize the objects more ambitiously and in different ways. The process that the elaborations undergo is not different from those observed during children's pretense play in the nursery school's doll corner or on the playground (Monighan-Nourot, Scales, Van Hoorn, & Almy, 1987). As recent studies reveal, play continues to be the mode through which children come to learn even later in life (Dauite, 1989; Dyson, 1987).

In addition, the methodology used in this study, which embedded a well-defined structure in the materials for children to "discover" in their play, can be used to inform the "implicit curriculum" utilized by educators (Monighan-Nourot et al., 1987). Teachers who are interested in helping children expand their world while playing could construct materials according to the principles that they are interested in conveying to the children (e.g., geometrical or aesthetic principles). An important advantage of attending to implicit curricula is that teachers must take the child's point of view when constructing them, because their success depends on how well they appeal to the sensitivities and concerns of young children. The sensitive teacher might expand these structures or settings further by incorporating the children's achievements and accomplishments during play. It is time, then, for both psychologists and educators to realize that play is, among other things, a powerful form of learning, which must be fostered and utilized rather than driven away from the classroom.

References

Dauite, C. (1989). Play as thought: Thinking strategies of young writers. *Harvard Educational Review, 59*, 1–23.

Dyson, A. Haas. (1987). The value of "time off task": Young children's spontaneous talk and deliberate text. *Harvard Educational Review, 57*, 396–420.

Erikson, E. H. (1972). *Play and development*. New York: Norton.

Forman, G. E., & Hill, F. (1980). *Constructive play: Applying Piaget in the preschool*. Monterey, CA: Brooks/Cole.

Forman, G. E., Wolf, D., Scarlett, G., Shotwell, J., & Gennari, J. (n.d.). *The development of three dimensional symbolization with blocks*. Cambridge, MA: Harvard Project Zero, Harvard University.

Guanella, F. M. (1934). Block building activities of young children. *Archives of Psychology, 174*, 1–92.

Hulson, E. L. (1930). Block construction of four-year-old children. *Journal of Juvenile Research, 14*, 188–288.

Inhelder, B., & Piaget, J. (1969). *The early growth of logic in the child*. New York: Norton.

Johnson, H. M. (1933). *The art of block building*. New York: John Day.

Klein, M. (1955). The psychoanalytic play technique. *New Directions in Psychoanalysis*. London: Tavistock.

Langer, J. (1980). *The origins of logic: Six to twelve months*. New York: Academic Press.

Langer, J. (1986). *The origins of logic: One to two years*. New York: Academic Press.

Monighan-Nourot, P., Scales, B., Van Hoorn, J., & Almy, M. (1987). *Looking at children's play: A bridge between theory and practice*. New York: Teachers College Press.

Pratt, C. (1948). *I learn from children*. New York: Simon & Schuster.

Reifel, S., & Greenfield, P. M. (1982). Structural development in a symbolic medium: The representational use of block constructions. In G. E. Forman (Ed.), *Action and thought: From sensorimotor schemes to symbolic operations* (pp. 203–233). New York: Academic Press.

Wolf, D., & Gardner, H. (1979). Style and sequence in early symbolic play. In N. R. Smith & M. B. Franklin (Eds.), *Symbolic functioning in childhood* (pp. 117–138). Hillsdale, NJ: Erlbaum.

Vereecken, P. (1961). *Spatial development: Constructive praxia from birth to the age of seven*. Groningen, The Netherlands: Wolters.

CHAPTER 13

Perspectives from the Field
Play and Paradox

PATRICIA MONIGHAN NOUROT

In recent visits to classrooms of young children ages 3 to 7, I have seen a wide variety of constructive materials and, more important, a wide range of teacher and child behaviors in regard to constructive play. Teachers in many of these classrooms seem to have taken special care to equip the environment with rich arrays of constructive materials, from the "basics" such as blocks and Playdoh, to more elaborate materials such as Legos, pattern blocks, popsicle sticks, and ceramic clay. This equipment is often purchased at the teacher's own expense, especially in public school settings, where the notion of blocks and other play materials as the primary "textbooks" of a classroom for young children rarely receives administrative or financial sanctions. The very presence of these materials serves as an eloquent testimony to teachers' dedication to providing play in their classrooms.

It is also important to note that the availability of constructive play materials is only one variable that reflects a teachers' commitment to play in the curriculum. Large class sizes, with regard to both adult-child ratios and the sheer amount of space available for play, are obstacles that many early childhood educators must circumvent in order to offer play as a regular component in the children's schedule. For example, in one public school kindergarten, the principal requires that there be table space for all 33 children to sit at one time, a requirement that severely limits the teacher's efforts to arrange opportunities for block play, table toys, and dramatic play in her classroom.

Despite apparent obstacles, how such materials are used by children in their learning and by teachers to support their program goals is an important source of information about playful curriculum in action and is the focus of this chapter. In writing this, I reflected on the paradoxes I have observed in watching both children and teachers construct meaning in playful activity in the classroom.

I have touched upon one of these paradoxes: the freedom for both teachers and children to consolidate and extend their understandings of the world and relationships through play. This is in contrast to the limitations inherent in the physical environment, the daily schedule, and the external requirements of curriculum goals. Less obvious, but equally important, are paradoxes concerning the relationships of both individual and collective symbol making, and how children's symbolic construction may reflect what they know in terms of both their inner and outer worlds—what Froebel (1887) called "forms of life" and "forms of beauty." Related to this is the paradox centering on the children's agenda for learning in play vis-à-vis the teacher's efforts to shape children's play. Here the teacher as observer and researcher of children's play and as an active agent in children's learning also presents a paradox that rings true for those in the classroom.

Viewing Play in Classrooms

In Ann's kindergarten classroom there are wooden and cardboard blocks stacked casually in a corner, and people, animal, and vehicle accessories in a basket on a nearby shelf, along with a set of Legos. Playdoh is available occasionally, and is used mainly in a teacher-directed activity focused on the formation of the letters of the alphabet. "Art" activities are product-oriented, usually consisting of teacher-made models and specific instructions designed to, in Ann's words, "Teach them to follow instructions." Sand and, infrequently, water-play occur outdoors and are generally supervised by a teacher's aide or a parent rather than the teacher.

During "free choice" time, usually about 30 minutes at the end of the kindergarten day, children pull out the blocks and other constructive materials onto the rug. Some play with paints, paper, and glue at tables.

Ann's approach to the play of the children in her classroom is benign. She says that she sees free choice time as a relief from her duties as teacher, a time to leave children to their own devices while she confers with the adults in the room. When asked why play is important she notes that it allows children to "work through" their feelings and to discharge their excess energy and frustrations.

Constructive and dramatic play are seen by Ann as rewards for having finished the "real work" of the day's curriculum. Her comments to me during free choice time focus on the obvious enjoyment of the children as they engage in the playful construction of objects, roles, and situations. Ann does not appear to see the learning that occurs during constructive or dramatic play. She smiles and nods at Jake as he carefully creates an intricate pattern of red, blue, and green paper squares in a collage, but she makes no comment. She seems oblivious to the elaborate escape from a burning building engineered by Sally and Maria. Hundreds of opportunities for teacher observation, elaboration, assessment, and communication go unheeded by Ann, although she defends free play as an essential component of her daily curriculum.

In a preschool program in another county, head teacher Joe has become interested in how play contributes to the learning of basic skills that are part of the required curriculum, for example, identifying colors and shapes and comparing sizes. Joe watches as Frank, Pedro, and Jacob work on a roadway and bridge leading to the airport of blocks. The boys have run out of rectangular blocks and are using triangular blocks to form equivalent shapes to extend the road. Joe sees this as an opportunity to teach shape and size (as it is!) and kneels down, pointing to various blocks in turn as he repeatedly asks, "What shape is this?" or "Can you find a smaller block?" He continues, "Put your finger on the square block, Pedro." After a few moments of questions, the boys leave the block area, one by one, and begin to wander in search of a new activity. Joe wonders aloud why they've lost interest in the road.

Both Ann and Joe are caring, well-intentioned teachers. Each senses that constructive play has an important place in development for children, and they incorporate opportunities for play in their classroom curricula. But neither is well enough informed about the development of play and its relationship to constructing knowledge to use it effectively. Ann unwittingly neglects play, and Joe inadvertently destroys it with his efforts to intervene and assess.

Children Play What They Know

As Nicolopoulou points out in Chapter 9, both Piaget (1945/1962) and Vygotsky (1978) offer frameworks for viewing the role of play in development. Piaget's theory guides teachers and researchers to see how imitation, play, skills, and concepts are interwoven in children's symbolic expression. Nicolopoulou's work, in particular, emphasizes that symbolic development does not represent only the assimilative end of the spectrum, but illustrates the interaction between children's assimilative play schemes and their accommodative imitation schemes.

Children "play what they know," as Reifel and Yeatman point out in Chapter 11. What they know represents a complicated array of elements drawn from children's sociocultural knowledge base and the information they perceive in their play contexts. These sociocultural elements make up the raw material of constructive play. How an apartment building looks and the evenness of a road are images from children's experiences that they bring to their constructions. In such constructions children both imitate what they have seen and heard and transform these images to meet their own needs.

This is a form of knowledge that Froebel (1887), who first introduced block play into the education of young children, terms the "forms of life." These forms are elements of children's past experiences and perceptions of the outside world that comprise the images that children use in their symbolic expression.

Nicolopoulou's study of constructive play (Chapter 12) brings to mind another element of symbolic construction. This is the form of knowledge that Froebel called "forms of beauty," encompassing the child's knowledge of order, pattern, symmetry, and balance of form. According to Froebel, the use of these aesthetic forms in play offers children symbolic vehicles for expressing their inner experiences and feelings. An emphasis on these forms of beauty seems to characterize the "patterners" of Nicolopoulou's work and that of Wolf and Gardner (1979).

Both the forms of life and the forms of beauty are important in observing children's constructive play. One takes as its source the outside world of the child's experience, one the child's inner world. Moreover, these forms of expression interact in children's constructive play, as in Nicolopoulou's example of a child's construction of form and color coalescing into a life form the child has experienced. The labeling of the "Christmas Tree" in one 4-year-old's play began to shape her intention, replacing an emphasis on forms of beauty with an emphasis on forms of life. Recently I observed a child who began with the intention of creating a pond for her park and then shifted her frame to one of form as she became absorbed in creating a circular patterning of shades of blue and green.

Herein lies one of the major features of play for young children: flexibility of goals. Play allows children to shift fluidly in and out of varying forms of representation and to pursue subgoals as their projects progress. This interaction between form and content as understood by children can be seen in their early literacy learning as well as in their constructive play with objects. In using "invented" or self-constructed spelling, children reflect on the structural features of letter and numeral shapes as well as their understandings of the sound-symbol relationships associated with the shapes. "Does the 'G' or the 'C' have a moustache on it?" asks Jake at the writing table. "You make 'R' by putting a foot on a 'P,' " says Katherine, as she draws a "P" and then adds a line to make a letter in her name. "Does 'once upon' have a 'w' or a 'l' at the start?" comments Francie to herself as she begins "Wnsapn a tim . . ." on her paper.

Understanding how these elements of inner knowing and outer knowing weave together in children's play is important in unraveling the apparent paradoxes inherent in the play of young children. Teachers who are both sensitive observers and well informed concerning the characteristics of the development of play are prepared to understand the two "dynamic" theories of play described by Gilmore (1971). Psychodynamic theory views play as an avenue for children to master feelings and frustrations through repetition and reconstruction of painful or mysterious events. Play represents wish fulfillment for unrealizable impulses, similar to Vygotsky's view of the origin of play. Isaacs (1933) interpreted this view of play for teachers through her examples and guidance for observing children's mastery of their emotions through play.

In the dynamic view of play drawn from Piaget's work, play is a self-focused activity in which children impose their own organizations on experience ("assimilation") and consolidate their past behavior. They may also adapt their internal organizational structures to meet the demands of the external world ("accommodation"). The dynamic exchange between these processes serves a key function in the development of children's intellect, as children construct meaning through the use of individual and, later, collective symbols. In Piaget's view the emotional or affective aspect of play is secondary to the cognitive aspect (Kohlberg & Fein, 1987).

Within the constructivist viewpoint, based on the theory of Piaget, constructive play can be seen to contribute to the development of both physical and logico-mathematical knowledge. Physical knowledge is seen in such activities as buttressing a bridge or creating an entrance to an airport through which vehicles can fit. These kinds of constructions require children to call upon their images of physical experiences. Logico-mathematical knowledge is represented and constructed in activities such as Jake's collage of different colored squares or Frank, Pedro, and Jacob's road extensions using triangles to form equivalent size rectangles.

Social knowledge is represented and transformed in children's play as well. For example, in one kindergarten classroom, children constructed "garages" for their boats in an imaginary harbor they had built in the block area. The children said the garages were "to keep the ships in at night and so they won't get wet when it's raining." The kindergarten teacher gave the children time and opportunities to transform their social knowledge about boats and harbors through field trips to real harbors and by providing books and pictures for them to view. Gradually new terms like "slips" and "docks" crept into their vocabulary and their block representations (Robinson, 1989).

In each case, elements of children's previous experience, whether in the physical, logico-mathematical, or social world, transact in complex ways to produce variations of both form and content that provide the keen observer and teacher of children with information about how children are thinking, communicating, and solving problems.

The Child's Agenda and the Teacher's Agenda for Play

The paradox of teacher intervention in play, exemplified by contrasts between Ann's and Joe's classrooms, is not new. Since the time of Froebel and the first kindergartens, controversies about the role of the teacher in observing, prescribing, and guiding constructive play have occurred (Monighan-Nourot, 1990).

Many teachers, like Ann, intuitively understand the role of play in children's expression of inner conflicts and unrealized wishes. Such insights may result in a "hands-off" attitude toward play in which play's role as catharsis or diffusion of excess energy is paramount.

But understanding that play is a multifaceted experience and that it contributes to the development of knowledge, concepts, and academic skills as well as to interpersonal harmony is only a first step. Joe sees that play opens opportunities for children's social knowledge, such as the labeling of shapes, and logico-mathematical knowledge, such as the comparison of sizes. What remains unclear for him are the strategies that lie midway between guidance and prescription, between facilitation and didactic teaching, which enable teachers to use play effectively to plan curriculum and assess development.

This paradox—balancing knowledge of the possibilities for learning inherent in play with total freedom for the child to play without adult intervention—plagued the earliest early childhood educators.

Froebel's "gifts," many of which were variations on small unit blocks, were accompanied by detailed descriptions for teachers of the strategies and educational goals designated for each "gift." The timing and sequence of the introduction of activities to children were specified for the teacher (Froebel, 1896). This curriculum was coupled with Froebel's philosophical orientation to play as the spontaneous expression of children's understandings of life and the vehicle through which children develop a sense of harmony and interconnectedness with the universe.

Kindergarten teachers who implemented Froebel's curriculum in their classrooms often succumbed to the pitfall of rigidly prescribing a sequence of activities with the materials. Their vague understanding of Freobel's intended balance between child expression and teacher direction was exacerbated by overcrowded classrooms, so that teacher demonstrations replaced individual experiences with the gifts, and a "facade of activity without substance" characterized the life of many classrooms (Cuffaro, 1986).

The firm understanding of child development and its expression in children's play was a legacy left by the early childhood educators of the early 1900s. It became increasingly undermined, however, as teachers were less well prepared to understand the significance of children's own activity as the source for learning and development.

Such transformation of play to rigid curriculum surrounded the implementation of play-based curricula into Head Start programs in the 1960s. A lack of coherent philosophy and a concomitant focus on program expansion led to limited preparation of teachers in theories of child development and a reliance on paraprofessionals as teachers. This was, in part, a consequence of the laudable goal of many local Head Start programs that Head Start should represent opportunities for adult employment as well as children's schooling, and also reflected the concern of many parents that play was not the vehicle for education they envisioned for their children. When in the 1970s, attempts were made to make curriculum more coherent and to teach the role of play to teachers, most programs failed to see play as an avenue for learning. Instead, play was more often viewed as a reward for good behavior and the completion of teacher-directed tasks (Omwake, 1979).

Sound familiar? These problems persist today in early education, fueled by teachers' superficial understandings of child development and misconceptions of "developmental stages," poor communication with parents, large class sizes, and demands for accountability that emphasize prescriptive skill-based curricula.

What tools do theory and research offer the practitioner that might be of help in overcoming these obstacles to a child-centered, yet educationally sound, use of play in classrooms for young children?

Groups of Children at Play

Piaget's theory and the work of Wolf and Gardner (1979) offer teachers important insights into the development of individual children as they begin to employ symbolic representations to interpret meaning in the world around them. However, neither perspective offers guidance to teachers about the symbolic behavior of groups of children.

Here lies the valuable contribution of Vygotsky's (1978) work to the repertoire of the early childhood educator. Vygotsky's theory helps us understand how teachers may use their knowledge of children's developmental stages to "stretch" children's understandings and representations about their thoughts, feelings, and experiences. His notion of the "zone of proximal development," the area between a child's actual and potential levels of functioning, is useful to teachers considering the development of children in group settings. This "zone" is filled through children's social interactions with others. One of the avenues for this interaction occurs in the context of adult-child relationships, the details of which are beautifully spelled out by Saxe, Gearhart, and Guberman (Chapter 10) in their description of parent-child problem solving. Strategies for teachers to ascertain the child's-eye view of the situation or problem presented are implicit in that study. Examples of how adults may ask questions, provide nonverbal facilitation, or provide direct instruction may be drawn from a careful reading of Chapter 10.

A key element in teachers' efforts to "up the ante" (Bruner, 1986) on children's thinking is the teacher's knowledge of the child's present level of thinking. This knowledge is coupled with a detailed understanding of stages of normal development in cognition and socialization and cultural patterns of symbolic expression (Heath, 1983). When these elements are present in the teacher's repertoire, the teacher may effectively direct the child's stretch toward the next step in his or her development. For example, Meg, a kindergarten teacher, observed that Nick had sorted a set of plastic bread wrapper fasteners to make a picture of an "eagle." He proudly presented this as his strategy, while other children in the group sorted objects by color, shape, or other observable attributes. Meg, knowing that graphic collections represented an early stage of children's classification skills, was able to design experiences for Nick that stretched him into classifying by attributes in his interactions with her.

Another means of extending Nick's thinking would be to set up a play activity that invited classification, such as a pretend shoe store or a bakery. As Vygotsky (1978) tells us, another avenue to the zone of proximal development is through children's play with their peers.

Play creates a zone of proximal development of the child. In play a child always behaves beyond his average age, above his daily behavior; in play it is as though he were a head taller than himself.

As in the focus of a magnifying glass, play contains all developmental tendencies in a condensed form and is itself a major source of development.

Though the play-development relationship can be compared to the instruction-development relationship, play provides a much wider background for changes in needs and consciousness. Action in an imaginative sphere, in an imaginative situation, the creation of voluntary intentions, and the formation of real-life plans and volitional motives, all appear in play and make it the highest level of preschool development. (p. 102)

Both of the classroom strategies based on Vygotsky's theory, adult-child interaction and child play, presume a particular view of child development. In this view, the teacher regards the child's present level of development as an indication of the child's potential for the next step rather than as an indication of the child's "unreadiness" to perform certain tasks or encounter certain problems. It is important for researchers and teachers to work together so that teachers may be informed, not only about the norms of development, but about the potential for next steps that each level represents. Only in this way can we move beyond the limited concept of development as readiness (or unreadiness), which has pervaded early childhood practice in recent years (Bredekamp, 1987).

Managing Play in the Classroom

Another aspect of classroom practice that may be addressed by Vygotsky's theory is the management of classroom behavior. Teachers who afford opportunities for children to make choices about their play and work in classrooms report fewer discipline problems than teachers who force children to engage in the same activities at the same time. As Reifel and Yeatman (Chapter 11) point out, children will voluntarily adhere to rules and goals when they are engaged in purposeful play. And, as Corsaro and Schwarz (Chapter 16) illustrate, children develop sophisticated strategies to maintain focus and concentration on their play.

In a kindergarten classroom I observed, the children were engaged in block activities, map making, costume making, and mural painting around the theme *Rosie's Walk*, a book they had been reading and interpreting together. At one point the teacher looked at the three adults in the room with 29 children and said, "Well, what shall we do now?" We laughed as we noted that the children would not even miss us if we left. At this point, the teacher's aide took the opportunity to work individually with a child who had been absent, the teacher sat down to write an anecdotal observation of the group constructing in the block area as they labeled their "farm" through invented spelling, and I continued to circulate through the classroom.

Another point that I believe is illustrated by reading both Nicolopoulou's work and the study by Reifel and Yeatman is how the collective nature of making meaning operates in the classroom alongside, and as a complement to, children's individual symbolic constructions. What begins as one child's project may shift goals and incorporate information about structure and content from interaction with peers. I have seen this clearly in a recent study of kindergarteners' "storyplay" experiences (Nourot, in press). Storyplay is a technique originated by Paley (1981) in which children dictate stories and then invite their classmates to participate as actors, as the child-author directs the play.

Over the course of several months, collective symbols emerged in the biweekly enactment of stories. In one classroom gates were conventionally represented by two children arching their arms and facing one another. These gates marked separations between settings contained in the story, such as between "the neighborhood" and "the dark woods." Journeys from San Francisco to a neighboring community were marked by passing through the gate (the "Golden Gate"?). As teachers, we may not know the original source in the "forms of life" that these symbols represent, but we can watch with awareness and sensitivity their evolution within the peer culture as children negotiate and elaborate meanings.

Not only are the forms of symbolic play born of children's observations and experience, but so, too, is the content. Vygotsky's theory reminds us that the primary impetus for children's symbolic play is their emotional lives. What is important to the child may be worked through or may be understood by successive enactments or constructions. Concerns that are vaguely understood or emotionally charged form the base for play. Real-life experiences (such as a visit to a hospital emergency room), developmental fears (such as separation from parents), or cultural events (e.g., trick or treating) are represented in the group constructive and dramatic play of young children. Although teachers do not always agree on how to handle emotionally charged or sensitive issues that emerge in children's play, no one can disregard their importance in allowing adults to grasp what is significant and meaningful in children's lives. For example, several preschool teachers I have talked with are struggling with children constructing "crack" houses in the block areas and buying drugs with pebbles representing cash. In the San Francisco Bay Area teachers are reporting dramatic re-enactments of the recent earthquake.

Play is dominated by block construction and destruction, trikes crashing and falling into the water, and rescues by imaginary firefighters of children trapped in cars. Here we see the symbolic distancing skills, delineated by Piaget's theory, used in the service of compelling needs to understand and communicate meaning about powerful feelings.

Keeping Track of Development Through Play

Finally, I turn to the assessment of development. At a time in early childhood education when "developmentally appropriate practice" often conflicts with measures of assessment of children's progress, teachers' understanding of stages, processes, and styles of development is essential (Kamii, 1990). This understanding must reflect both sequences of age-appropriate development and attention to the cultures and emotional concerns of children. Who knows better than the average early childhood teacher that knowledge is not constructed in a vacuum and that, in fact, much of what we see the children in our classrooms learning has its source outside the teacher's planned curriculum?

Teachers have an opportunity to shape and understand complex processes of learning by acknowledging the paradoxes presented in this chapter: the freedom to construct meanings and the limitations placed on those constructions by the environment (e.g., nature and availability of materials, time, or space), the individual and collective nature of symbols, the interaction between the accommodative forms of life and the assimilative forms of beauty, and finally, by the child's agenda for constructing meaning and the teacher's agenda for shaping that construction. Such assessment strategies as the compilation of "portfolios" of children's artwork or photographs of their symbolic constructions, as well as observation, draw on teachers' understandings of the paradoxes revealed in play.

Going back to our examples at the beginning of the chapter, Ann struggled with these paradoxes by simply separating her concerns as a teacher and facilitator of learning from the children's concerns as they played. She walked away from confronting these paradoxes. Joe, on the other hand, attempted to deal with one paradox, that of the teacher's agenda in contrast to the child's, but his limited understanding of play blinded him to the possibilities inherent in the other paradoxes presented in play.

A recent observation from a kindergarten–first grade combination class serves as a positive example. The teacher Keiko sat at a table, helping a child write the name of her family on a picture. Other children were engaged in self-selected activities. Pao Ku took out several rectangular blocks, attempting to build an upright rectangular building, with two blocks as the base, one on each side, and two end-to-end across the top. As he reached the "top" of his construction, he attempted unsuccessfully to have the two blocks meet in the middle. Without support they fell. He slowly dismantled his construction, examining each piece, and eventually rebuilt it with one block at the base, one on each side, and one block bridging across the top. He then proceeded to run toy cars under and over his "overpass," making appropriate motor and horn noises. The whole process took nearly 10 minutes as he discovered his own solution to the problem. During that time, Keiko observed him carefully, writing her observations on a small "Post-it" pad she carries for such purposes. She noted the tactics he used to resolve the questions he set for himself. Later she commented that earlier in the year, he would have walked away from such a problem or asked a teacher to "fix it" for him. She was delighted with the growth she had seen. I was inspired by the keen observation skills and sensitivity of a teacher who could see the growth in a child's activity and knew when to stand back and let the learning happen.

As several authors in this part of the book have noted, the nature of play itself is paradoxical. It serves both the intellect and the emotions, the development of the individual and the group, the ends of the teacher and those of the child. The sensitive uses of play in early childhood classrooms to plan curriculum and to extend and assess development represent both excellence in the art of teaching and knowledge about the science of research.

References

Bredekamp, S. (Ed.). (1987). *Developmentally appropriate practice in early childhood programs serving children from birth through age 8* (expanded ed.). Washington DC: National Association for the Education of Young Children.

Bruner, J. S. (1986). *Actual minds, possible worlds.* Cambridge, MA: Harvard University Press.

Cuffaro, H. K. (1986, October). *Blocks as "textbooks" of the early childhood curriculum.* Paper presented at Progressive Education: A Reassessment Conference, New York.

Froebel, F. (1896). *Pedagogies of the kindergarten* (J. Jarris, Trans.). New York: Appleton.

Froebel, F. (1887). *The education of man* (W. N. Hailman, Trans.). New York: Appleton.

Gilmore, J. B. (1971). Play: A special behavior. In R. E. Herron & B. Sutton-Smith (Eds.), *Child's play* (pp. 343–355). New York: Wiley.

Heath, S. B. (1983). *Ways with words: Language, life, and work in communities and classrooms.* New York: Cambridge University Press.

Isaacs, S. (1933). *Social development in young children.* New York: Schocken.

Kamii, C. (Ed.). (1990). *Achievement testing in the early grades.* Washington, DC: National Association for the Education of Young Children.

Kohlberg, L., & Fein, G. (1987). Play and constructive work as contributors to development. In L. Kohlberg with R. De Vries, G. Fein, D. Hart, R. Mayer, G. Noam, J. Snarey, & J. Wertsch (Eds.), *Child psychology and childhood education* (pp. 392–441). New York: Longman.

Monighan-Nourot, P. (1990). The legacy of play in American early childhood education. In E. Klugman & S. Smilansky (Eds.), *Children's play and learning: Perspectives and policy implications.* New York: Teachers College Press.

Nourot, P. M. (in press). Storyplaying in the kindergarten. In L. Bird, K. Goodman, & Y. Goodman (Eds.), *The whole language catalogue.* New York: American School Publishers.

Omwake, E. B. (1979). Assessment of the Head Start preschool education effort. In E. Zigler & J. Valentine (Eds.), *Project Head Start: A legacy of the War on Poverty.* New York: Macmillan.

Paley, V. (1981). *Wally's stories.* Cambridge, MA: Harvard University Press.

Piaget, J. (1962). *Play, dreams and imitation in childhood.* New York: Norton. (Original work published 1945).

Robinson, V. B. (1989, July). *The contributions of Piaget's theory to developmentally appropriate education for children.* Paper presented at the International Congress on Piaget and New Challenges to Sciences and Education, Lisbon, Portugal.

Vygotsky, L. S. (1978). *Mind in society: The development of higher psychological processes* (M. Cole, V. John-Steiner, S. Scribner, & E. Souberman, Eds. & Trans.). Cambridge, MA: Harvard University Press.

Wolf, D., & Gardner, H. (1979). Style and sequence in early symbolic play. In N. R. Smith & M. B. Franklin (Eds.), *Symbolic functioning in childhood* (pp. 117–138). Hillsdale, NJ: Erlbaum.

Part IV

**PLAY AND
THE SOCIAL WORLDS
OF CHILDREN**

CHAPTER 14

Children's Construction of "Childness"

JENNY COOK-GUMPERZ

In these final chapters we explore the ways in which children's early sense of a social self begins to develop both inside the home and family, and outside in the world of the nursery school and child care center. This chapter and the others that follow discuss how children in the course of their own activities develop a growing sense of their own social self in relation to others and to the activities of others.

Children's social experiences include not only the world inside of their immediate family and with their peers but also a world of unknown others—the public domain—which can and does have a meaning for and an influence on their world. In this chapter I am going to focus particularly on how children use language and discourse categories to build up an understanding of that public world, and how they make use of this understanding in their daily relationships at home and school.

Corsaro and Schwarz, in Chapter 16, look in detail at the world of children's peer groups and the powerful influence of peer-negotiated social understandings on children's nursery schools. Nucci and Killen, in Chapter 15, provide a glimpse over a longer time span, from the nursery school years through middle childhood, at the development of two distinct ways of understanding the social world. That understanding is developed first through a private morality—a sense of right and justice—and second through a social sense of convention, of what can or cannot be done in any public situation. We could perhaps refer to this as a public morality. These studies provide different inputs into the general issue of how children learn about the social world and learn to be socially competent beings. This issue is once again being seen as an essential part of the early childhood curriculum. Corsaro and Schwarz' chapter, in particular, speaks to how children's self-generated social activities in play provide a framework for early childhood school practice.

Children's Sense of "the Social Self"

It is well known to most mothers and some researchers that when children are asked by an adult to do something that seems to them too difficult or unsuitable, a child's likely response to the request is "I can't do that, I'm only a kid." The first time this happens adults may be surprised that children use a generic social category to describe their own sense of their social selves, that is, their sense of their own "childness." But on reflection we realize that as adults we make frequent use of similar reasoning, opposing the category of "adult" to that of "child." It should be no surprise to us when our children do the same.

I should point out right away that since there is no general term to describe children's self-generated social categorization, it was necessary to invent the word *childness*. Many of the expressions that involve descriptions of children and their activities are either pejorative, such as "childlike" or "childish," or else refer either to *childhood* as part of the life cycle or to *children* as a generic group. The understanding that children have of themselves as a social category, which they themselves use to express their own sense of group membership, requires, I think, a special term. We may ask why we assume that children are unlikely to reflect upon their own social definition. Perhaps it is because we know that childhood as a social phenomenon is a construction of adults, and that the history of this phenomenon can be traced over several centuries (Pollack, 1983). We, as adults, can still be surprised that socially inexperienced children can be aware of, and can use productively, their own sense of what it means to be a child. Increasingly, the adult world of educators, historians, and social planners is showing an interest in the active social categorizations and productions of children, as the chapters in this volume show. How this sense of *childness* is developed by children and how they use their own sense of self as a child is an area of inquiry that research on discourse and social development is only just beginning to explore. Research reported in this part of the book presents varied views of children's newly emerging sense of social self and of what it means to be a child from the perspective of those committed to looking at children's own ways of making sense of their world.

Children and Childhood in the Public World

Perhaps we should first look briefly at a contrasting position, at how the concept of childhood usually enters into the discussions of educators and social planners; that is, at the language of social planning *for* children, *by* adults. In a report on child care policies, presented during a recent Canadian seminar on childhood and implications for child care policies, Jens Qvortrup (1988) and his collaborators from the European Centre for Social Welfare Training and Research suggested the need for changes in the way social policies for children are conceived and discussed. They pointed to the essentially adult focus of many terms and statistics on which policies are based. (From a slightly different disciplinary perspective Grubb makes a similar point in Chapter 2.) In reporting their research on "childhood as a social phenomenon" Qvortrup and colleagues call for a future research agenda that provides a greater degree of child-centeredness for social policy decisions. They suggest that for the "language" of social policy to reflect this child-centeredness, thinking must change not only at the programmatic level but even in such matters as the statistics that are a major part of any policy analyst's or social planner's vocabulary. Using Danish and German statistics on families with children in different households, they argue that traditional bias in public statistics makes it difficult for research to focus explicitly on the children themselves when only households or families are counted. From the point of view of the social planner, and also the educator as a planner of child care, curriculum, and after-school children's services, children are subsumed within the wider social category of family or family unit. Families typically consist of one or two parents and their children. The family or household complex is most readily considered the relevant social unit—one in which the separate existence of the child is merged with that of the adults who give the child a public name and provide the support services of normal child rearing. Thus, the "named" family unit makes the child bureaucratically viable yet *socially invisible*. As Qvortrup (1988) and his colleagues point out,

> It is important to bear in mind this notion of dependency [of children] in public statistics. It resembles assessments of children as costly and valueless. It was introduced at about the same time as [other] historical events [such as] the transfer of children from manual to schoolwork, the strengthening of the family ideology, and the definition of childhood through psychology. It joins the main trends in the evaluation of childhood by adult society, and thus it is part of its language of power. (pp. 16–17)

Even simple statistical counts, such as the percentage tables used in most public statistics, make a telling illustration of Qvortrup's point about the need to consider the children's perspective. Although the research using these statistics appears to deal in social facts, it is important to remember that these apparent facts are based on ideologically motivated decisions about what to count and how to define the unit to be counted. Public statistics usually represent the traditional view of families and children, and so are unlikely to view children as separable social beings.

From a very different viewpoint, studies of children's worlds from a developmental and qualitative perspective make a set of assumptions very different from those involved in quantitative arguments. From the qualitative perspective, children's worlds are viewed as the sociocognitive construction of children's interactional practices and thus are essentially child focused. Whether the emphasis is on cognitive and moral development (Nucci & Killen), on the uses of interactional strategies and discourse (Corsaro & Schwarz), or the development through discourse practices of sociocognitive categorizations (this chapter), the assumption here is that children and their developing understanding of a shared peer and adult world are the basis for any theoretical discussions of children's competence and position in the world.

While theoretical perspectives that elucidate the basic premises of children's developing social understanding may differ, all assume that the developing child is the interactional center of a set of human relationships that provide the context for further knowing (Dunn, 1988). In this brief chapter only a glimpse of other research perspectives is possible in order to create a context for looking at children's play, peer group understandings, and moral and other sociocognitive forms of discourse.

Children in their Social World: The Presentation of Self

We need to ask several questions about children's social development that are not often considered applicable to the young and naive apprentices that children are assumed to be. In Goffman's (1959) sociological notion of the presentation of self in everyday life, he suggests that there are two ways of considering the presentation of self in public situations: either as a consciously engineered public self or as an unconsciously controlled and expressed self; these are discovered interactionally as the *signals given or given off* in the course of everyday interactions. We do not assume in theories of development that children are subject to the same kinds of consciously stage-managed public persona that are attributable to adults. But we still need to ask how children put together their sense of self as social beings. Can young children have an awareness of a public presentation of self? Most of the work in children's early social development begins from the position that children's social understanding grows out of their early interactional experience in the family. We assume that children's early social experiences provide them with an awareness of a social world that is immediate, present, attainable, and supportive. The social events that take place in their as yet short lives give them a basis for developing hypotheses about the way the world works both inside and outside the immediate domain of the home, play group, or nursery school.

The growth of children's social understanding can be explored from several different theoretical positions. These perspectives on children's understanding of the social world provide a glimpse of the way in which social knowledge can be understood both by adults and by children. Key concepts from these different research perspectives provide us with further insight into a researcher's view of children's cultures.

Upon entering into the children's world, anthropologists and folklorists focus on how they as adults understand the experiences that children receive and exchange. From this perspective the child is the experienced member of this children's culture, and the adult is the stranger. The culture that children create in games and play is of their own making (Kelly-Byrne, 1989).

From the point of view of the folklorist, children's own cultural activities are often presented as a closed transmission system that is passed between generations of children. In *The Lore and Language of Schoolchildren* Iona and Peter Opie (1959) present a compelling view of this children's culture as an oral one, capable of being transmitted across long periods of time (even a century or more), and from generation to generation. They suggest that children's games and play provide children with a world view that is not mediated by adults, except, as they point out in the quotation below, for adults' tendency to suppress it.

> The schoolchild's verses are not intended for adult ears. In fact part of their fun is the thought, usually correct, that adults know nothing about them. Grownups have outgrown the schoolchild's lore. If made aware of it they tend to deride it; and they actively seek to suppress its livelier manifestations. Certainly they do nothing to encourage it. (pp. 1–2)

By contrast with the Opies' vision of an underground "children's culture" that flourishes only as a counterculture apart from that which is adult sanctioned, the research perspectives that have had greatest influence on the theoretical shaping of views of children's social development are the developmental and constructivist approaches reviewed by Corsaro and Schwarz. These perspectives provide a view of children's social development based on conceptualizing children's sense of the social from a far more abstract point of view. Not only are rich ethnographic or folkloric details subsumed within general categories, but the theories focus on "the individual child's accommodation to an autonomous world" in which social development is conceived of as the child's "private internalization of adult skills and knowledge" (Corsaro & Schwarz, Chapter 16). These theoretical perspectives present the view of the child as an apprentice, mini-psychologist, or scientist struggling with the construction of an abstract set of categories with which to reproduce the adult social world.

Contrary to the constructivists' structural viewpoint, the research perspective of the developmental psychologist focuses on children's entry into the relational dynamics of families and other social groups of which they become members. The child's understanding of social relations emerges from a contextually embedded awareness of others that the child develops during his or her early life in the family. While focusing on the child's growing social understanding, many developmentalists assume that the child's immediate interactional experience provides the essential frame for any knowledge of the world. Research perspectives that concentrate on the cognitive understanding of the social world also explore the ways in which children acquire social representations of the adult world. From such studies we can see that, as Nucci and Killen illustrate in Chapter 15, the social representations of the public domain held by adults and by children cannot be clearly separated from each other. The developmental expectation remains that children grow into an adult world and that they are necessarily apprentices to adult skills. However, from the interactional perspective both interactional sociologists and child developmentalists are aware that children's construction of their own social self and their understanding of their own childness can be a focus for exploring children's social activities.

How Childness Is Constructed

Again we can ask the question, How do children come to understand their own self-definition as a child? We suggest that one way of considering the beginnings of an understanding of the social self is to explore children's own ways of describing and dealing with their categories of social experience in their conversations and other discourse. In our explorations we found that a key understanding of what was important socially for children revolved around the categorizations of "child" versus "adult," large as opposed to small, and quite soon the emerging gender categories that also begin with the opposition of girls to boys. I suggest that these essentially oppositional categories (Leach, 1970; Ortner & Whitehead, 1981) form part of children's social reasoning from their earliest encounters in the public domain of the school, that is, in the nursery school, and continue to play an important part in their developing social understanding. As belonging to a peer group plays an ever more significant part in children's social life, children's self-generated social categories take on other language forms, such as nicknaming or the naming of "club" (or gang) membership (Harre, 1976, 1979), and these categories enter into children's daily discourse both inside and outside the school. In Corsaro and Schwarz' detailed analysis of two culturally different nursery schools, we can see the beginnings of these social discourses at work, and in Nucci and Killen's analysis of moral development terms, a sense of the character of children's social reasoning becomes clearer.

Further consideration in recent research of how social categories develop in children's early experience suggests that children's family experiences have great importance for their general understanding of social categories. They build on their awareness of the psychodynamics of their family roles (Dunn, 1988; Schutze, Kreppner, & Paulsen, 1986). The author's recent research suggests that the dynamics of interpersonal relations can be seen as influencing both children's linguistic categorizations of self and also their communicative practices (Cook-Gumperz, 1990). Children's developing social categorizations involve the interactional specifics of the family relationships they experience, as well as express the power dynamics of these intimate personal relationships. They focus on the different social and psychological qualities of biological givens in their relationships. For example, children use notions of such elements as "big" and "small" as a way of symbolically defining the social difference between child and adult. Secondly, since the arrival of the firstborn child makes two adults into parents, and the secondborn makes a sibling of the first child, birth order plays an important part: Firstborns and only children particularly have an awareness of their own special social advantages and disadvantages in parent–child interactions; secondborns have a special social role in relation to first children. These facts present a social reference point and new social possibilities for both the children and the family group. Work on family social relationships by Judy Dunn and collaborators (Dunn, 1988; Dunn & Kendrick, 1982) has shown how children build the social categorizations of self/other relations into sibling/family discourse.

In the following episode from Dunn and Kendrick (1982), a little girl and her father discuss her social characteristics in comparison with those of her baby brother. Dunn comments on the ease and playfulness with which children as young as 2 years or so use social information, particularly she suggests, "those [features] that involve *playing* with dimensions of self/identity. [These examples] demonstrate particularly forcefully the confidence with which the elder child applied dimensions such as gender, age, size, or good/naughty to [him- or herself] and to the baby sibling."

> In the first example, "a little girl *plays* with the father about the gender identity of herself and of her brother."
> *C:* (playing with her teddy) to father, (F): Teddy's a man.
> *F:* What are you?
> *C:* You're a boy.
> *F:* Yeah. What are you?
> *C:* A menace.
> *F:* Yeah, a menace. Apart from that are you a boy or a girl?
> *C:* Boy (laughs).
> *F:* Are you? What's Trevor?
> *C:* A girl (laughs).
> *F:* You're silly.
>
> Another conversation, which took place between a mother (M) and a 26-month-old (C), illustrates that children seem very clear about gender identity even when they are not verbally advanced.
> *C:* (throws comic book at B)
> *M:* You giving Joyce your comic, are you?
> *C:* No.
> *M:* Are you a monkey?
> *C:* No. Me not monkey. Me boy. Joyce girl.
> *M:* Is she?
> *C:* Joyce baby.
> *M:* She's not a baby now, is she?
>
> Many of the self-categorizing comments made in the context of conversation about the sibling were, unsurprisingly, about the big/small, or big/baby dimension:
> *C:* (to M) I'm a pudding.
> *M:* Are you a pudding? And who is Robert?
> *C:* Robert is a pudding too. He's a baby pudding.

The boy in the next example corrected the observer when she referred to his 8-month-old sibling as a "big brother":

Ian W: (to O) *Little* brother. (pp. 110–111)

In all of these examples we can see how children use and play with their own and others' "childness" within daily interactions; as Dunn and Kendrick comment, these episodes demonstrate a far greater sophistication toward children's own social self than they have previously been given credit for. Further, it seems that children combine their experience of the psychodynamics of their family life with their notion of *oppositional categories;* that is, children use natural oppositions that enter into their perceptual world in such forms as size (small/big; tiny/large) and color (blue/red) and transform them into social categories (boys/girls; us/them; child/adult) that exist as binary oppositions (Ortner, 1974).

Childness in the Discourse
of the Nursery School and the Home

In this last section let us look at a couple of examples of how children construct their social self and use this knowledge to make sense of events that happen in their daily life.

First, a brief extract from Corsaro's (1985) nursery school study illustrates this point well by showing how children search for and find a social category into which to place a strange adult. Corsaro, the stranger (adult researcher), was neither child nor parent but nonetheless shared their social activities and so needed a social position and, perhaps even more important, *a name.* Corsaro describes how during his time in the nursery school the children shifted from asking him who he was, to asking him if he was a teacher or a parent; only after attempting to place him in a known category did they settle on a distinctive name for him.

For the next several days, children in both sessions began to react to my presence (ask who I was) and invite me to play. Although I was able to observe, and in many cases participate in, peer activities, the process was a gradual one. For nearly the first month, the children were curious about me and why I was around every day.

Children's questions provide data on attempts at identification. They do not, however, directly support the contention that the children had accepted me into peer activities. The reference, or nickname, "Big Bill," which surfaces near the end of the first month of participant observation, indicates a marking of the size difference between me and the children, but also differentiates me from other adults.

In addition to the questions and the nickname, there were three other types of data which demonstrated my acceptance as a peer. First, I was allowed to enter ongoing peer activities with little or no disruption. In most instances, the children simply acknowledged my entry by addressing me in the course of unfolding events. In only a few cases were activities stopped and my presence questioned.

A second cue to the children's perceptions was my lack of authority. Given the nature of the research, attempts to control behavior were few and produced only when I felt there was a chance that a certain activity might lead to physical injury. On these occasions my "Be careful" warnings were always countered with "You're not a teacher!" or "You can't tell us what to do!"

A third type of data is more indirect, but occurred with a great deal of consistency. Throughout the school year, the children insisted I be a part of the more formal peer activities. At birthday parties, for example, the children demanded I sit with them (in a circle) rather than on the periphery with the teachers and parents. Also, several of the children demanded their mothers write my name, along with the names of the other children, on cookies, cupcakes, and valentines which were brought to school on special days. (pp. 30–31)

The solution reached by the nursery school children was to build upon the natural "oppositional" categories just discussed and add the attribute "big" to the personal name of this adult who was not quite an adult and could be almost a "peer" member of some activities.

In a second, brief example, this time from the author's research, we can see the same oppositional understanding of big/little as a social coding of adult–child relations emerging in the course of a conversational interchange in a typical game sequence of two girls, age 3.6 months, who are regular afternoon playmates in each other's homes. The two are engaged in playing some version of "Mummies and Babies" while the mother of one of them is packing away winter clothes into storage boxes. While all three are together in a small room, the interaction between the two girls, Laurie and Sally, is an exclusive event, carried on in the special heightened voice tones that mark "play voice" (see, for example, Auwater, 1986; Cook-Gumperz, 1987; Cook-Gumperz & Gumperz, 1976). The mother (D), engrossed in her activities, nonetheless anticipates that she is a third-party listener in the conversation, making it necessary for the two girls to reformulate her social position in their game world.

L: Natcha natcha. . . . What are you doing mama?
D: I'm still sorting through these things.
L: *No* I mean dattie.

D: You mean Sally is your mummy?

L: Yeah . . .

S: Cause she's not little.

L: No she's *big* (with emphasis)

In this short interchange the two girls are using a symbolic "size = age coding" as a way of reasoning for the impossibility of the adult being the correct addressee in their *game world*. Laurie's final comment and tone imply the sense of an "obviously anyone knows this" reasoning.

Conclusion

In these two examples we see the very beginning of a social categorization process at work. As Corsaro and Schwarz' comparative study of Italian and U.S. nursery school children shows, the issue of whether the discourse realization of fundamental social categorizations is universal or not is only beginning to be studied in interactional discourse work. The universal importance of looking at children's self-definition and categorization as part of their development, however, can be universally acknowledged.

References

Auwater, M. (1986). Development of communicative skills: The construction of fictional reality in children's play. In J. Cook-Gumperz, W. Corsaro, & J. Streeck (Eds.), *Children's world and children's language* (pp. 205–230). Berlin: Mouton.

Cook-Gumperz, J. (1987). Keeping it together: Text and context in children's language socialization (rev.). In S. Berentzen (Ed.), *Ethnographic approaches to children's worlds and peer cultures.* Report 15 (pp. 44–70). Trondheim: Norwegian Centre for Child Research.

Cook-Gumperz, J. (1990). *Belonging and sharing: Talk about intimacy in young children.* Unpublished manuscript.

Cook-Gumperz, J., & Gumperz, J. (1976). Context in children's talk. In N. Waterson & C. Snow (Eds.), *The development of communication* (pp. 30–31). New York: Wiley Interscience.

Corsaro, W. (1985). *Friendship and peer culture in the early years.* Norwood NJ: Ablex.

Dunn, J. (1988). *The beginnings of social understanding.* Cambridge, MA: Harvard University Press.

Dunn, J. & Kendrick, C. (1982). *Siblings: Love, envy, and understanding.* Cambridge, MA: Harvard University Press.

Goffman, E. (1959). *The presentation of self in everyday life*. New York: Anchor Doubleday.

Harre, R. (Ed.). (1976). *Life sentences: Aspects of the social role of language*. New York: Wiley.

Harre, R. (1979). *Social being*. Boston: Basil Blackwell.

Kelly-Byrne, D. (1989). *A child's play life: An ethnographic study*. New York: Teachers College Press.

Leach, E. (1970). *Levi-Strauss*. London: Fontana Great Masters Books.

Opie, I., & Opie, P. (1959). *The lore and language of schoolchildren*. London: Oxford University Press.

Ortner, S. (1974). Is female to male as nature is to culture? In M. Z. Rosaldo & L. Lamphere (Eds.), *Women, culture and society* (pp. 67–87). Stanford, CA: Stanford University Press.

Ortner, S., & Whitehead, H. (1981). *Sexual meanings: The cultural construction of gender and sexuality*. New York: Cambridge University Press.

Pollack, L. (1983). *Forgotten children: Parent–child relations from 1500 to 1900*. New York: Cambridge University Press.

Qvortrup, Jens, in cooperation with Brady, M., Sgritta, G., & Wintersberger, H. (1988). Childhood as a social phenomenon: Implications for future social policy. In H. Philip Hepworth (Ed.), *Seminar report from Canadian seminar on childhood implications for child care policies* (pp. 1–29). Vienna, Austria: European Centre for Social Welfare Training and Research.

Schutze, Y., Kreppner, K., & Paulsen, S. (1986). The social construction of the sibling relationship. In J. Cook-Gumperz, W. Corsaro, & J. Streeck (Eds.), *Children's world and children's language* (pp. 129–145). Berlin: Mouton.

CHAPTER 15

Social Interactions in the Preschool and the Development of Moral and Social Concepts

LARRY NUCCI
MELANIE KILLEN

Early childhood has long been considered a critical time in the formation of children's moral and social values. It has also been generally acknowledged that peer interaction plays an important role in the social development of young children (Piaget, 1932; Youniss, 1980). Beyond these generally accepted truisms, however, considerable disagreement exists regarding the manner in which programs of early childhood education might interface with children's natural patterns of social interaction to contribute to children's moral and social growth. Indeed, few areas of schooling at any level are as rife with controversy as moral education (Nucci, 1989). Disagreement surrounds both the definition of morality as well as assumptions about the processes by which moral and social development take place. Fortunately, however, recent advances in the study of moral and social development in young children have yielded findings that may help educators address some of these issues. The research indicates that children's conceptions of morality form a domain distinct from their understandings of other forms of social right and wrong, such as societal convention (Turiel, 1983). Moreover, the research demonstrates that these distinct conceptual frameworks emerge in early childhood from correspondingly distinct patterns of social interaction. Of particular interest for readers of this volume are findings that the observed domain-specific patterns typify peer interactions in play contexts, as well as adult–child interchanges. The aims of this chapter, then, are twofold. The first is to review the extant literature pertaining to the relationship between social interactions and the emergence of moral and societal concepts in early childhood. The second is to consider the implications of this research for programs of early childhood education.

Moral and Societal Concepts in Early Childhood

As we stated earlier, one of the significant recent advances in the study of children's social development has been the discovery that children's concepts of morality are distinct from their conceptions of social convention (Nucci & Turiel, 1978; Smetana, 1981; Turiel, Killen, & Helwig, 1987). Within the framework of that research, morality pertains to interpersonal actions such as hitting and hurting, and the distribution of limited resources that have nonarbitrary consequences for the rights or welfare of persons. Moral issues, then, are treated as categorical and universalizable; specific moral concepts (e.g., it is wrong to hit and hurt another; one should share with others) are thought to be structured by underlying conceptions of justice, rights, and welfare (beneficence). Whereas morality deals with issues inherent in interpersonal relations, social conventions such as modes of dress, forms of address, sex roles, manners, and aspects of mores regarding sexuality are behaviors whose propriety is determined by the social system in which they are formed. Because the specific behaviors are themselves arbitrary (e.g., boys instead of girls could be designated to wear dresses as a way of distinguishing between the sexes), conventions are seen as alterable and context dependent. Through accepted usage, however, these conventional standards serve to coordinate the interactions of members in social systems by providing a set of expectations regarding appropriate behavior. In turn, the matrix of social conventions and customs serves as a basic element in the structuring and maintenance of the general social order. Thus, concepts about social convention are structured by underlying conceptions of social organization (Turiel, 1983).

Evidence in support of the claim that morality and convention form distinct conceptual domains has been reported in more than 30 studies. Recent thorough reviews of this research can be found in Turiel, Killen, and Helwig (1987) and Helwig, Tisak, and Turiel (in press). While much of that research focuses on middle childhood and adolescence, studies with children as young as 2-½ years (Smetana & Braeges, 1987) have reported that subjects distinguish between matters of morality and social convention. In studies with preschool age children (Nucci & Turiel, 1978; Nucci, Turiel, & Encarnacion-Gawrych, 1983; Siegal & Storey, 1985; Smetana, 1981, 1984), it has been found that subjects view moral transgressions (e.g., hitting and hurting, stealing) as wrong irrespective of the presence of governing rules, while conventional acts (not remaining seated during snack time) are viewed as wrong only if they are in violation of an existing standard. Interviews with preschool children have also found that individuals view conventional standards as alterable, while moral prescriptions are viewed as universal and unchangeable. Furthermore, the justifications children provide for such judgments appear to be concordant with the moral or conventional nature of the issues under consideration. That is, children evaluate moral acts such as hitting as wrong on the basis of the intrinsic negative consequences that occur from inflicting harm on others. On the other hand, children evaluate transgressions of social convention in terms of their normative status as determined by the commands of authority, governing rules, or the prevailing social consensus. The distinction young children make between moral and social conventional issues is nicely illustrated by the following excerpts from an interview with a 4-year-old girl regarding actual transgressions she was observing in her preschool (taken from the raw data for Nucci, Turiel, & Encarnacion-Gawrych, 1983):

> *Moral Issue:* Did you see what just happened? Yes. They were playing and John hit him too hard. Is that something you are supposed to do or not supposed to do? Not so hard to hurt. Is there a rule about that? Yes. What is the rule? You are not to hit hard. What if there were no rule about hitting hard; would it be all right to do then? No. Why not? Because he could get hurt and start to cry.

> *Conventional Issue:* Did you see what just happened? Yes. They were noisy. Is that something you are supposed to do or not supposed to do? Not do. Is there a rule about that? Yes. We have to be quiet. What if there were no rule; would it be all right to do then? Yes. Why? Because there is no rule.

The capacity to distinguish between moral and conventional issues exhibited by young children becomes increasingly stable and generalized with age (Turiel et al., 1987). Prior to about 8 or 9 years of age, children do not consistently employ all the criteria available to them when distinguishing between the two classes of events (Shantz, 1987; Siegal & Storey, 1985; Smetana, 1981). In addition, younger children appear to be unable to extend their domain distinction to unfamiliar issues (Davidson, Turiel, & Black, 1983). With age, however, children appear to generate a stable conceptual framework for interpreting social events, and by middle childhood apply distinctively moral and conventional criteria to both familiar and unfamiliar issues.

This picture of young children's moral and social concepts is at variance with the view that has dominated the field of early childhood education for the past half century. In their seminal work, Piaget (1932) and later Kohlberg (1969) characterized the moral thinking of children in early to middle childhood as authority and rule based. According to these earlier views it is only at the higher stages of moral development that morality (justice) is differentiated from and displaces convention as the basis for moral judgments.

As this cursory review indicates, however, early conceptual development is more differentiated than previously believed. As we have seen, not all rule violations are treated alike; evaluations vary depending on the specific social and moral aspects of the transgression. In addition, the findings indicate that preschoolers have the capacity to critically evaluate actions in the moral domain independent of the views of authorities. Thus, it would appear that the adult–child relationship is more complex than as depicted in earlier developmental accounts (Piaget, 1932), which described the relationship as unilateral and heteronomous. One implication of this is that the characterizations of child–child and adult–child interactions may need to be recast in terms of complementary rather than competing roles in terms of the child's social development. Moreover, if early conceptual development is more differentiated than previously believed, then early social experience may also be more differentiated. This expectation is based on the developmental hypothesis that social knowledge is constructed out of social action (Turiel, 1983). Let us then turn to the research examining young children's patterns of interaction in the context of moral and social conventional events.

Responses to Moral and Social Conventional Transgressions

Initial studies of moral and social conventional interactions among children in preschool or day care settings focused on events entailing transgressions. This was because the social give-and-take surrounding transgressions provides children information regarding the status of social actions and the attendant responsibilities of the participants. Such interactions have been characterized as forming a kind of social grammar in which children negotiate, test, and clarify social norms (Much & Shweder, 1978; Sedlak & Walton, 1982). With minor differences among studies, the observational procedures entailed recording a descriptive narrative of observed events and the sequence of actions and statements on a behavioral checklist. Copies of the narrative descriptions were provided to judges at the completion of the observations. The judges then classified events as moral or conventional on the basis of criteria derived from the definitions of the two domains. In two studies (Nucci & Turiel, 1978; Nucci et al., 1983) children who had witnessed events were interviewed to elicit their domain placement of the observed transgressions. (An example of such an interview was presented earlier.) Over 80 percent of the time children's domain placement of events in these studies corresponded with the adult judges' classifications of events as moral or conventional. Once the judges had classified the events, analyses were conducted of the correspondence between observed behaviors and event domain.

In the study employing the youngest subjects (Smetana, 1984), observations were made of interactions among toddlers attending day care classrooms. Two age groups were observed, 13 to 27 months old (M = 20.76), and 18 to 40 months old (M = 30.08). Findings from this study indicated that social interactions in the context of moral and conventional transgressions differ qualitatively by the second year of life. Both the toddlers and their teachers initiated responses to moral transgressions. In both age groups, the child victims of moral transgressions responded in ways that provided direct feedback to the transgressors about the effects of their actions. Included within the toddlers' responses were statements indicating the consequences of actions, such as the pain experienced or the loss incurred. Such verbal reactions were provided more frequently by the older children. In addition, the toddlers reacted to moral transgressions through attempts at physical retaliation and through emotional reactions such as crying. Finally, these young children occasionally sought out adults to address their grievances.

Adult responses to moral transgressions complemented those of the children and often followed them in temporal sequence. Their responses also focused on the consequences of acts to the victim. Adults interceded by adjudicating rights in a moral dispute, by pointing out to the transgressor the effects of his or her act on the victim, and, less often, by attempting to divert the victim's or transgressor's attention from the act.

Adults, but not children, in this study responded to the violations of conventions. Smetana (1984) noted, for example, that when one 3-year-old boy chose to wear a girl's pink bathing suit to go wading, his teachers responded to the act as a transgression, although the boy and his friends appeared to be oblivious to this breach of decorum. This finding should not be too surprising in that conventional acts do not in themselves lead to a particular set of consequences for the actor or for others. Thus, knowledge regarding such breaches cannot come from experiences with the act itself, but rather come from experiences regarding the normative status of the act. For the day care toddler, this experience comes in the form of adult commands to refrain from norm-violating behavior, and, less frequently, from statements pertaining to aspects of social organization, such as rules and statements regarding the disorder or disruption the act created.

Three studies (Much & Shweder, 1978; Nucci & Turiel, 1978; Nucci et al., 1983) have examined child and adult responses to moral and social conventional transgressions at the preschool level. Children in these studies ranged from 3 to 5 years of age. In each of these studies, as in Smetana's (1984) observations with toddlers, it was found that moral and conventional transgressions elicited differing forms of response. As was the case with toddlers, both children and adults in the preschool studies responded to moral transgressions. Preschool children, like toddlers, responded to moral breaches with statements of injury or loss, emotional reactions, and attempts at retaliation, and by involving adults. As one would expect, these older children provided a greater proportion of explicit statements regarding the loss or injury experienced, and they had fewer emotional outbursts (such as crying) than were observed with toddlers. Despite their increased verbalization, the preschool children in these studies did not respond to moral transgressions by invoking rules or social standards for objecting to the acts.

Like the children, adults did not respond to moral transgressions through appeals to rules or normative expectations with nearly the frequency with which they employed such forms of response in reaction to breaches of convention. As in the toddler study, the adults observed in the preschools provided responses that complemented those of the children. That is, adult responses to moral transgressions focused on the harmful or unfair effects of the act on the victim.

In one of the preschool studies (Nucci & Turiel, 1978), as in the toddler study, there were no observed child responses to breaches of convention. However, the other two studies (Much & Shweder, 1978; Nucci et al., 1983) did report child responses to violations of social convention. These latter studies distinguished between general conventions, such as gender-related clothing norms (for example, dresses for girls, not boys) and conventional school regulations (such as designated play areas). Both children and adults were found to respond to general conventions. Almost all responses to school regulations, however, came from adults. Children's responses in the study conducted by Nucci and others (1983) focused on social rules ("Boys don't play with baby dolls!") and requests for adult intervention. Much and Shweder (1978), using a somewhat different procedure (they analyzed linguistic bouts rather than employing a behavioral checklist), also reported that children's discussions of conventional transgressions dealt with social expectations and norms.

Adult responses to convention in all three preschool studies, as in the toddler study, focused on aspects of the social order. Relative to the adult responses to toddlers, teachers in the preschools provided considerably fewer simple commands and increased the rate at which they provided rule statements and other responses indicating that acts were deviant (e.g., "That's not the way a girl should sit") or disorderly (e.g., "It's getting too noisy in here").

In sum, the findings from these initial studies focusing on responses to transgressions, provided evidence that preschool children's experiences in the context of moral events differ from the form of social interactions in the context of breaches of social conventions. These findings with preschool age children were corroborated in subsequent research conducted with school age children (reviewed in Nucci, 1985). Further, these studies illustrated that adult–child interactions in the context of moral and conventional transgressions, far from being disjointed from the structure of child–child interchanges, complement the forms of peer interactions within the two domains.

Peer Versus Adult–Child Interactions Revisited

While domain analyses of peer and adult–child interactions have provided evidence of their complementarity, observational studies of children's social interactions have also revealed evidence of the differential contributions peer and adult–child interchanges make to children's moral and conventional understandings. This research has particular bearing on our understanding of the unique role play has in children's social development.

As we noted earlier, young children infrequently address breaches of conventional school rules. In fact, it is not until middle childhood that children begin to respond regularly to peer violations of institutional norms (Nucci & Nucci, 1982). On the other hand, even young children attend to and construct conventions to structure their own patterns of interaction in play contexts and respond to breaches of such peer norms (Killen, 1989). Corsaro and Schwarz (Chapter 16) clearly illustrate that children develop and transmit from one generation to another methods of play and rituals not structured by adults. In a similar vein, Killen and Turiel (in press) observed that children as young as 3 years of age will over the course of eight weekly meetings generate "entrance and exit rituals" to structure their patterns of interaction in an unsupervised setting. Thus it appears that although adults and preschool age children both respond to matters of social convention, their focus is on different elements of the conventional environment. In each case, the interactions surround the conventions of a particular "society." The adult emphasis is on the norms of the institution (the school) and the conventions established by the adult culture. Preschool age children, on the other hand, seem only tenuously connected to these adult norms, and spontaneously respond for the most part to breaches of convention that structure their play patterns or rituals of engagement.

In the moral domain the differential features of children's interactions with adults versus peers are not so much in the foci of engagement as in the shifts that occur in forms of peer exchanges as a result of the presence or absence of a supervising adult. These differences were uncovered in a recent series of studies examining the ways in which children and adults respond to and resolve children's social conflicts (Killen, 1989; Killen & Turiel, in press; Rende & Killen, 1989; Slomkowski & Killen, 1989). In contrast with the studies discussed earlier, which focused solely on responses to transgression, this series of studies attempted to characterize the overall nature of conflictual interactions. In order to study the impact of adults on such interactions, children in these studies were observed in two social settings. One setting was school-time free play with a supervising teacher present throughout. The second was a semi-structured peer group setting in which child triads met in a room at a table and were instructed to play with the approximately 20 toys available to them. An adult sat in a corner in a nearby room and observed through a window. Unlike the teacher in the school free-play sessions, the adult observer in the peer group setting remained uninvolved in the children's activities. After one session, children in this context generally ignored the adult observer, whom they could see through the window. Children were observed in each setting in weekly sessions over a period of weeks or months, depending on the specific study.

Results from the first of these studies (Killen & Turiel, in press) indicated that children generated more resolutions to conflicts in the peer group sessions (36%) than in the school free-play setting (19%). However, more conflicts were left unresolved in the peer group sessions (60%) than during school free play. The higher number of resolved conflicts in the school setting appeared to be due to the involvement of the teachers, who intervened in 58% of the conflicts in the free-play context. In a subsequent study (Killen, 1990), analyses were conducted of the forms of conflict resolution. Out of the 177 conflicts observed in the peer group context, 69% involved compromising and bargaining, 24% involved reconciliation by the instigator, and 7% involved appeal to adults (though no actual adult intervention was possible). Out of the 193 conflicts observed in school free play, 60% involved reconciliation by the instigator, 23% involved direct and sole intervention by an adult, 9% involved compromising and bargaining, and 7% involved appeal to adults (numbers rounded). Reconciliation by the instigator referred to instances where the instigator immediately adhered to the protests of the respondent, whereas compromising and bargaining referred to extended discussions between the participants about the conflict. In this study, then, more active and extended discussions regarding conflicts took place among children in the peer group than in the adult-supervised school play setting. In effect, the presence of adults served to truncate the exchanges among children in the school context, while moving the interactions toward efficient, if not expedient, resolution. These results are in keeping with earlier findings (Killen & Turiel, 1985) that child-generated resolution of conflicts occurred less than 20% of the time when supervising adults were present.

The communicative and functional give-and-take entailed in moral conflict resolution has been shown to be an important contributor to moral development inasmuch as it requires participants to consider the perspective and needs of others in relation to their own needs and desires (Berkowitz, 1985; Camras, 1984; Eisenberg & Garvey, 1981). William Damon (1988), who has conducted extensive studies of the development of children's moral conceptions of distributive justice, has recently emphasized the role that natural exchanges concerning the distribution of toys and other goods play in moral development in the preschool years. Such interactions were among those witnessed in the Killen (1990) study, as illustrated in the following exchange among 4-year-olds in the peer group setting where no adults were present.

L, M, and R enter the room and sit down to play with the toys at the table.

L: I need the work things . . . I want the work things. (L grabs a few of the toys.) (To M) You can have the train. Can I have the work things? (Grabs a toy truck.) Can I have this piece?

R: No. (R pulls back the truck and looks upset.)

M: I'll give you one of the trains. (To R) I'll give you one of the trains if you give that to L. Okay?

R: No.

L: I want all of the work things.

M: (To R) Then I won't give you the train.

R: I don't want the train. Hey, M, you want to trade cars?

M: No . . . I don't want another car.

L: (To M) Can I have this train?

M: Okay. (Looking at the pile of toys that each one has) You guys have more.

R: I have the cookie monster too. (M looks a little upset, but is distracted by R.) Look, this moves (playing with one of the trucks).

L: Well, this is the Oscar thing.

R: Look, this moves.

M: Hey, look, watch this. (M grabs the truck from L and shows him how it works. L watches and is not bothered that M has taken his toy. M gives it back to L.)

L: How do you work it?

(There is some discussion about the trucks and how they work.)

M: I don't want this truck anymore.

R: I know (she takes a toy from L's pile).

L: (To M) You can have this one (hands her a toy).

R: Now, I only have two.

L: And I only got one.

M: Me too.

R: I know . . .

M: Let's share this one (holds up an unclaimed toy).

R: No (putting M's hand down). Since you (referring to M) have two, you (L) can have this (gives L a toy). (All three seem content and continue to play.)

The negotiations depicted in the preceding excerpt involved children in the very social actions that form the basis of moral understanding. In order to simultaneously maintain their relationship with one another and obtain toys for their own use, the children were drawn into a series of social actions that entailed expressing their wishes to others and taking the needs of others into account. In effect, the children were drawn naturally into the action precursors of moral reciprocity (Piaget, 1932). In pointing out this example of how children's spontaneous social interactions may contribute to their moral development, we are not implying that childhood should be viewed as a Rousseauian idyll. We need only remind the reader that the majority of observed conflicts in the peer group settings went unresolved (Killen & Turiel, 1985). We also wish to note at this point that schools and teachers varied in their willingness to permit and support these more extended forms of peer interaction (Killen, 1990). An unresolved question is how teachers through their conscious efforts can best build upon children's spontaneous forms of social interaction to contribute to their moral and social growth. It is to these issues of early childhood education that we will now turn our attention.

Implications for Early Childhood Education

If even very young children distinguish between matters of morality and social convention, then early childhood educators should be cognizant of this distinction in the design of preschool curricula and teaching practices. In saying this we are not claiming that all social issues can be classified as falling neatly into one domain or the other. (For a thorough discussion of domain overlap, see Turiel et al., 1987.) Nor is it our intention that preschool education attempt to "sharpen" children's conceptions of issues as matters of either morality or societal convention. What we are suggesting is that early childhood educators consider how aspects of their classroom environment and practices differentially map onto the forms of social experience associated with the development of children's moral and conventional understandings.

At the level of the formal curriculum, such an approach would entail "domain analyses" of such things as the content of stories read to children intended to foster moral values, to determine whether in fact a story was concerned with issues of justice and human welfare, or if the supposed moral content of the story really conveyed a particular set of conventions. A domain-consistent discussion following the reading of a story concerned primarily with moral issues would focus on the needs of characters in the story and the impact of various actions on the welfare of given characters. One implication of the research on children's social concepts is that emphasizing social rules or norms would not be particularly effective in contributing to children's moral development. This view has received some empirical support from a recent study (Nucci & Weber, in press) in which eighth-grade students in an American history course were directed to discuss moral issues such as slavery in terms of societal norms and values, or in terms of the underlying human welfare and justice issues. Students whose discussions focused on social rules and societal organization were found to have lower moral reasoning scores at the end of the course than students whose discussions emphasized the justice and welfare dimensions of moral issues.

Such formal curricular activities would hopefully not form the main source of moral and social educational experiences in the preschool. If the research on young children's social development has taught us anything, it is that the primary source of social knowledge for young children is their direct interactions with others. In the preschool one element of that experience under the control of the teacher is the set of events children encounter in the guise of classroom structure, climate, and teacher responses to social transgressions. While it is beyond the scope of this chapter to thoroughly discuss all the issues entailed by these features of what Philip Jackson (1968) has called the "hidden curriculum," we will take up some of the implications that the research on children's social interaction presents for this aspect of early childhood education. Put simply, the results of our studies on children's and adults' responses to social transgressions imply that children construct their moral knowledge in part from feedback in the form of adult statements focusing on the effects of acts on others, while their conceptions of social convention seem to come from feedback regarding social rules or social expectations. From this it follows that teacher responses to transgressions should be generally concordant with these patterns. While there have been no studies to evaluate the efficacy of such an approach, there is evidence that children and adults prefer such domain-concordant responses to moral and conventional violations.

Killen and LaFleur (in preparation) presented preschool children, teachers, and parents with a set of hypothetical social conflicts and asked them to rate the adequacy of potential ways in which a teacher might respond to each situation. Some of the conflicts entailed moral issues (e.g., hitting, not sharing); others dealt with social conventions (e.g., standing rather than sitting at the snack table, playing with the Lego blocks in the sandbox). After the description of each conflict, a range of possible resolutions was presented, and the subject was asked to choose the best resolution of the conflict. The resolutions (like the conflicts) varied along moral and social conventional dimensions. Results from interviews with parents indicated that they preferred as ideal resolutions intrinsic moral explanations for moral events (e.g., "The teacher tells Joe not to hit Jane because it hurts her"), and social order explanations in response to social conventional conflicts (e.g., "The teacher tells Joe not to stand at juice time because it might create a mess at the table"). Preliminary analyses of children's preferences show similar trends. Interestingly, however, preschool children, but not their parents, preferred "letting children work it out on their own" as a resolution for moral conflicts. The general pattern of the Killen and LaFleur results are in line with findings that elementary school students rate as more adequate those teachers who employ domain-consistent responses to moral and conventional transgressions (Nucci, 1984). This general pattern of results, spanning from preschool through seventh grade, suggests that children attend to the informational content of teacher responses to transgressions, and that domain consistency is an important variable in such contexts.

While teacher behaviors are important, the research on children's social and moral development makes abundantly clear that much of preschool education takes place through peer interactions in the context of children's play. The young child's functional knowledge of convention comes through interactions in the context of child-generated play conventions and rituals. Similarly, the child's functional knowledge of moral reciprocity emerges in large measure through the give-and-take of interchanges with peers. What we have also learned, however, is that adult–child interactions serve a complementary role to that of peer interaction. It is formalizing that complementarity that constitutes the artful integration of social development research into the practice of early childhood education.

References

Berkowitz, M. (1985). The role of discussion in moral education. In M. W. Berkowitz & F. Oser (Eds.), *Moral education: Theory and application* (pp. 197–218). Hillsdale, NJ: Erlbaum.

Camras, L. A. (1984). Children's verbal and nonverbal communication in a conflict situation. *Ethology and Sociobiology, 5,* 257–268.

Damon, W. (1988). *The moral child: Nurturing children's natural moral growth.* New York: Free Press.

Davidson, P., Turiel, E., & Black, A. (1983). The effect of stimulus familiarity on the use of criteria and justifications in children's social reasoning. *British Journal of Developmental Psychology, 1,* 46–65.

Eisenberg, N., & Garvey, C. (1981). Children's use of verbal strategies in resolving conflicts. *Discourse Processes, 4,* 149–170.

Helwig, C., Tisak, M., & Turiel, E. (in press). Children's social reasoning in context. *Child Development.*

Jackson, P. (1968). *Life in classrooms.* New York: Holt, Rinehart, & Winston.

Killen, M. (1989). Context, conflict, and coordination in social development. In L. T. Winegar (Ed.), *Social interaction and the development of children's understanding* (pp. 119–146). Norwood, NJ: Ablex.

Killen, M. (in press). Social and moral development in early childhood. In W.M. Kurtines & J.L. Gewirtz (Eds.), *Handbook of Moral Behavior and Development: Theory, Research, and Application.* Hillsdale, NJ: Lawrence, Erlbaum & Associates.

Killen, M., & LaFleur, R. (in preparation). *Parents' and preschoolers' judgments about social conflict resolutions.* Wesleyan University, Middletown, CT.

Killen, M., & Turiel, E. (in press). *Conflict resolution in preschooler interactions. Early Education and Development.*

Kohlberg, L. (1969). Stage and sequence: The cognitive-developmental approach to socialization. In D. A. Goslin (Ed.), *Handbook of socialization theory and research* (pp. 347–480). Chicago: Rand McNally.

Much, N., & Shweder, R. (1978). Speaking of rules: The analysis of culture in the breach. In W. Damon (Ed.), *New directions for child development: Vol. 2. Moral development* (pp. 19–40). San Francisco: Jossey-Bass.

Nucci, L. (1984). Evaluating teachers as social agents: Students' ratings of domain appropriate and domain inappropriate teacher responses to transgressions. *AmericanEducational Research Journal, 21,* 367–378.

Nucci, L. (1985). Children's conceptions of morality, societal convention, and religious prescription. In C. Harding (Ed.), *Moral dilemmas: Philosophical and psychological reconsiderations of the development of moral reasoning* (pp. 137–174). Chicago: Precedent Press.

Nucci, L. (Ed.). (1989). *Moral development and character education: A dialogue.* Berkeley, CA: McCutchan.

Nucci, L., & Nucci, M. S. (1982). Children's social interactions in the context of moral and conventional transgressions. *Child Development, 53,* 403–412.

Nucci, L,. & Turiel, E. (1978). Social interaction and the development of social concepts in preschool children. *Child Development, 49,* 400–407.

Nucci, L., Turiel, E., & Encarnacion-Gawrych, G. (1983). Children's social interactions and social concepts: Analyses of morality and convention in the Virgin Islands. *Journal of Cross-Cultural Psychology, 14,* 469–487.

Nucci, L., & Weber, E. (in press). The domain approach to values education: From theory to practice. In W. Kurtines & J. Gewirtz (Ed.), *Handbook of moral behavior and development* (Vol. 3). Hillside, NJ: Erlbaum.

Piaget, J. (1932). *The moral judgment of the child.* Glencoe, IL: Free Press.

Rende, R., & Killen, M. (1989). *Social interactional antecedents of object conflict in young children.* Unpublished manuscript, Wesleyan University, Middletown, CT.

Sedlak, A., & Walton, M. D. (1982). Sequencing in social repair: A Markov grammar of children's discourse about transgressions. *Developmental Review, 2,* 305–329.

Shantz, C. U. (1987). Conflicts between children. *Child Development, 58,* 283–305.

Siegal, M., & Storey, R. M. (1985). Day care and children's conceptions of moral and social rules. *Child Development, 56,* 1001–1008.

Slomkowski, C., & Killen, M. (1989). *Children's conceptions of friendship in relation to conflict resolution and peer exchanges.* Unpublished manuscript, Wesleyan University, Middletown, CT.

Smetana, J. (1981). Preschool children's conceptions of moral and social rules. *Developmental Psychology, 52,* 1333–1336.

Smetana, J. (1984). Toddler's social interactions regarding moral and conventional transgressions. *Child Development, 55,* 1767–1776.

Smetana, J., & Braeges, J. L. (1987). *The development of toddler's moral and con-*

ventional judgments and their relation to language development. Poster presented at the biennial meetings of the Society for Research in Child Development, Baltimore.

Turiel, E. (1983). *The development of social knowledge: Morality and convention.* Cambridge, MA: Cambridge University Press.

Turiel, E., Killen, M., & Helwig, C. (1987). Morality: Its structure, functions, and vagaries. In J. Kagan & S. Lamb (Eds.), *The emergence of morality in young children* (pp. 155–243). Chicago: University of Chicago Press.

Youniss, J. (1980). *Parents and peers in social development.* Chicago: University of Chicago Press.

CHAPTER 16

Peer Play and Socialization in Two Cultures
Implications for Research and Practice

WILLIAM A. CORSARO
KATHERINE SCHWARZ

Over the last 20 years we have seen growing interest in the importance of play and child-initiated activity in early education theory and practice. Much of this interest can be tied directly to the influence of Piaget and the constructivist view of child development. Constructivist theory influenced the design of early education programs in important ways. Recognizing the child as an active explorer and discoverer, programs stressed more free and unstructured play in well-designed, rich, and challenging learning environments. However, recent research and theoretical developments in childhood socialization point to some inherent limitations in constructivist theory.

Constructivism, most especially as presented in Piaget's work, is a theory of the individual child's accommodation to an autonomous world. There is an image of human development that "locates all of the sources of change inside the individual, the solo child" (Bruner, 1986, p. 149). One manifestation of this adherence to individualism is an overwhelming concern with the endpoint of development, or the movement from immaturity to adult competence.

There is a need for theories of children's social development to break free from the individualistic doctrine that sees social development solely as the private internalization of adult skills and knowledge. Childhood socialization should be understood also as a social and collective process. In this view, it "is not just that the child must make his knowledge his own, but that he must make it his own in a community of those who share his sense of belonging to a culture" (Bruner, 1986, p. 127). This interpretive approach views development as a process of children's appropriation of their culture. Children enter into social systems and, by interacting and negotiating with others, establish shared understandings that become fundamental social knowledge on which they continually build. Thus, the interpretive model refines Piaget's linear notion of stages by viewing development as a productive–reproductive process of increasing density and reorganization of knowledge that changes with the children's developing cognitive and language abilities and with changes in their social worlds.

A major change in children's worlds is their movement outside the family. In interacting with siblings and playmates, participating in organized play groups, and attending nursery schools, children jointly produce an initial peer culture. Such experiences launch children on a path involving their production of and participation in a series of peer cultures in which childhood knowledge and practices are gradually transformed into the knowledge and skills necessary for participation in the adult world.

Our research has focused on peer culture in the preschool years. Through ethnographic study of peer interaction in nursery schools in the United States and Italy, we have identified common features of peer culture and have described basic patterns of cultural production and reproduction in these schools (Corsaro, 1985, 1988; Corsaro & Rizzo, 1988). We have discovered, in line with Bruner (1986), that *collective negotiation* is central to these cultural processes. Although we have recognized the importance of adults (especially parents and teachers) in such negotiations, we have concentrated primarily on the analysis of peer interaction and culture. In this chapter we examine the role of teachers more directly, and develop further the notion of early childhood education as a reproductive partnership (see Corsaro, 1985).

Teacher–Child Culture Contact in Preschool Settings

Although peer culture most often emerges in children's spontaneous play, its production is often a reaction to the adult world. Adult ideas, materials, rules, and restrictions can be seen as frames or boundaries within which features of peer culture emerge and are played out. Some of these frames or boundaries are carried to preschool settings in the children's perceptions and understandings of the adult world that have developed from interactions in the family; others originate in the preschool and are tied directly to particular features of the setting and curriculum and are built up and maintained by teachers (Corsaro, 1985; Fernie, Kantor, Klein, Meyer, & Elgas, 1988).

Preschool teachers are in a unique position regarding contact between peer and adult culture. While parents' contact with peer culture is frequent, it is primarily restricted to interpersonal interaction between parent and child, except when parents negotiate with more than one of their own children (i.e., siblings) or with their child and one or a small group of playmates. Things are quite different for preschool teachers. Most of their interactions with children involve talking to, explaining, questioning, negotiating, reprimanding, and sharing with groups of children. In addition, most of the children in such groups share a history of being together as well as both a local (preschool) and more general peer culture.

Preschool teachers' interactions with children also differ from those of kindergarten and elementary school teachers. Preschool children are negotiating and producing an initial peer culture whose shared content (values, concerns, artifacts, and activities or routines) is relatively small and rapidly expanding, so that negotiations regarding shared meaning are often strained and conflictual. As a result, preschool children often call on their teachers to enter into disputes. Consequently, preschool teachers may have greater influence upon the peer relations and culture than do teachers of older children who are less likely to ask for such assistance. In addition, because preschool programs are often more unstructured and promote spontaneous play, peer culture and the adult world (as presented in school rules and educational procedures) are not clearly bifurcated as they are in kindergarten and elementary school (see Rizzo, 1989). Preschool teachers, then, are partners in children's production of an initial peer culture and their movement toward the eventual reproduction of the adult world.

Here we examine this reproductive partnership by analyzing teachers' contacts with peer culture in nursery schools in the United States and Italy. We focus on two specific instances of teacher entry into peer culture and analyze the teachers' intervention strategies, the dynamics of interaction between the teachers and children, and the overall effects of the intervention in terms of children's peer culture, childhood socialization, and educational practice.

Data and Method

The data for the following analysis were collected in two long-term micro-ethnographic studies of peer interaction in nursery schools. In the description of the data collection procedures the first person will be used to refer to the first author (Corsaro), who carried out the ethnographic research in the United States and Italy. The first study was conducted in an American nursery school that is part of a child study center staffed and operated by a state university for education and research. The school is located in a large metropolitan city near the university campus. There were two groups of approximately 25 children each at the school. One group attended morning sessions and ranged in age from 2.10 to 3.10 years. The second group (which had been at the school the year before) attended afternoon sessions and ranged in age from 3.10 to 4.10 years at the start of the school term.

A detailed discussion of field entry and data collection procedures for this study is presented elsewhere (Corsaro, 1981, 1985), and we provide only a summary of the data collection process here. Data collection moved through a series of phases. The first phase involved unobtrusive monitoring of activities in the school from a concealed observation area. These observations were important in learning a great deal about the children (e.g., their names, play activities, frequent playmates, etc.) and the schedule and normal routine of the school day. After three weeks, this initial phase was followed by three months of participant observation. I employed what I term a "reactive" method of field entry, allowing the children to react to and define me and gradually draw me into their activities. I was also careful to avoid any behavior that might have led the children to define me as another authority figure. This strategy was successful as the children came to see me as an atypical adult and in many ways a "big kid" (many of the children referred to me as "Big Bill").

My participation during this phase was primarily restricted to a peripheral role. I never initiated activities, but did respond when children asked me to take on certain roles in their play (e.g., I pretended to eat sand cakes and pies, helped build constructions with blocks, etc.). Although clearly I was not a full participant or seen as a peer, I was accepted into the children's culture and routinely included in activities that the children produced only in the absence of the teachers and other adults (see Corsaro, 1985).

During my fifth month at the school, I began the third phase of data collection with the introduction of the video equipment. For the next five months an assistant videotaped peer interactive episodes twice a week while I remained involved with the children. On other days during this period I continued participant observation and the collection of field notes. I recorded 633 interactive episodes in field notes and 146 episodes on videotape (around 25 hours of video data; see Corsaro, 1985, for a description of the "interactive episode" and other details). Although I collected some episodes of teacher-directed activities, most of the data focused on peer play and culture. These materials were supplemented with informal interviews with the teachers, parents, and children throughout the 10-month period.

The second study was conducted in a *scuola materna* in a large city in northern Italy. The *scuola materna,* a preschool education program that exists throughout Italy and is usually administered by local governments, provides child care and educational programs for children 3 to 6 years of age. Attendance in the program is high; in the city of the school I studied in 1983 over 90 percent of the children aged 3 to 6 attended regularly. The *scuola materna* studied was staffed by five teachers; 35 children attended each weekday for approximately 7 hours (9:30 until 5:30) though some children returned home at 1:00. The general methodological procedures, involving participant observation, audiovisual recording, and micro-analysis of peer interaction, were similar to those employed in the American study.

In some ways field entry was more easily accomplished in the Italian setting because of my earlier experience in the American school. In addition, my limitations in conversational Italian (my comprehension was good and improved, but I made numerous grammatical and pronunciation errors when speaking) led the children to see me as an incompetent adult. Over time it became apparent to the children that I could communicate better with them than with the teachers. As a result the children saw themselves as having a special relationship with me—a relationship that was different from the one I had with the teachers. The children could talk with me and I with them with little difficulty, but they saw that my communication with the teachers was more problematic. In some respects, the children saw our relationship as contributing to a partial breakdown of the teachers' control, an important aspect of children's peer culture (Corsaro, 1985, 1988). As a result of these aspects of field entry, I was able to quickly establish myself as a peripheral member of the peer culture in the *scuola materna.*

In the *scuola materna* I collected around 325 interactive episodes in field notes over a seven-month period. During the last few months of this period I collected approximately 40 episodes of peer interaction on audio- or videotape, and 15 additional episodes on videotape during a six-week return visit a year later. These materials were supplemented with informal interviews with parents, the teachers, and the children themselves.

Teaching Styles and Curriculum in the American and Italian Schools

The American and Italian nursery schools shared a number of features regarding educational philosophy and practice. Both schools stressed child-initiated activities with ample time allotted for free play inside the schools and in the outside play yards, and the American and Italian teachers shared a philosophy of limited intervention in the children's activities during free play. Although free play was stressed, there were designated times for teacher-directed activities and projects in both schools. Teachers were also more likely to become involved in peer activities in certain areas of the school (e.g., arts and crafts) than in other areas.

While the teachers shared a general educational philosophy, there were important differences in actual practice in the two schools. All of these differences were related to a general teaching strategy. The Italian teachers emphasized a strong group orientation among the children, while the American teachers attempted to foster an orientation of the individual child within a group. This difference was manifested in both the style and content of educational practice. First, while meeting or group times occurred in both settings, the activities during such periods differed in important ways. In the American school the teachers often went beyond group songs or games, to encourage children's individual performances (e.g., to sing, tell a story, show and tell, etc.). Although all the children were given an opportunity to perform, these activities singled out individual students as having specific talents to contribute to the group. In the Italian school such individual performances were rare. The teachers did, however, often introduce games or songs in which subgroups of children (two to four) would perform with encouragement from the rest of the class. These activities usually continued until all the children had participated in a particular subgroup.

This individual versus group orientation was also evident in the design and execution of various class projects. For example, both schools had projects involving discussions and artistic depictions of holidays and seasons of the year. The artistic component of such projects in the American school involved children creating individual artwork at designated work tables with teachers. This method encouraged a great deal of talk between the teachers and students (e.g., children's requests for aid and evaluation, teachers' questions, encouragement, and praise), but sustained peer interaction was rare at the work tables. Individual artistic productions from such projects were then displayed in the school or taken home for similar display.

Although the Italian children produced a wide variety of artwork, few individual productions were displayed publicly. Rather, there were group discussions during which children decided on individual contributions to collective artistic projects such as murals and collages. When actually producing their individual contributions children worked together at tables while the teachers worked at another table nearby. When children wanted help or to display their work to the teachers, they went to the teachers' table. As a result, the children carried on lively peer discussions about the project and their individual contributions, while at the same time they had the opportunity for individual help from teachers.

Finally, the individual versus group orientation was also manifest in the teachers' strategies for intervening in children's play and culture. The Italian teachers were much less likely than the American teachers to intervene in order to extend play, enforce school rules, or settle disputes. Additionally, when children complained about the behavior of a playmate or requested help to settle a dispute, Italian teachers were more likely to send them back to settle things on their own.

Here we examine this issue of teacher intervention, which is a central process in the contact between children's peer culture and adult culture in nursery schools. We first examine an intervention episode in an American school, in which the teacher enters into the children's activities in an attempt to settle a dispute over the sharing of a play area, at the request of two children whose participation is resisted. We then go on to consider an example from the Italian data, where a teacher first hesitates, and then decides to intervene in a play activity that clearly violates a specific school rule.

It's Only for Police

In previous work (Corsaro, 1985, 1988), we noted the tendency of nursery school children to claim ownership of play areas in which interactive events are emerging and to try to protect the activity from attempts by other children to gain access. The protection of interactive space is related to both the social contextual demands of the nursery school and children's developing communicative abilities. Because they are in the process of developing the linguistic and cognitive skills necessary for communication and discourse, establishing and maintaining interaction with peers is not an easy task for young children. The nursery school is an ideal setting for facilitating children's development of such social skills. It is a setting in which children not only learn to initiate and construct interactive events with peers, but also attempt to maintain these events amidst many possible disruptions. The children's desire to maintain peer activities in spite of frequent disruptions from multiple sources is the basis of their tendency to protect interactive space.

On the surface, children's protection of interactive space seems uncooperative or selfish to adults. Preschool teachers who lack sensitivity to the complexities of peer culture often intervene in access disputes by demanding that children share play areas and materials and by reminding children that the exclusion of playmates is not friendly behavior.

This type of intervention is highly frustrating to children since they are not refusing to cooperate or resisting the idea of sharing. On the contrary, the children wish to continue to share the interactive experience that is already underway *with each other*. This is not to say that teachers should not intervene in access disputes. Rather some sort of intervention is almost always necessary. However, when preschool teachers who have a keen awareness of peer culture decide to intervene in access disputes, they must face several conflicting demands. They want children to be aware of and use general rules regarding sharing and to be sensitive to the needs and feelings of other children. But these general, adult rules and values must be articulated with the local interactive scene and with specific features and concerns of the peer culture (Cicourel, 1974; Corsaro, 1986). Therefore, to intervene successfully in children's access disputes, teachers must be knowledgeable of peer culture and sensitive to subtle features of the ongoing interactive scene.

To illustrate this process we present and analyze a videotaped example of an American preschool teacher's attempt to intervene in an access dispute (see Figure 16.1 for an explanation of the notational devices used in the transcripts). This is a typical example in which two children have made a claim on an area (the climbing bars) and decided on a play theme (role play as policemen). After they have been playing for about 10 minutes another child attempts to enter the area, resulting in the following dispute.

> Steven (S) and Jonathan (J) have been playing police on the climbing bars. Graham (G) has made numerous attempts to enter the bars, but Jonathan and Steven have resisted, insisting that he can't come in because the bars are only for policemen. Graham has solicited the assistance of another child, Antoinette (A), and she also has been unsuccessful in her efforts to gain access to the bars. Antoinette has left the area of the bars after telling Graham that she is going to tell the teacher that Jonathan and Steven are refusing to share. The following transcript begins as Antoinette and the teaching assistant (T) return to the scene.
>
> 1   *S–J,T:*   Nobody's coming in our police quarters.
> 2   *T–S:*   What?
> 3   *S–T:*   No people can come in our police quarters. We're policemen.
> 4   *T–S:*   How about the other side?
> 5   *S–T:*   No—
> 6   *T–S:*   All the policemen I know are very friendly.
> 7   *S–T:*   That's part of the police quarters too.
> 8   *T–S:*   The policemen I know let people visit.

9   *J–T:* That part's Matthew's and that part's ours. It's—it's all of ours. [A moves up ladder and enters bars as T talks to J and S.]

10   *T–J,S:* Well, most policemen let visitors come to their house and I think you should be (that kind) too.

11   *J–T:* No.

12   *T–J,S:* Well, if—if you hurt the visitors, then they're gonna come get me.

13   *S–J:* Look, he's coming in. [G has started up ladder, and A is now inside the bars.]

14   *J–G:* Oh no you can't. [Moves over to block G]

15   *A–J,S:* I already come in.

16   *J–A:* Oh yeah. [T moves close to bars near J.]

17   *T–J,S:* Jonathan and Steven. You must share the police house. I was hoping that you would decide to be friendly, but (   ). [J moves down ladder toward G.]

18   *G–J:* Go back. I'm gonna tell teacher again. Go back.

19   *S–J:* [Both in bars] (   ) We won't let any visitors come in our police quarters. [T moves off camera.]

In this sequence of the episode the teacher promptly responds to Antoinette's request that she intervene in the access dispute. When the teacher and Antoinette reach the bars, Steven immediately claims ownership in line with the play theme. Rather than insisting on the boys' acceptance of the general rule regarding sharing, the teacher indirectly suggests that the contested area could be partitioned (4). This suggestion is rejected by Steven (5, 7), so the teacher quickly shifts to another tack, which advises that policemen (like all good adults) are friendly (6) and that Antoinette and Graham could be visitors to the police quarters (8). In these two turns the teacher shows a sensitivity to the importance of

FIGURE 16.1. Notational Devices Used in Transcripts

NOTATION	MEANING	EXAMPLE
—	Interruption by self or others.	"It's—it's all of ours."
( )	Probable transcription. (If blank, unintelligible speech.)	"Can I go (up)?"
\\	Beginning or ending of overlapping speech.	A: "He wants the carton—\\" M: "\\He doesn't want\\ to give me the carton."

role play themes and ownership of play areas in peer culture. She also nicely links the general rule of sharing and being friendly to specific features of the local scene (i.e., the large physical dimensions of the bars and the boys' definition of the bars as police quarters).

Steven and Jonathan resist the teacher's suggestions (9), claiming that the area is theirs primarily because they were the first to claim it, along with another child (Matthew, who has left the area). During the boys' discussion with the teacher, Antoinette snuck into the bars and Graham now begins to climb in as well. When Steven and Jonathan block Graham's entry, the teacher threatens to force them to share (12, 17). However, instead of carrying through with this threat, the teacher leaves the area, moves a short distance from the bars, and continues to monitor the activity. Although we cannot be sure of the teacher's motives, it seems she wants the children to work things out themselves rather than having to enforce the general rule about sharing. Perhaps with Antoinette already in the bars, the teacher believes that Steven and Jonathan will give in and accept Graham as well.

Graham does eventually gain entry to the bars, but not without long and highly complex negotiations that involve further intervention by the teacher (see Corsaro, 1985, pp. 138–149, for a detailed discussion of these negotiations and a presentation of interviews conducted with Jonathan and Graham in an attempt to capture the children's interpretation of these events). These negotiations begin with Jonathan (the police chief in the play theme) sending Steven off to have his lunch, promising that he will get Antoinette out of the bars. Steven grudgingly accepts this plan and goes off to another part of the bars and pretends to eat lunch. Jonathan, meanwhile, talks to Antoinette about her older brother and then whispers that she can stay and play in the bars. Steven now returns, threatens Antoinette, and balks at Jonathan's attempt to send him back to have some more lunch. During the discussion between Jonathan and Steven, Antoinette leaves the bars, consults with Graham (who is still waiting on the ground), and climbs the ladder back into the bars with Graham trailing behind her. Steven resists their entry and this leads the teacher to intervene a second time.

20	S–A:	Oh no. [Steven moves to block A's entry to bars.]
21	J–S:	Oh Steven I said she could come in.
22	S–J:	But, I don't want her to come in. [T returns.]
23	T–J,S:	Me too. Can I go (up)?
24	S–T:	No you can't.
25	A–T:	You're too big.
26	T–A,S,J:	Me or Antoinette.

27	*S–T:*	You can't come in. You can't come in. You can't come in.
28	*T–S:*	All right then let—then let Antoinette in.
29	*S–T:*	You can't come in. You can't come in. You can't come in.
30	*T–S:*	Antoinette can go in and I won't go in, OK?
31	*J–T:*	OK.
32	*T–J:*	OK. [A now moves into the bars, and T leaves.]
33	*A–G:*	[G still on ladder] Come on. Come in, come on very fast. [G moves into the bars.]

The teacher, who had been monitoring the children's interaction, returns to the bars as Steven again resists the entry of Antoinette and Graham. She arrives just as Jonathan and Steven are continuing their debate about accepting Antoinette into the play area (21, 22). The teacher's tactic here is interesting in that instead of requesting entry for Antoinette and Graham, she makes her own personal entry bid (23). While Antoinette does not take this request seriously (pointing out that the teacher is too big to go into the bars, 25), Steven immediately denies the teacher's request as he did the earlier bids of Antoinette and Graham. Anticipating Steven's negative reaction, the teacher then offers a compromise (Steven and Jonathan either accept her or Antoinette into the bars, 26–28). Steven refuses (29). However, when the teacher offers the compromise for a third time, Jonathan accepts, and first Antoinette and then Graham scurry into the bars (30–33). Once Antoinette and Graham are in the bars, the dispute moves to a quick resolution. Steven says they are bad guys, which is a role assignment that could allow them to fit into the police theme. Jonathan picks up on this suggestion and says they could be thieves. Jonathan then goes on to offer a definitive resolution to the conflict.

34	*J–S:*	Hey, I think—I think—(all of us) can have a talk about it. We can have a talk.
35	*S–J:*	We can—we need to talk about it.
36	*J–S:*	OK.
37	*G–A,S,J:*	[G sees a plane.] Look at plane guys. [All turn to look at plane.]
38	*S–J,G,A:*	We got to talk about it.
39	*G–S:*	(Good we have) Come down here.
40	*A–G:*	Hey come on let's go. I'm going all the way to the top. [A climbs up]
41	*J–S:*	We need to talk about it so—ah—let—let—Steven why don't we cooperate and why don't (you agree to be a nice policeman).
42	*S–J:*	o—o—OK. [J reaches over bar offering hand to S]

43   *J–S:*   Here, shake hands. [J and S shake hands]
44   *J–S:*   Hey I shook it from (over this bar).
45   *S–J:*   (get) those robbers.
46   *S–J:*   (We get   ) robbers who steal the jewels.

It is clear that the children reach a resolution to this access dispute that is in line with the teacher's earlier suggestions about the importance of sharing. We now consider some of the main features of the teacher's intervention strategies in this example. Underlying the teacher's actions is a general belief that every child in the group has certain rights and privileges and can expect to be treated fairly by his or her playmates. This principle is in line with the American teachers' emphasis on the importance of the individual child within the group. The teacher's specific intervention strategies manifest the general principle in several ways.

The teacher immediately responds to Antoinette's request for intervention. She does not send the child back to try to deal with the problem on her own, suggest strategies that she might employ, or even question her regarding the history and specific details of the dispute. The immediate response communicates that the exclusion of one's playmates is a serious matter. In fact, there is evidence to suggest that the children are also aware of this general principle and anticipated the teacher's reaction. For example, when Graham first asked Antoinette for help he suggested that they (with Antoinette in the lead) fight their way into the bars. Antoinette responded that she had a special way, which was to tell the teacher. Also, when Antoinette and Graham return to the bars with the teacher, Steven and Jonathan are not surprised by the teacher's intervention. Instead, they are prepared to resist, offering a wide range of justifications for their defense of the play area.

Although the teacher promptly intervenes in the dispute, she does not strictly impose the principle of sharing upon the children. Instead, she makes a number of indirect suggestions (see lines 4 and 6 above) and threats (lines 12 and 17), which display her willingness to negotiate a solution within certain limits that are in line with the general principle (i.e., that the children be open to compromise and that they not use physical force to exclude others). The teacher's amenability to negotiation is important because it widens the parameters of possible contact between adult and child cultures. In fact, as the negotiations proceed, the teacher's intervention strategies display a clear sensitivity to specific elements of peer culture.

First, the teacher endorses the role play theme of police and then suggests that the children attempting access could play a part within this theme (lines 6, 8, and 10). Although she could have suggested a more active role for Antoinette and Graham (e.g., robbers rather than visitors), she did encourage the boys to link specific features of the play to the general rule of sharing, by suggesting that allowing visitors would be consistent with the police theme. Second, when Antoinette gains entry into the bars, the teacher temporarily withdraws and gives the children a chance to work out the problem on their own. The timing of the teacher's retreat is important in that she has helped one child physically gain access and left the defenders of the play area with suggestions that could serve as a compromise to settle the dispute. Finally, when the teacher returns she uses a childlike tactic. She first says that she also wants to enter the bars and then offers to sacrifice her own desire to play so that Antoinette can be accepted (lines 23–30). Although the children are aware that the teacher is an adult and does not really want to play in the bars, her suggestion does carry symbolic weight. She is willing to bargain like a peer. Jonathan is quick to respond to this ploy, and Antoinette and Graham enter and are soon after integrated into the play theme.

Overall, this instance of teacher intervention displays a pattern of adult–child culture contact in which children are encouraged to reflect upon the social significance of their everyday activities. Through a complex series of negotiations the teacher and children articulate the general values of sharing and individual rights with situational features related to the production of basic routines of peer culture (playing police and defending interactive space).

We will make one final point before moving on to the Italian data. Although the teacher monitored the children's interaction for a short period after she left the area, she did not witness the above resolution of the access dispute. As a result, she was not aware that the children eventually did many of the things she had earlier suggested (i.e., sharing and deciding to be nice policemen). This pattern of delayed acceptance of teacher (or adult) suggestions was common in the peer culture of the American nursery school children. The pattern reflects the children's tendency to first resist adult control, but later use information and ideas provided by adults to deal with problems within the peer culture. For this reason teachers should not expect to see immediate results when intervening in children's activities. Evaluations of the effectiveness of various intervention strategies should be based on observations of children's behavior over time and across play settings.

Arriva La Banca

All nursery schools have a set of rules that embody expectations regarding the children's behavior. Children's resistance to school rules represents their desire to gain control over their lives and is an important element of peer culture. Such activity is normally produced in a style that is easily recognizable to members of the peer culture. For example, it is often highly exaggerated (e.g., making faces behind the teacher's back), or is prefaced by "calls for attention" of other children (e.g., "look what I've got" in reference to possession of a forbidden object).

Although recurrent, predictable, and recognizable in terms of its general nature, specific instances of children's resistance to adult rules are often highly complex and dynamic. In the nursery school, children run up against a range of rules that they perceive as arbitrary and unfair. Over time the children develop a shared sense of the injustice of these rules and then proceed to concoct an impressive repertoire of types of resistance.

A wide variety of strategies or "secondary adjustments" (Goffman, 1961) to evade adult rules were produced by children in the nursery schools in both Italy and the United States (see Corsaro, 1985, 1990). One type of secondary adjustment involved the children's use of what Goffman has referred to as "make-dos" to get around rules regarding the use of particular objects or play materials. That is, the children would use "available artifacts in a manner and for an end not officially intended" (Goffman, 1961, p. 207). For example, there were no toy weapons in either school, and the use of pretend weapons was prohibited. However, children would often shoot at each other from a distance simply by pointing their fingers and cocking their thumbs. Children would also convert objects like sticks and broomstick horses to swords or guns and would actually construct weapons with building materials like Lego (Corsaro, 1985).

In this section we examine the intervention strategies employed by an Italian teacher when a group of children create a highly innovative "make-do" in connection with their play with a forbidden object. When the children went to the outside yard of the *scuola materna* each afternoon, the teachers used a large plastic milk carton to carry play materials. Not surprisingly, some of the children found the carton to be an attractive play alternative. On an earlier occasion, a child placed the carton on her head, was pushed by another child, fell, and suffered a minor injury. After this incident, the children were not allowed to play with the carton. However, one day we recorded an episode of peer play on videotape during which several children placed a bucket fillet with rocks in the carton. Then two children, one at each end, picked up the carton and marched around the school with the others, chanting: "Arriva la banca!" ("Here comes the bank!"). The children had created a whole new dimension in banking, a bank that makes house calls. A number of other children immediately responded to this innovation, asking for money. Soon the teachers and the researcher (Corsaro) became involved, encouraging the children to count out the money (rocks) carefully and follow normal banking procedures. Later, when three children were still playing with the travelling bank near the researcher, the following incident occurred:

> Three children, Alberto (A), Matteo (M), and Luisa (L) are playing with the travelling bank, and the researcher, Bill (B), is sitting nearby. A dispute over the carton develops between Alberto and Matteo.
> 1 *B:* Che è successo? (What happened?)
> 2 *A:* Vuole la cassetta—\ \ (He wants the carton—\ \)
> 3 *M:* \\Non mi vuole\\ dare la cassetta [whiny voice]. (\\He doesn't want\\ to give me the carton.)
> 4 *B:* Si—ahh—gioca con tutti. (Yes—ahh—play with everyone.)
> 5 *L:* Ciao. (Hello.) [Luisa moves closer and addresses the researcher]
> 6 *B:* Gioca con tutti—ciao Luisa. (Play with everyone—hello Luisa.) [The boys fight over carton and Alberto falls to the ground with the carton on his head. Now the teacher enters and separates the boys.]

At this point the teacher has entered into the dispute over the carton. Before we go on to examine her intervention strategy, it is necessary to provide some additional relevant background information. First, the teacher had noticed the children's earlier play with the carton and had actually encouraged it by asking for money from the bank. I had noticed that the teacher had also been monitoring the play before she intervened in the dispute over the carton. Second, I was aware of the rule that restricted the children's play with the carton, but I did not know that it originated after an injury, as I was not at the school when this occurred. I did suspect that the rule was tied to safety concerns. Finally, this is the first serious dispute that occurred over the possession of the carton during this lengthy play episode of the travelling bank. It is also the first time one of the children had placed the carton on his head, creating the possibility of an injury. These facts undoubtedly affected the teacher's decision to intervene at this point. Let us now see how the intervention progressed.

> 7 *T:* È già finita all'ospedale una bambina con la cassetta, ve lo, ricordate? (One little girl already ended up in the hospital because of the carton, do you remember?) [Luisa shakes head yes]
> 8 *T:* Vero, la Carla M. [last name], cose è successo? [waits for an

answer but does not receive one]. Tu stavi piangendo, cos'è successo? [Addressing M] (Right, Carla M., what happened? You were crying, what happened?)

9 *A:* Allora davo la cassetta io. (Then I was the one giving the carton.)

10 *T:* Piangevi perché non ti dava la cassetta o perché ti aveva fatto male? (You were crying because he didn't give you the carton or because he hurt you?)

11 *M:* Perché non—(Because—)

12 *T:* Perché non ti dava la cassetta? (Why didn't he give you the carton?)

13 *A:* —cassetta. (—carton.)

14 *T:* E beh c'è bisogno di piangere? E tu, perché fai il prepontente? Quella cassetta qui, vi ricordate la Carlina, il segno che ha qui? Carla! Carla M., vieni qua! Ché Bill non c'era e non lo sa. La Carla con questa, è all'ospedale. (Hey well do you need to cry? [to Matteo, and after a pause she then addresses Alberto] And you, why are you being a bully? This carton here [points to the edge of the carton], do you remember when Carlina, the mark that she has here? [She points to a place on her forehead where Carla sustained her injury] Carla! Carla M. come here! [She motions Carla to come over] Cause Bill was not here and he does not know. [as Carla arrives the teacher turns to the researcher and says] Carla because of this [taps carton, researcher says Ah] to the hospital.

15 *B:* Quando? (When?)

16 *T:* Eh—in—settem—ottobre, quando tu non c'eri. (Ah—in—September—October, when you weren't here.)

17 *B:* Ah, si. (Ah, yes.)

18 *T:* Perché, se la son tirata così. (Because, they had pushed like this.) [she displays by moving the carton to her forehead]

19 *B:* Ah. (Ah.)

In this sequence (lines 7–19) the teacher is encouraging the children to link a past event (Carla's injury while playing with the carton) to their present behavior (fighting over the possession of the carton). This is the first phase of a complex intervention strategy in which the teacher subtly and indirectly invokes the rule that playing with the carton in a certain manner is a forbidden activity. In line 7 the teacher is creating circumstances that are relevant to her eventual evocation of the rule (see Wootton, 1986, for a discussion of the linguistic organization of rule statements). She summarizes the past event, stating the outcome (a little girl ended up in the hospital) and cause (the carton), and ends her turn with the tag, "Do you remember?" The children are now primed for a series of more direct questions about the event and its relevance to the rule. The teacher begins with the identification of the injured girl (Carla) and then asks what happened to her (8). When she does not receive an answer, the teacher switches from her more general goal (the evocation of the rule) to address local concerns (Matteo's crying). She does this through several questions to Matteo and Alberto (lines 8, 10, and 12). Given their responses (9, 11, 13), she decides that it is not a serious matter, and playfully chides Matteo for his oversensitivity and warns Alberto not to be a bully (14).

Having dealt with the local problems, the teacher returns to the rule regarding play with the carton (14). She picks up the carton and asks if the children remember the scar that Carla has from her accident. Before the children can answer, the teacher calls for Carla to join the group. While they wait for Carla, the teacher reminds the children that the researcher (Bill) was not present when the accident occurred so he does not know what happened. When Carla arrives the teacher again summarizes what happened, when it happened, and how it happened (lines 14, 16, and 18). Although we cannot be sure if the teacher's recreation of the event is primarily for the researcher or the children, it is clear from the last segment of the teacher's intervention that the children are communally reliving the experience.

20   *T:* Lo sapevo—(I knew—)
21   *A:* Chi è stato? (Who did it?)
22   *T:* Lo so io chi è stata. Non si dice chi è stato. (I know who she was. We don't say who did it.) [She smiles and taps Matteo and Alberto and Luisa on the head as she says this]
23   *T:* Quindi non si fa con la cassetta, \ \ è un brutto gioco. \ \ (So, we don't play with the carton, \ \ it's an awful thing to play with.\ \)
24   *M:* \ \Ecco.\ \ (\ \ Here. \ \) [M says this as he places rocks into the bucket]
25   *T:* Giocateci, usandala così. (Play with it, using it like this.) [She places the carton on the ground indicating that they can play with it only in that manner.]

This last segment begins with Alberto interrupting the teacher and asking who pushed Carla and, thus, was responsible for her injury (21). It is clear from this question, and from the other children's nonverbal orientation to the discussion on the videotape, that the children were carefully listening to the teacher's recreation of the past event. Alberto's question displays a curiosity typical in the peer culture: the desire to have information about the mischief of a fellow playmate. The teacher refuses to supply such information in an interesting and complex conversational turn (22). To capture this complexity it is necessary to discuss a few things about Italian grammar and the English translation. First, Alberto's question, "*Chi è stato?*" could be literally translated as "Who was it?" or more loosely, as we have translated it here, "Who did it?" In either case, Alberto's use of the ending "-o" on the past participle ("*stato*") indicates masculinity, in line with the grammatical rule that the masculine be used in cases where the identity of the subject is unknown. The teacher's response is composed of two contrasting declarative sentences. In the first she uses the feminine ending "-a" for the past participle, implying that the culprit was a girl. More important, however, she states emphatically that she *knows who it was*. She does this with the construction "*Lo so io*," employing the first-person pronoun ("*io*") redundantly and strategically placing it after the verb ("*so*"). In Italian, person is expressed through verb endings, and any use of personal pronouns is for emphasis. Additionally, when the personal pronoun is placed after the verb there is a sort of double emphasis. In short, in this first sentence the teacher is drawing Alberto's attention to the fact that she knows who did it. In the second sentence she contrasts this emphasis with the general principle or rule of not "telling on others" or "dwelling on the past misbehavior of others" ("We don't say who did it"). This sentence is interesting because it is stated as a general rule, with the teacher using the impersonal construction "*Non si dice*" and switching from "*stata*" back to "*stato*" to protect the identity of the responsible party. The teacher reinforces her beliefs in this regard by smiling and tapping the three children on the head.

The teacher then goes on to provide the moral of the recreation of the past event (line 23, "So, we don't play with the carton, it's an awful thing to play with"). At this point she starts to leave with the carton, but changes her mind and places it on the ground. She then tells the children they can play with it, but only if they use it as a container. The carton must stay on the ground and the children can put things in it, but not carry it around with them. We can see how the teacher in this intervention subtly invokes the children's awareness of the rule, its source, and its purpose.

As we did in the American example, we now consider some of the more general implications of the Italian teacher's strategies. Underlying the teacher's actions is a philosophy that stresses the rights and welfare of the group. This philosophy is manifested in several ways. First, when the children initially began playing with the carton, the teacher decided to relax the normal restriction of play with a potentially dangerous object and to monitor the activity from a distance. Thus, the creative use of the plastic carton temporarily suspended its threat to the general welfare of the children. However, once a struggle over the carton occurred, its potential danger reappeared and the teacher intervened in the play. The teacher's hesitancy in enforcing the rule displays both awareness and appreciation of the creativity and autonomy of communal aspects of the peer culture.

Second, once the teacher entered into the activity, she did not immediately enforce the rule, but rather subtly drew the children's attention to the reason for its existence. She did this by encouraging the communal recreation of the event that brought about the establishment of the rule. This recreation involved questioning the children, providing needed information to the researcher, and even examining the scar of the child injured as a result of the inappropriate play with the carton. Recreations of past events (both verbal and artistic) were common in the *scuola materna,* and may be seen as a way of instilling strong communal values and bonds.

Third, the teacher resisted the children's requests that she identify the particular child responsible for the earlier accident. This resistance displays her emphasis on the importance of the rule for the general welfare of the group as opposed to the need to restrict the untoward behavior of particular individuals. In short, her message is not that "so-and-so's behavior was bad and that you [as an individual child] should not repeat it," but rather that "what happened to Carla could happen to any member of the group so we should all be careful in playing with the carton."

Conclusions

Earlier we discussed the importance of understanding socialization as a social and collective process. From this interpretive perspective childhood socialization is viewed as children's production of, and participation in, a series of peer cultures in which childhood knowledge and skills are gradually transformed into the knowledge and abilities necessary for participation in the adult world. This emphasis on peer culture does not, however, deny the importance of adults in the socialization process. On the contrary, peer culture can be seen as primarily involving children's attempts to use, practice, and eventually more firmly grasp information first presented to them by adults. In terms of early education, formal instruction and teachers' intervention into peer activities are important points of culture contact. It is during such contacts that children are encouraged to reflect upon the general social significance of their everyday activities.

In this chapter we have examined teachers' intervention strategies when confronting two typical situations in preschool settings: disputes over access and children's violation of school rules. In both cases we saw the value of the teachers' knowledge and appreciation of peer culture for dealing effectively with disruptive behavior, making children aware of adult rules and concerns, and preserving the positive aspects of peer play.

Finally, by examining data from two cultures, we were able to see how differing educational philosophies affected the teachers' intervention strategies. In the American school, the teacher's strategies reflect the importance of the individual child within a group. In contrast, the Italian teacher's intervention strategies reflect the importance of being a member and contributing to the general welfare of a group. Although there is a need for further exploration of the significance of this finding, it demonstrates the importance of cross-cultural studies for research and practice in early childhood education.

References

Bruner, J. S. (1986). *Actual minds, possible worlds*. Cambridge, MA: Harvard University Press.

Cicourel, A. (1974). *Cognitive sociology*. New York: Free Press.

Corsaro, W. (1981). Entering the child's world: Research strategies for field entry and data collection in a preschool setting. In J. Green & C. Wallat (Eds.), *Ethnography and language in educational settings* (pp. 117–146). Norwood, NJ: Ablex.

Corsaro, W. (1985). *Friendship and peer culture in the early years*. Norwood, NJ: Ablex.

Corsaro, W. (1986). Discourse processes within peer culture: From a constructivist to an interpretive approach to childhood socialization. In P. & P. Adler (Eds.), *Sociological studies of child development* (pp. 81–101). Greenwich, CT: JAI Press.

Corsaro, W. (1988). Routines in the peer culture of American and Italian nursery school children. *Sociology of Education, 61*, 1–14.

Corsaro, W. (1990). The underlife of the nursery school: Young children's social representations of adult rules. In B. Lloyd & G. Duveen (Eds.), *Social representations and the development of knowledge* (pp. 11–26). Cambridge, MA: Cambridge University Press.

Corsaro, W., & Rizzo, T. (1988). *Discussione* and friendship: Socialization processes in the peer culture of Italian nursery school children. *American Sociological Review, 53*, 879–894.

Fernie, D., Kantor, R., Klein, E., Meyer, C., & Elgas, P. (1988). Becoming students and becoming ethnographers in a preschool. *Journal of Research in Childhood Education, 3*(2), 132–141.

Goffman, E. (1961). *Asylums.* Garden City, NY: Anchor.

Rizzo, T. (1989). *Friendship development among children in school.* Norwood, NJ: Ablex.

Wootton, A. (1986). Rules in action: Orderly features of actions that formulate rules. In J. Cook-Gumperz, W. Corsaro, & J. Streeck (Eds.), *Children's worlds and children's language* (pp. 147–168). Berlin: Mouton.

CHAPTER 17

Questioning the Schoolroom

A Teacher's Perspective

REBECCA TRACY

I walk through the long schoolroom questioning;
—W. B. Yeats, "Among School Children," 1926

Preschool teachers are frequently not free to observe their classrooms as fully as they would like. Adequate staffing would permit teachers to do more observation, but funding constraints keep staff–child ratios skimpy in most programs. Child development research can provide theoretical "maps" to direct our inquiries so that as teachers we make the best use of the limited time at our disposal.

I am a head teacher in a university child care program that provides full-day care for children of faculty, staff, and students. I work with a staff that includes both professional teachers and undergraduate student assistants. Staff training is an ongoing responsibility, and in our university setting we can make effective use of current research findings. When I move outside the university, however, to teach in a community setting, I encounter not only indifference to reports of research, but a level of negativity toward the practices of research that is fairly pervasive among child care providers.

This attitude, combined with the fact that most research emanates from academic settings that are perceived as remote from the practical world of child care, creates a sense that the research community is separated, even isolated, from the teaching community. This is unfortunate both for the researchers, who could make use of the teachers' intimate knowledge of the children, and for teachers, whose perceptions and understanding could gain authority if backed up by current research (Cochran-Smith & Lytle, 1989).

In considering this fragmentation of effort—both teachers and researchers are invested in the growth and well-being of young children—I would like to propose an analogy between the professional disciplines of child development/early education and the process of modern regional development. Just as economic developers rely on maps and field reports about the land and people they are preparing to work on, so teachers can be aided by child development research and case studies, which function as maps to the modes and patterns of children's thought.

While developing children are in important ways different from a developing region, "products or outcomes" for both are generated by the subject population through the agency of outside influences and interests: social maturation or "school readiness" by the child under the guidance of parents and teachers; cocoa, rubber, or transistor radios by the people of the developing region under the direction of the development authority (nowadays probably a multinational corporation or the World Bank). Thus, we speak of a child's play as "productive" or "unproductive," using the language of economics to describe interactions that are satisfying to the participants and that also follow some sort of social protocol. What is ultimately "produced" in the preschool classroom is a child who knows how to play and work with others, follow simple directions, attend to a story, and take care of him- or herself in the bathroom: in short, a child who is "ready for kindergarten."

Teacher Observations: The Constraints

In their spontaneous play and response to classroom materials, children already practice many of the skills teachers feel obligated to "teach." Children discriminate among shapes as they work with blocks; they use complex grammatical structures as they argue over play procedures; they generate rules that reflect the rules and directives of the adult world. In the substances of children's play, teachers have a rich source of raw material to use in building a curriculum based on the children's interests as well as on larger social needs. What is actually going on in the playhouse or the sandpile? Research offers us ways to look at our classrooms; it can direct our thinking in useful ways, as maps and field reports direct a regional developer.

We need these maps and field reports because it is very difficult to do sustained observations in a busy child care classroom. We are constantly pulled away, diverted by the physical and emotional needs of our children and by parents who may come and go at varying times. "Tie my shoes!" "She hit me!" "Teacher, I need string for this . . . ," "Mrs. Brown, did you get my note about George's nosebleed yesterday?" Here is a jacket sleeve turned inside out, a phenomenon both cognitively and physically difficult for a child, and here is a 3-year-old in diapers who must be taken to the bathroom regularly. All conspire to frustrate our need to listen carefully to the other children busy at their play. Yet we have a professional responsibility to observe and to remember what we see; Jones (1990) reminds us that "classroom observations are required—they are not optional."

Audibility is a constraining factor. We cannot always hear what the children are saying, even if we are watching. One analysis (Perry, 1989) used three video cameras and three microphones to capture the complex dynamics of sustained group play. Paley (1989) uses a tape recorder systematically to capture children's dialogue and narrative. But in a 10-hour child care day we can't always walk around with a tape recorder, so we miss what the shy child finally says to the girls who grudgingly admit her into their "families" scenario (or they to her). Teachers may hear and see only a fraction of what is going on among the children.

Staffing levels are often too low to leave anyone free to observe in a reflective manner. This is a fiscal and hence a political issue. As practitioners, we have to insist that our classrooms are staffed with enough adults so that someone is free to observe. The role of "floater"—an unassigned teacher—is frequently seen as one who helps where needed, but it can also include the function of "looker and understander." We have to know the content of the children's play so that we can respond in ways that extend the children's thinking. A skillful—and unharried—observer is the key to gathering that information.

Research: The Practical Benefits

In considering the nature of child development research, it is helpful to distinguish between quantitative research—the systematic statistical analysis of child behavior or cognitive performance, with inevitably generalized findings—and more ethnographic case studies or field reports that document particular children's social, linguistic, or cognitive responses to their environment, like Corsaro's (Chapter 16) or Perry's (1989). Of the two research modes, the first seems to generate negative or ambivalent responses among the child care providers I have observed. The second, closer to the traditional methods of the nursery school teacher who observes children and gathers evidence of their growth and development from their activity, is more familiar and more likely to interest teachers. Both, however, can benefit our early childhood programs.

If play is an important avenue for children's learning, and if teachers are not able to fully assess the substance of classroom play due to demands on their time and attention, then who is in a position to know what the children are learning? Rather than merely assume or speculate that children are learning something from their self-generated activity, we can get help from the ethnographers of early childhood. We need access to research that brings technical knowledge of children's cognitive development to bear on the observed dynamics of their behavior.

Parents want to know about their child's progress; for a young child, that progress is largely charted through observations of play and other social behavior. Monighan Nourot (Chapter 13) comments on the kindergarten teacher with her pad of "Post-it" notes always ready, keeping track of the growth and change she perceives in the children's play. Such investigative techniques are a form of direct teacher-initiated research. We can be most effective, as we communicate our observations to parents, if we also have a research-supported knowledge of child development and are familiar with studies that support our observations. In other terms, we need to have the maps of the region at our disposal.

We need access to current research in child development because as teachers we are expected to be knowledgeable when we interpret our work to parents or visitors, or when we justify our needs and our existence to funding agencies. The latest research, the new studies, the longitudinal project—our awareness can support us professionally in a whole range of situations. A teacher who is well informed about new developments in the field can speak authoritatively in defense of lower staff–child ratios before a school board or legislative committee. A teacher who has taken the trouble to read up on social cognition is better able to help a mother deal with her child's aggressive behavior. In each case, the children stand to benefit from our knowledge.

Negativity Toward Research

Teachers' negative attitudes toward research take three forms. One is a disinclination to read about research. Fatigue is a factor; teachers who spend eight hours a day with preschool children are very tired by evening and unlikely to curl up with a professional journal or technical report.

Many early childhood teachers take evening or weekend classes to qualify for a permit or credential. Some do not find this productive time, but rather something they are required to do. They need, and are eager to learn, practical classroom ideas: discipline techniques, songs for circle time, art and science project ideas. Interest flags when the instructor moves to the theoretical realm.

"After reading David Elkind's article on 'Child Development and Early Childhood Education: Where Do We Stand Today?' (1982), I was thoroughly confused," a teacher wrote in his class journal.

> I could tell that it was a very scholarly article from an academic standpoint but it left me feeling overwhelmed. Is it really that complicated and involved, I wondered. My sense was: how can I use or apply any of that information in my practical work life? Maybe I was just tired when I started to read. . . . The terms for describing concepts are too fancy for my taste: I don't remember them and question why specialties and fields of study endeavor to be so "special." I really like interacting and getting ideas from other professionals who work with children, and I find it constructive and supportive. Maybe someday I'll read this article again and love it, but today it just seems so cold and formal. (Mermis, 1990)

Another teacher in the same class wrote of her "anger" at having to read about research that, for her, ignores the complex motivations that drive the 2-year-olds she works with. Neither of these teachers found any relevance to their work in Elkind's article, which in fact calls for closer links between early childhood research and teaching practice. It appears that immediate, real situations take precedence for hard-worked teachers over theory or statistical data. But when theory is presented in the context of such situations it can become meaningful for the practitioner.

A second consideration is the way in which "testing" and research are associated in the imaginations of many preschool teachers. "How do they know what else is going on in a child's life? Maybe that kid wasn't feeling good that day!" is a common response when we read about low test scores. Caring about children's well-being, child care providers may tend to view research as something that distorts, rather than reflects, the lives of children.

A third form of negativity can surface when researchers propose to work in a classroom, and stems from the teacher's own professional pride and desire to maintain control over the classroom setting. I have heard teachers comment: "Nobody knows my kids as well as I do. I'm with them eight or nine hours a day, more even than their parents!" While this perception is at odds with a professional obligation to work in partnership with parents, it suggests a deep-seated territoriality that exists in some early childhood settings. Sensitively approached, this commitment to children can be a resource for a researcher rather than a constraint.

Teachers also worry in a practical way when researchers enter their classrooms. Will routines be interrupted, will some children get lots of attention while others get none? Will furniture have to be moved to make room for testing procedures? Will the staff room be tied up during the day? Such concerns are linked to a wish to minimize stress for staff and children.

A Tool for Staff Development

How do the findings of child development research reach our preschool classrooms, infant groups, and family day care homes? Slowly, for the most part, as our work is perceived to be very separate from academic research. If we go to a teachers' conference we may hear something to share with others in our staff meetings. Books come to us recommended by word of mouth (". . . and it's available in paperback!"), the research they contain perhaps already outdated. Teaching-oriented journals like *Young Children, Zero to Three,* and *Child Care Information Exchange* are shared and photocopied. *Young Children*'s regular feature, "Research in Review," usefully embodies the implications of research for teaching practice. Newspaper articles that report on child health and development are circulated and posted for parents to read or copied into program newsletters.

The research that helps us tends to be issue-oriented. For example, an analysis of teachers' repeated use of male-generic pronouns in teaching and storytelling settings (Gelb, 1989) was useful to our staff in planning a nonsexist curriculum. Dyson's "Symbol Makers, Symbol Weavers" (1990) gives us technical language and research-based authority for discussing with parents the complex developmental stages by which children enter literacy.

In a child care center, one teacher may act as information broker for the staff, bringing in newspaper clippings or reporting on a conference. An effective staff development plan tries to ensure that all teachers have access to conferences, classes, and new ideas. Interpreting theory in terms of current classroom problems is a key function: How do these findings relate to John's unhappiness when his mother leaves? Should we reorganize music time in view of this new study?

Programs for little children are conservative because youngsters react poorly to changes in routine. If a particular process or schedule seems to be working for most of the children, we resist change. But we also do our own research, making small adjustments ("Let's bring out the clay earlier in the day—it may calm the children down."), or observing the behavior of individual children ("Can we discover any patterns in when and whom Alicia bites, and what is causing the tension for her?"). We question our own classrooms and collect data that are useful to us and to the children. We are less likely to make changes in response to theoretical or generalized information.

Unless research can shed real light on children's behavior, it may be perceived as irrelevant, too technical, or too mathematical (statistical tables and terminology are unfamiliar to many). Implications for teaching practice need to be very clearly stated by people who present research findings to teachers. Effective interpretation requires knowing something about one's audience and about the realities of life in child care centers and family day care homes: the noise level, the constant cleaning up, the need to provide staff breaks, the needs of the children for comfort and attention as well as stimulation and food—not to mention the anxieties of parents who need reassurance that this is a good place for their child.

From the standpoint of early childhood practitioners, researchers seem to have a luxurious life observing in the classroom. They are not responsible for bathrooms or teaching the alphabet or conducting story time; their responsibility is to observe and document child language and behavior. Their observations can be of great potential use to teachers, who become very invested in their perceived role of guiding children through the day. Teachers channel, manage, organize, interrupt, and sometimes frustrate children's behavior. "Leave us alone!" called out a 2½-year-old as the teacher approached quietly. "We don't want to go to the bathroom! We don't want to go to circle time!" To this child, the teacher was someone who had thwarted his desires too often. An observer's perspective would have been very helpful to the teacher at that point.

Researchers can watch and document and not interfere in the children's lives. They have precious opportunities to see what really goes on among children in social settings, or to find out how children learn and process information. This is vital information for teachers, a resource for helping us to improve our programs and to work effectively with children and parents.

References

Cochran-Smith, T., & Lytle, S. L. (1989, February). *Teacher research: Rethinking the genre.* Paper presented at the University of Pennsylvania, Graduate School of Education, Ethnography and Education Forum.

Dyson, A. H. (1990). Symbol makers, symbol weavers: How children link play, pictures and print. *Young Children, 45*(2), 50–57.

Elkind, D. (1982). Child development and early education: Where do we stand today? In J. Brown (Ed.), *Curriculum planning for young children* (pp. 4–11). Washington, DC: National Association for the Education of Young Children.

Gelb, S. A. (1989). Language and the problem of male salience in early childhood classroom environments. *Early Childhood Research Quarterly, 4*(2), 205–215.

Jones, E. (1990). *The teacher's role in children's play: A dialogue.* Presentation (with C. A. Kuster & S. Wallick) at the California Association for the Education of Young Children conference, San Jose.

Mermis, R. (1990). Unpublished journal. Berkeley, CA.

Paley, V. G. (1989). Must teachers also be writers? Occasional Paper #13, Center for the Study of Writing, University of California, Berkeley.

Perry, J. (1989). *Teacher strategies in an early childhood education play setting.* Unpublished doctoral dissertation, School of Education, University of California, Berkeley.

Afterword

BARBARA SCALES
MILLIE ALMY
AGELIKI NICOLOPOULOU
SUSAN ERVIN-TRIPP

This book's dialogue about young children's play, its significance in their development, and the ways to nurture it has nearly ended. But first we wish to address those who have been its readers and who have participated in the dialogue.

We hope that the ideas in the book can reach policy makers. Many of them recognize the inevitability of increased institutionalized child care. Whether such an increase is in the long run benign or deleterious will depend in large part on their decisions. While the book does not directly address policy makers, it provides an abundance of evidence and ways of looking at play that can be used to inform those decisions, encouraging support for the provisions (staff, space, equipment, etc.) necessary for play.

Researchers, especially those from the diverse disciplines related to child development, can find in child care and early education not only a wealth of data but also opportunities for new views of children within their particular social context, that is, in their play. Such resources become available, as this book shows, when researchers understand the complex realities of child care settings and are able to appreciate them from the viewpoints of the staff.

Early childhood practitioners, as several chapters have reiterated, are in many respects a vulnerable group, underpaid, undervalued, and put upon often by bureaucratic administrations and sometimes by parents. But they are also a potentially powerful group for they hold many of the keys to understanding and expounding the significance of young children's play. Their input is often essential to establishing the validity of research. The concerns early childhood educators express about various aspects of children's play in their classrooms are concerns that need to be shared and reflected on. Many are concerns that need to be investigated so that the best solutions can be found and the body of knowledge and theory about early childhood play made more substantial and reliable. Such knowledge not only contributes to the practitioner's status as a professional, but adds intellectual stimulation and satisfaction and the zest of play and experimentation to the work.

Finally, we hope that readers will find ways to continue the dialogue. We ourselves, discussing and reflecting on the various chapters, have clarified points of view, gained new insights, and found new possibilities for collaborative efforts to defend children's play against possible encroachment. We have enjoyed the dialogue, occasionally playful in itself. We hope our readers can do likewise.

Index

About the Editors
and the Contributors

Millie Almy (Editor), Professor Emerita at the University of California, Berkeley, has been a student of early childhood development, education, and care for over 50 years.

Marian K. Altman, Principal, Jefferson School, Berkeley, California, taught in kindergarten and also in sixth grade before becoming an administrator. She has long been involved in activities relating to parents and to the community.

Lyda Beardsley's varied experience includes teaching in private preschool, in public child care centers, and in elementary school. At the University of California, Berkeley, she has been Director of Child Care Services. She is the author of *Good Day/Bad Day: The Child's Experience of Child Care.*

Jenny Cook-Gumperz is Research Sociologist at the University of California, Berkeley. Her areas of specialization include language socialization, family interaction, inter-ethnic communication, and gender identity perception. Early childhood educators have found Cook-Gumperz' grasp of the ways that the socio-ecological features of settings influence children's language and communication particularly useful.

William A. Corsaro is Professor and Chair of the Department of Sociology, Indiana University, Bloomington. He is currently finishing a book on the peer culture of Italian preschool children and has recently begun a study of cultural values, child care policy, and children's peer cultures. He is the author of *Friendship and Peer Culture in the Early Years* and coeditor of *Children's World and Children's Language.*

Anne Haas Dyson, who has taught 4-year-olds as well as in first and second grades, is Associate Professor in the Graduate School of Education, University of California, Berkeley. She is also a project director in the Center for the Study of Writing and the author of *Multiple Worlds of Child Writers: Friends Learning to Write.*

Susan Ervin-Tripp (Editor) is Professor of Psychology at the University of California, Berkeley. Her major interests are in psycholinguistics, bilingualism, child language, and pragmatics. She also brings a broad perspective to the theoretical and public policy implications of research on play.

Wendy Fong, teacher in the Chinese Bicultural program at Jefferson School, Berkeley, California, holds an Early Childhood Specialist credential. She has been a preschool director and mental health worker.

Maryl Gearhart received her doctorate in developmental psychology at the City University of New York. She is currently Assistant Research Educationist, Center for the Study of Evaluation, Graduate School of Education, University of California, Los Angeles. Her extensive research experience includes analysis of home, peer, and classroom interactions.

Celia Genishi, Associate Professor at Teachers College, Columbia University, has spent much time as a researcher in bilingual settings, particularly at the early childhood level, where she has observed children's play, language, and learning. She is the author, with Anne Haas Dyson, of *Language Assessment in the Early Years*.

W. Norton Grubb, an economist and historian who specializes in public policy, is the coauthor of *Broken Promises: How Americans Fail Their Children*. He is Professor in the Graduate School of Education, University of California, Berkeley.

Steven R. Guberman is currently in the Ph.D. program in psychology at the University of California, Los Angeles. His major area of emphasis is developmental psychology. His other areas of interest are cognitive psychology and psychocultural studies.

Melanie Killen is Assistant Professor of Psychology at Wesleyan University. She is the author of "Social and Moral Development in Early Childhood," to appear in the *Handbook of Moral Behavior and Development,* edited by Kurtines and Gewirtz.

Patricia Monighan Nourot, whose teaching experience spans preschool, child care, and the primary grades, is Assistant Professor of Education at Sonoma State University, Rohnert Park, California. She is coauthor of *Looking at Children's Play: A Bridge Between Theory and Practice*.

Paul Mussen, a developmental psychologist, is Professor Emeritus at the University of California, Berkeley. He has written many articles and books related to children's social and personality development and is the editor of the four-volume *Handbook of Child Psychology.*

Ageliki Nicolopoulou (Editor) is a developmental psychologist pursuing several lines of research in the field of socio-cultural and socio-historical psychology; one of her areas of interest is the role of play and fantasy in education and development. She is Research Associate in the Laboratory of Comparative Human Cognition and Lecturer in Communication at the University of California, San Diego.

Larry Nucci's research focuses on the development of moral and conventional thinking in children and the effects of social interaction in that development. He uses both clinical and observational methods. He is Professor of Educational Psychology at the University of Illinois at Chicago.

Stuart Reifel's interest in early childhood play goes back to his experience as a teacher in nursery school and as director of a kindergarten program. His research has centered on spatial representation, particularly in block play. He is Associate Professor, Curriculum and Instruction, University of Texas, Austin.

Geoffrey B. Saxe's interests are in cognitive development and education. His research, which has included the study of children's early number play, has often been comparative across cultures and has taken him to diverse settings, including Brazil and Papua New Guinea. He is Professor of Education, University of California, Los Angeles.

Barbara Scales (Editor), organizer of the symposium, is Head Teacher at the Harold E. Jones Child Study Center at the University of California, Berkeley. Dr. Scales, who began her career as an artist, has been studying the social ecology of the preschool, often with collaborators from other disciplines, for several years. She is coauthor of *Looking at Children's Play: A Bridge Between Theory and Practice*.

Katherine Schwarz is a doctoral student in the Department of Sociology, Indiana University, Bloomington. She is interested in the effects of social welfare policies on women's employment and child care.

Doris O. Smith is Coordinator of Early Childhood Programs, California State University, Fresno. She has provided consultation in kindergarten and primary issues throughout the state, drawing on a broad background of teaching experience and preparation in early childhood education and in human development. She holds a doctorate in educational administration.

Rebecca Tracy is a Head Teacher in the University of California Child Care Services, Berkeley, California. Her graduate preparation includes special education as well as early childhood education. She frequently conducts inservice training workshops on a variety of topics, including toy making, cross-cultural child rearing, and coping with separation distress.

June Yeatman is a Lead Teacher in the University United Methodist Church Early Childhood Center, Austin, Texas. Her experience includes work with infants, toddlers, and 3- and 4-year-olds in family day care as well as nursery school.